THE BEST OF
LONDON
PARKS
AND SMALL GREEN PLACES

D1352296

If you want to know how...

Our Greatest Writers
and their major works

This book will take you to the heart of some of the great literature of the English language. Our major writers are presented in order of their birth, and discussed through carefully selected extracts, informed comment and key bibliographic detail; giving you the opportunity to discover some of the finest writers of the English language and be able to speak about them and their writing with confidence.

'A perfect tool for upping your literary IQ.' – The Good Book Guide

'Excellent...a useful, well-written book.' – The Teacher

Holiday Courses for Long Weekends and Short Breaks
A Guide to the Best Holiday Courses in the UK and Ireland

This unique guide is full of fascinating and often unusual things you can do throughout the UK and Ireland for a long weekend or a mini-break.

You could choose to: make bread at the foot of the Pennines, enhance your photographic skills in the Lake District or paint watercolours in the grounds of a Scottish castle.

Most of the courses chosen are set in areas of outstanding natural beauty or particular cultural interest, and will leave you coming home feeling refreshed, energised, and enriched from having gained a new skill or developed an existing interest.

howtobooks
Send for a free copy of the latest catalogue to:
How To Books
3 Newtec Place, Magdalen Road,
Oxford OX4 1RE, United Kingdom
email: info@howtobooks.co.uk
http://www.howtobooks.co.uk

THE BEST OF
LONDON
PARKS
AND SMALL GREEN PLACES

Louise and Simon Read

howto books

Published by How To Books Ltd,
3 Newtec Place, Magdalen Road,
Oxford, OX4 1RE, United Kingdom.
Tel: (01865) 793806. Fax: (01865) 248780.
email: info@howtobooks.co.uk
http://www.howtobooks.co.uk

British Library Cataloguing in Publication Data
A catalogue record for this book is available from
the British Library.

Produced for How To Books by Deer Park Productions, Tavistock
Prepared by *specialist* publishing services, Milton Keynes
Cover design by Baseline Arts Ltd, Oxford
Printed and bound by Cromwell Press, Trowbridge, Wiltshire

Note: The material contained in this book is set out in good
faith for general guidance and no liability can be accepted
for loss or expense incurred as a result of relying in particular
circumstances on statements made in the book. The laws and
regulations are complex and liable to change, and readers should
check the current position with the relevant authorities before
making personal arrangements.

CONTENTS

London Location maps

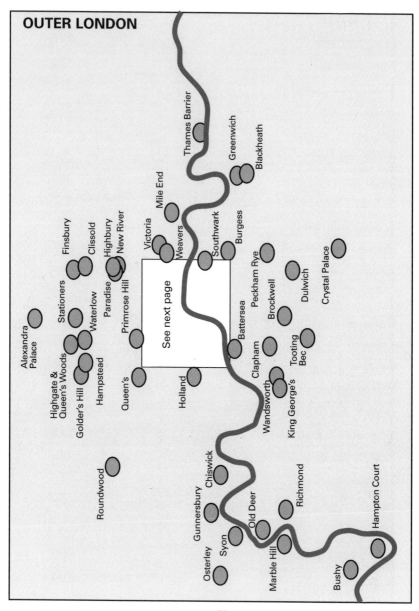

OUTER LONDON

Thames Barrier

Greenwich

Blackheath

Mile End

Victoria

Finsbury

Clissold

Highbury

New River

Weavers

Southwark

Burgess

Paradise

Primrose Hill

Peckham Rye

Brockwell

Dulwich

Crystal Palace

Stationers

Waterlow

Battersea

See next page

Alexandra Palace

Highgate & Queen's Woods

Golder's Hill

Hampstead

Queen's

Holland

Clapham

Tooting Bec

Wandsworth

King George's

Roundwood

Chiswick

Gunnersbury

Old Deer

Richmond

Hampton Court

Osterley

Syon

Marble Hill

Bushy

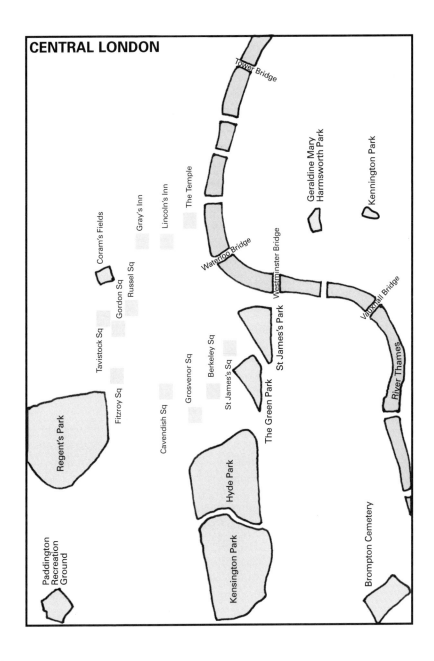

Introduction

'Parks are the lungs of London,' said William Pitt as he addressed Parliament in the 19th century. By 1850 half the population lived in cities and it was widely agreed that public spaces were needed for health and recreation. Within a few years London had established itself as one of the greenest cities in Europe. Today it has more parks and open spaces than any other city in the world.

There are parks for everyone: athletes and beekeepers, children and coffee addicts, fishermen, gardeners, golfers, music lovers, romantics, shoppers, skaters, sports fanatics, sunbathers, swimmers, walkers and wildlife enthusiasts. There are parks with views, woodland walks, places to picnic, deck-chairs to siesta in, benches to relax on and historic houses to visit. Despite this, practical information about the parks is hard to find. Millions visit them each year but few are aware of the sheer number of parks and superb facilities on offer.

The idea for this book came to us on a sunny evening in the Parliament Hill café on Hampstead Heath. We had passed it many times before but did not know that it stayed open until 9pm in the summer and that the view across the rolling lawns was better than that from any pub (and cheaper). Having lived just a few minutes walk away, we wondered how many other unknown delights were going on in London's parks and thought that other people must feel the same.

This book is the result of those thoughts. It is a fun, practical guide to the best of London's parks. Every region of London is covered. Each entry is packed with information including park maps, facilities, cafés, sports, walks, local clubs, history and nearby sights and places of interest. We have rooted out information, tips and highlights that even the park offices do not know about and secrets that will surprise many Londoners.

We have also detailed the local clubs and societies using the parks with their training times and contact details. This guide will entice the most urban person into the green lungs of London. It brings the parks to life.

LITTLE KNOWN FACTS

Battersea Park is famous, but relatively few know about the 33.5m Japanese Peace Pagoda, the free rowing lessons or the best Italian cappuccino. Many have heard of Hampstead Heath, but not about the magnificent 800ft pergola, the secret Hill Garden, the free swimming with hot showers, the highest natural point in London or one of the best athletic tracks in the city. Regent's Park is famous, but less well known are its beekeeping talks, the 'adopt a hive' scheme or the little-visited Secret Garden.

Few except local Londoners know of the best small parks: Waterlow Park near Highgate, with its magnificent views and café, Postman's Park a few minutes from St Paul's Cathedral, a tiny gem with a beautiful memorial to everyday heroes, St George's Gardens in Bloomsbury and Roundwood Park in Brent.

We have visited and listed the best squares and other small spaces hidden within the city: the oases of green perfect for a lunchtime picnic, or for an escape from the office or the high street. Also included are the magnificent modern parks such as Thames Barrier Park and Mile End Park, with their high tech ecology centres and pools of reflective water. We have also found the 'green corridors' that run across London, away from the traffic and noise: Regent's Canal, the Parkland Way, the New River Walk and the Thames foot-tunnels with their thousands of glazed tiles.

UPDATES

If you know of a park that you think should be included in future editions, or of details that need adding or changing, please contact us at the email address shown below. Your feedback will help to keep the information as up to date as possible.

We have visited over 60 parks for this first edition. There were many more that we would like to have visited but for reasons of time and space could not. We hope you enjoy exploring London's parks as much as we have.

If you need help planning your journey to any of the parks then try the excellent journey planner on www.tfl.gov.uk.

LAYOUT

The parks are listed in alphabetical order. The larger parks include a map and on pages viii and ix there are two outline maps of London that provide a general indication of the location of all of our parks. At the back of the book we have summarised a few of our personal highlights: the best park cafés, views, wildlife, flowerbeds, designs and facilities.

Simon and Louise Read

email: londonsparks@mac.com

Alexandra Park

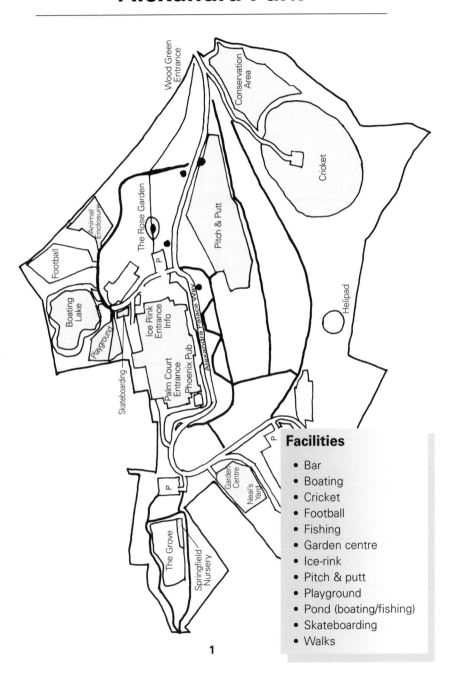

Wood Green Entrance

Conservation Area

Cricket

The Rose Garden

Animal Enclosure

Football

Pitch & Putt

Boating Lake

Playground

Skateboarding

Ice Rink
Entrance
Info

Palm Court Entrance

Phoenix Pub

Alexandra Palace Way

Helipad

Garden Centre

Neal's Yard

The Grove

Springfield Nursery

Facilities

- Bar
- Boating
- Cricket
- Football
- Fishing
- Garden centre
- Ice-rink
- Pitch & putt
- Playground
- Pond (boating/fishing)
- Skateboarding
- Walks

1

VISITOR INFORMATION

Alexandra Palace Way, Wood Green, N22 7AY

There is an information office in the BBC Tower Reception.

Palace: 020 8365 2121

Bus: W3, W7, 84A, 144, 144A

Tube: Wood Green and then the W3 bus

Train: Alexandra Palace (from Kings Cross)

Website: www.alexandrapalace.com
Email: info@alexandrapalace.com

Alexandra Park is home to one of London's most famous Victorian Palaces, Alexandra Palace, and one of London's best views. The palace was built as an extravagant Victorian recreation centre, 'the People's Palace', in 1873 by Alfred Messon and John Johnson. This was North London's answer to the magnificent Crystal Palace in Sydenham (p62). It was named after the beautiful wife of Edward VII, Queen Alexandra, and was so popular that within 16 days of opening it had attracted over 124,000 visitors.

The palace, like Crystal Palace a few years later, then promptly burned down. Fortunately this project was revived and within two years it had been rebuilt, covering seven acres of land and boasting the largest banqueting hall in London. Despite the initial popularity it was never a commercial success, and was subsequently used as a World War I barracks, refugee camp and then a German prisoner of war camp. In 1936 its fortunes changed when the BBC used it to transmit their first ever public broadcast. The palace was used by the BBC for its broadcasts for many years.

The park's 80 hectares (196 acres) include exceptional views of London, a boating lake, an 18-hole pitch and putt course, café, football pitch, cricket pavilion and a pre-school nursery.

There is also an excellent ice rink and a garden centre. The palace hosts regular events such as antique fairs, classic car shows, craft exhibitions, fireworks, funfairs, super bikes and country food. The Parkland Walk (see p83) follows an old railway line and links Alexandra Palace with Finsbury Park (see p77). The palace and the park are a little tatty but fortunately are about to benefit from a £2.7m restoration project.

HIGHLIGHTS

- Eighteen-hole pitch and putt course
- Firework displays: the closest Saturday to 5 November is one of London's favourites
- Garden centre with café
- Ice-rink
- Parkland Walk (see p83): the green corridor linking Alexandra Palace to Finsbury Park
- Spectacular views of London: bring your binoculars

ANIMALS

The animal enclosure is downhill from the Boating Lake. The enclosure has deer and an educational visitor centre is planned.

Animal training

The Animal Care Project has 45 places per year for 16-24 year olds with learning or social needs to study for an NVQ in Animal Care: tel. 020 8365 3781 for more details.

BIRDS

Over 150 species of bird have been recorded in the last 30 years, including firecrests, crossbills and pied flycatchers. Contact the Conservation Officer for more details.

BOATING

The Boating Lake is one of London's prettiest park lakes and has a bronze lion called Leo overlooking it. The lake is due to reopen in 2005 following renovation and dredging. Boat hire costs approximately £4.50 per boat, contact the main parks number.

BUTTERFLIES

There are at least 24 species of butterfly recorded in the park including the Essex, large and small skippers, brimstones, white letters and purple hairstreaks.

CAFÉ

The Phoenix Bar

Tel: 020 8365 4356, open in summer Monday–Sunday 10.30–23.00 and in winter Monday–Thursday 11.30–20.00, Friday and Saturday 11.30–23.00, Sunday 11.30–22.30.

The Phoenix Bar is a rather scruffy pub with a view, and includes a large outdoor terrace. A nicer place for a coffee is at the garden centre (see below).

CONSERVATION

The two-hectare conservation area near the Wood Green entrance includes secondary woodland, meadow, areas of scrub and a pond. The woodland includes ash, oak, elm, holly and horse chestnut. There are plans to open an information centre and to extend existing conservation work. Volunteers meet at the information centre once a month (see below). The New River (see p180) runs along the eastern border of the park, and the Parkland Walk begins near the Grove (Muswell Hill) (see p83).

CRICKET

The cricket pitch is used by the Alexandra Park Cricket Club, which was formed in 1888. There are regular fixtures, tours and meetings and teams of all levels. Check the website www.apclub.co.uk, email info@alexandraparkcc.co.uk or telephone the chairman of the cricket committee, Dave Cattell, on 020 8343 2213, or 07970 996 063, or contact the main parks number.

FISHING

The Alexandra Palace Angling Association, managed by Kevin Pestell, runs fishing from the Boating Lake. The lake is full of fish including bream, chub, catfish, pike, carp, rudd, perch and roach. A season ticket costs £10 or a single session £2 (£1 for children). Anyone over the age of 12 also requires a rod licence, which is available from Post Offices for £23 (adults) or £5 (age 12–17). Contact Kevin Pestell on 0777 649 8473 or General Office 020 8365 2121. The National Federation of Anglers can be contacted on 01283 734735, website www.nfadirect.com.

GARDEN

The Rose Garden is opposite the entrance to the ice-rink. It is a quiet place to sit with a pond (currently being restored), box hedges and roses.

GARDEN CENTRE

Capital Gardens Ltd, tel: 020 8883 8088. Open Monday to Saturday from 09.00–18.00 and Sundays from 10.30–16.30.

This large garden centre has everything for gardens, a gift shop and a café (homemade chocolate brownies recommended).

GOLF

The park's 1920 18–hole pitch and putt course is open from Easter until the end of September from 10.00 until dusk. Nine holes cost £3.50 and 18 holes cost £4.50. Iron hire is £1. Tel. 07956 624355.

ICE-SKATING

Alexandra Palace Ice Rink has a range of courses and lessons for everyone from toddlers upwards, including disco evenings and pantomimes. There is also a junior ice-hockey club running regular events, matches and training (website: www.haringeyhockey.com). The rink is open weekdays from 11.00–13.30 and 14.00–17.30 and at weekends from 10.30–12.30, 14.00–16.30 and 20.30–23.00. Tickets cost Monday to Friday £4.50 (adult), £4 (children), Saturday and Sunday £6 (adult), £5 (children) and £19.50 (family). Tel. 020 8365 4386.

NURSERY

The Springfield Nursery in the Grove is a pre-school group for two- to five-year-olds.

It has a lovely sheltered area deep in the park and is open weekdays from 09.30–12.00. The cost is according to parental means. Tel. 020 8883 7173 (rarely answer).

PLAYGROUND

There is a rather run-down playground near the Boating Lake with a good range of games.

SKATEBOARDING

There is a free skateboarding park located between the ice-rink and the Boating Pond.

TOURS OF THE PALACE

There are guided walking tours of the palace on selected Sundays during the year. These include the original BBC studios, the Great Hall and the famous Henry Willis organ. Tours cost £4.50 per person, last about two hours and take place at 11.30 and 14.00. They must be booked in advance and are only available for over 12s. Tel. 020 8365 2121 for further details or check the park website.

WALKS

The Parkland Walk (p83) starts near the Grove end of the Park, below the Palm Court entrance. It runs along an old railway line and passes through Highgate Wood, over disused bridges, and along the lines of rooftops on its way to Finsbury Park. For further details contact 020 8348 6005.

The number of guided park walks is due to be expanded. Contact Matt Baker for further details, tel. 020 8365 2121.

Battersea Park

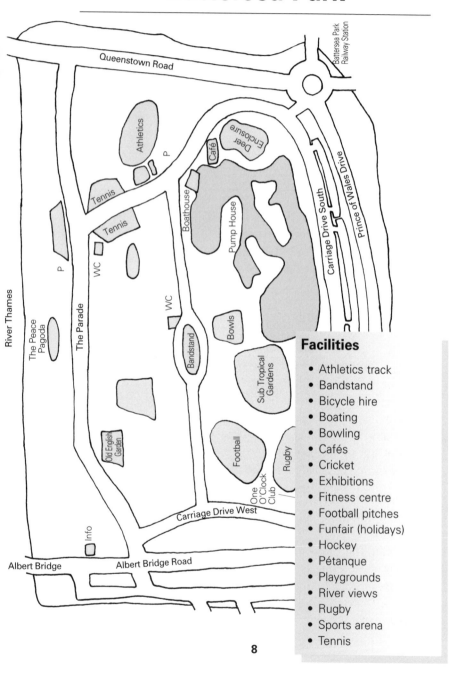

Battersea Park Railway Station

Queenstown Road

Athletics

Deer Enclosure

Café

P

Tennis

Tennis

Boathouse

Pump House

Carriage Drive South

Prince of Wales Drive

WC

WC

River Thames

The Peace Pagoda

P

The Parade

Bandstand

Bowls

Sub Tropical Gardens

Old English Garden

Football

Rugby

One O'Clock Club

Carriage Drive West

Info

Albert Bridge

Albert Bridge Road

Facilities

- Athletics track
- Bandstand
- Bicycle hire
- Boating
- Bowling
- Cafés
- Cricket
- Exhibitions
- Fitness centre
- Football pitches
- Funfair (holidays)
- Hockey
- Pétanque
- Playgrounds
- River views
- Rugby
- Sports arena
- Tennis

8

VISITOR INFORMATION

Albert Bridge Road/Queenstown Road, SW8

Tel. 020 8871 7530, website: www.batterseapark.org

Tube and train: Sloane Square is a 20-minute walk away (or catch the 137 bus), Battersea Park Station (from Clapham Junction or Victoria) and Queenstown Road Station are just five minutes' walk away.

Bus: 19, 39, 44, 45, 49 ,137, 170, 319, 345

Car: There is metered car parking within the park for 1,000 cars, by the Albert Bridge Road, Prince of Wales Drive, Queens Circus or Queenstown Road. This costs £1/hour every day from 9.00–17.00.

Battersea Park stretches along the south side of the River Thames between the Albert and Chelsea Bridges. The park's 83 acres were opened to the public by Queen Victoria in 1858 and it was soon renowned for its colourful sub-tropical gardens, riverside walks, bandstand concerts and fashionable cycling parades. During both World Wars anti-aircraft guns and shelters were stationed in the park and vegetable allotments were grown as part of Britain's 'Dig for Victory' campaign. For the Festival of Britain in 1951, the park was developed as a fun alternative to the cultural exhibitions on the South Bank. The Festival Gardens and Fountains can still be seen today. In 1985 a remarkable 33.5m Japanese Peace Pagoda was built overlooking the Thames. The park's riverbank walk still provides some of London's best views.

The park is packed with facilities. There is a 16-acre lake with rowing boats for hire and a lakeside Italian café. There are sculptures by Henry Moore, Eric Kennington and Barbara Hepworth. The fabulous Millennium Arena has an eight-lane athletics track, a fitness centre, sauna and aerobics room. There are classes in kickboxing, tai chi, yoga, body sculpt, Pilates and aerobics. There are also tennis courts, a bowling green, football, hockey, softball, rugby, cricket pitches and a pétanque pitch.

During bank holidays there is often a funfair or circus. All types of bicycles are available for hire throughout the year.

HIGHLIGHTS

- Japanese Peace Pagoda over looking the Thames
- Millennium Arena with athletics track and fitness centre
- Rare Cheviot goats with frost-proof ears
- The Riverside Walk: some of London's finest views
- Night-time view of the Albert Bridge
- Avenue of plane trees on West Carriage Drive
- Huge children's adventure playground

ANIMALS

The Victorian Deer Enclosure (near the Italian café and corner of Prince of Wales Drive and Queenstown Road) has a range of animals including rare Cheviot goats and several peacocks. There are only 200 Cheviot goats left in the world, 20 of which are in the park. The Cheviot was mentioned in the Doomsday Book. They are short sturdy animals with small frost-proof ears. The goats' hair was used for wigs in the 18th century and its skin, meat and milk were also made use of.

ART

The Pump House Gallery (next to the lake), tel. 020 7350 0523, is open Wednesday, Thursday and Sunday, 11.00–17.00 and Friday and Saturday, 11.00–16.00. The Victoria Pump House (1861) was built originally to house the lake's water pump, but is now a grade II listed building with free art exhibitions throughout the year. There is a shop selling cards, books, magazines and crafts. There is a good view of the lake from the second floor (and a toilet on the third floor).

BICYCLING

London Recumbents (near the Millennium Arena and Thrive Horticultural Centre), tel. 020 7498 6543, website www.londonrecumbents.com, email recumbents@aol.com, is open every day in school holidays and weekends, 10.00–16.30, variable weekdays. Bicycles for hire cost from £5/hour. Identification is required. The shop has a range of bicycles for all ages including speciality 'recumbent' bicycles and bicycles for people with special needs.

The park has been a popular place to bicycle since the 18th century.

BIRDS

The park is alive with the sound of bird song. An extensive variety of birds live in the park including black swans, cormorants, gulls, jays, magpies, mallards, owls, robins and sparrows.

BOATING

Boat hire and rowing lessons (near the café and deer enclosure): Blue Bird Boats, tel. 020 7262 1330 (central number), open March to October, 10.00–17.00.

The 6.5 hectare boating lake has rowing boats and pedal boats for hire from £5/hour. When the attendants are not too busy they will give free rowing lessons. A £5 deposit is required. There is a lakeside Italian café for a quick energy boost before and after rowing.

BOWLING

The bowling green (south of the bandstand near the lake) is the original Victorian bowling green where the Battersea Park Bowling Club plays. Non-members are also welcome.

CAFÉ

The Gondola Italian Café

(Near the Millennium Arena and Boating Lake) tel. 020 7978 1655, open every day 09.00–16.00.

This Italian café has outdoor seating by the lake opposite the Victorian Cascade. A good range of food is available including cappuccino (£1.60), tea (£1), toasted sandwiches (£2), cakes (£2.50), beer (£2.50), crisps (50p), lasagne (£4.90) and salads (£3.90).

CHILDREN AND PARENTS

Traditional and adventure playground with a safety surface, tel. 020 8871 7539, open 11.00–18.00 Monday to Sunday during holidays, 15.30–17.00 Tuesday to Friday and 11.00–18.00 Saturday and Sunday during term time.

The playgrounds are free but the Bouncy Castle costs 50p for ten minutes. There are both under and over fives' sessions. The tuck shop has drinks, crisps and ice-pops that cost 10p each.

One O'Clock Centre (near the corner of Albert Bridge Road and Prince of Wales Drive), tel. 020 8871 7541, open Monday to Friday 13.00–16.00.

This free informal meeting point is for the under fives to play and for their parents to meet. A range of toys and creative games are available. There are always two members of staff to facilitate play. Light refreshments are served.

FOOTBALL

There are two all-weather pitches at Battersea Park, and a number of teams using them for matches. The matches usually take place on Sundays with kick-off at 14.00. Contact the pitch booking number, 020 8871 7535 for further information about the matches or booking the pitch.

FRIENDS

The Friends of Battersea Park have monthly meetings, play an active role in shaping developments in the park and publish a quarterly magazine. Membership costs £7.50 per year. Contact Elizabeth Hood, tel. 020 7622 7658.

GARDENS

The Old English Garden (near the Parks Office and the Albert Bridge) was planted and constructed in 1912. Its design is typical of this period with geometrical patterns, dwarf box hedges, a goldfish pond and a sundial. There is a short woodland walk around the garden.

The Sub Tropical Gardens (on the west side of the lake, near the playgrounds) were planted in 1863 and were designed to be a microclimate of tropical plants including banana plants, palm trees and ferns. The garden was designed to challenge Kew, and was one of Victorian London's most famous sights. Although many of the original plants are gone it is still an interesting place.

HOCKEY

There are several local hockey teams using the Astroturf pitches in Battersea Park, all of which welcome new members. Matches take place on Saturdays from mid September until the end of March and there is evening training in the park from August. The park also hosts an annual Battersea Hockey Festival, held over a spring weekend (usually May). This festival is now in its ninth year and brings together teams from all around the world for matches, fun and socialising. There is a pitch-side marquee, festival parties in the evening, and all weekend bars. For further information about the hockey festival contact the London Wayfarers or Wanderers clubs (see below). For further information about booking an all-weather pitch contact 020 8871 7535 (pitch booking at Battersea Park).

Wanderers Hockey Club: www.wanderershockeyclub.co.uk

London Wayfarers Hockey Club: www.londonwayfarers.com

Spencer Hockey Club: www.spencerclub.org/hockey/

HORTICULTURE

'Thrive' is a national charity that provides horticultural work for people with mental health problems and other disabilities. The scheme has an excellent plant shop with a range of good value plants for sale. Volunteers are always needed.

The shop is open Monday to Friday 09.00–17.00, tel. 020 7720 2212, website: www.thrive.org.uk.

INFORMATION

Parks Office (near the Albert Bridge entrance), tel. 020 8871 7530, is open Monday to Friday 09.00–17.00.

The Parks Office has a range of free leaflets about the park including maps. They also have information on events such as the Teddy Bears' Picnics, funfairs, circuses, concerts and trade shows.

MUSIC

During the summer the Gondola Italian Café has free lakeside concerts on Tuesdays and Friday evenings from 19.00. The concerts include jazz, blues, rock, salsa and soul.

PEACE PAGODA

This remarkable 33.5m pagoda is dedicated to universal peace. The monks and nuns of the Japanese Buddhist Order of Nipponzan Myohoji built the pagoda in 1985 for the people of London. They used ancient Indian and Japanese designs and have built 70 other peace pagodas around the world including one in Milton Keynes. In Milton Keynes, however, they only obtained planning permission for one storey! The lower terrace walls are made of Portland stone from Dorset and the octagonal roofs are made from Canadian Douglas fir trees decorated with handmade Japanese tiles. There are four gilded statues of Buddha: facing south his birth in the Himalayas, facing east his enlightenment, facing north his first public sermon and facing west his death. One of the monks who maintains the pagoda (and cleans and polishes it every day) lives in the small house nearby and has information about Buddhism, tel. 020 7228 9620.

SCULPTURE

Barbara Hepworth's 'Single Form' is a memorial to Dag Hammerskjold near the south side of the lake. Henry Moore's 'Three Standing Figures' has been in the park since 1948 near the bandstand. Eric Kennington's '24th Division' is a three-figure war memorial to those lost in World War I. It was erected in 1922. Robert Graves, the poet, was the model for the soldier on the right, with a broken nose.

SPORT

The Millennium Arena (near Queenstown Road), tel. 020 8871 7537 is open weekdays 07.00–22.00 and weekends 07.30–19.30.

This new arena has an eight-lane athletics track, flood-lit tennis courts, an all-weather sports pitch, a fully equipped fitness centre, an aerobics studio, vending machines with a seating area and a clubroom. The athletics track costs £2 or £1.30 for under-16s or over-60s. Season tickets cost £78 or £39 for concessions. The air-conditioned fitness centre on the first floor has all the latest machines with televisions to keep you amused. There is also a sauna and clean changing rooms with lockers. Membership costs from £32 per month or £25 for off peak use. All members must attend an induction session costing £8. Non-members can use the facilities but have fewer benefits. Fitness classes cost £4.40 and are half price to members. The sauna costs £5.40 for non-members and is free for members. The aerobics studio has a range of classes including body sculpture, kick boxing, Pilates, tai chi and yoga. Next to the entrance of the Millennium Arena is a free eight station 'Trim Trail' for circuit training.

TENNIS

There are 19 flood-lit tennis courts attached to the Millennium Arena including three with Astroturf and 16 all-weather courts. There is a range of coaching sessions throughout the year, to suit all ages and abilities. Prices for courts start at £4 per hour. An annual registration card for telephone pre-bookings costs £14.25. Tel. 020 8871 7542. Open Monday to Friday 08.00–22.00 and weekends 08.00–20.00.

TREES

There are over 3,000 trees in the park from 50 different species. The black Italian poplar is the tallest tree on the west side of the lake at 37m high. There is also a huge North American black walnut at the north end of the Albert Bridge car park which is over 33m high. The most common tree in the park is the London plane.

WALKS

The Riverside Walk runs along the south side of the River Thames for the whole length of the park and has views over to neighbouring Chelsea. The walk is about a mile long and accessible to everyone. It passes the Peace Pagoda that was given to all Londoners by a Japanese Buddhist Order in 1985 (see p14). An excellent map of the park is available from the Parks Office near the Albert Bridge entrance.

Bishop's Park

Bishop's Avenue/Putney Bridge, SW6

Parks Development Officer: tel. 020 8753 4125

Tube: Putney Bridge

Bus: 14, 74, 220, 414, 430

Car: pay parking is available in Bishop's Avenue

Bishop's Park was named after the bishops who lived in the neighbouring Fulham Palace for more than 1000 years. The park was opened to the public in 1893 and includes a beautiful river walk shaded by enormous London plane trees. Fulham Palace itself has a 17th century botanical garden where the first magnolia in Europe was grown as well as early tulips, walnut, maple and cork oak tress. In the 17th century rare seeds were bought back from the Americas, India and the other colonies. The park has many facilities including an under fives' playground, café, garden centre, tennis courts, roller skating rink, sand pit, paddling pool and smaller gardens.

HIGHLIGHTS

- Riverside Walk under London plane trees
- Fulham Palace Gardens, one of London's prettiest
- Playgrounds

Facilities

- Basketball
- Café
- Garden centre
- Gardens
- Paddling pool
- Playground
- Playgroup
- Sandpit
- Roller skating
- Tennis

ALLOTMENTS

The Warren has been used by local residents for allotments since 1916.

Tel. 020 7731 6055 (Saturday and Sunday mornings).

CAFÉ

Jackie's Cottage Café
Open daily 10.00–16.00.

This is a small café serving many processed foods at low prices. The chips are made to order but the café has a cold rundown feeling. Bacon rolls £1.20, English breakfast £3.70, tea 60p, coffee 70p, chips £1 and hot dogs £2.

CHURCH

All Saints Church, Fulham: www.allsaints-fulham.org.uk, tel. 020 7736 3264.

This pretty church near Putney Bridge marks the beginning of the old mile-long moat that protected Fulham Palace from invasions. Its medieval tower is made from Kentish ragstone, and the church displays its long association with the bishops of London.

FOOTBALL

There is a football pitch parallel with the river past the old Ornamental Pond.

GARDEN CENTRE

The Fulham Palace Garden Centre is open Monday to Thursday 09.30–17.30, Friday and Saturday 09.30–18.00 and Sundays 10.00–17.00, tel. 020 7736 2640, website www.fulhamgardencentre.com. This garden centre has everything needed for gardens or window boxes. There are also gifts and cards. The profits go to the charity Inner City Youth.

FULHAM PALACE

Fulham Palace was home to the Bishops of London from 704 to 1973. The Tudor red brick courtyard and gardens are open to the public all year round. Tours of the inside of the palace and the gardens run on the second and fourth Sundays of each month at 14.00, cost £3, and meet in the Tudor Courtyard (phone the museum for details). The palace's botanical gardens had some of the rarest plants in the Europe during the 18th century. The gardens remain some of London's prettiest and wildest. Huge wisteria wind around the Victorian knot garden and exotic trees such as the Indian bean tree shelter the collapsing glasshouses and fruit trees. Fulham Palace, Bishop's Avenue off Fulham Palace Road, tel. 020 7736 3233 (museum) or 020 8753 4930 (palace bookings).

ORNAMENTAL POND

The Ornamental Pond was dug between 1893 and 1903 and originally contained swans that were donated by the King. An artificial beach was created by bringing vast quantities of sand from Kent to create the famous 'beach in Fulham'. The area has distinctive ornamental terracotta balustrades decorated with the coat of arms and monogram of Fulham Council. Unfortunately, owing to ever tightening health and safety regulations, the pond was drained several years ago. There are no plans to refill it.

PLAYGROUND AND PADDLING POOL

There are two playgrounds. The smallest is for under-fives and the larger one is for all age groups. There is a sand pit with a fantastic stone crocodile in the middle and an enormous neighbouring paddling pool. The Bishop's Park Parent and Toddler Group meets Monday to Friday from 10.00–12.00 in the building next to the playground, cost £2 per family. They aim to provide all children with the opportunity to learn through play. Tea and coffee is provided and all children get juice and a biscuit after song time at 11.30. The adventure playground has a range of games for older children.

SKATING

Opposite the café, there is a large flat area for roller-blading, skate boarding and basket ball practice.

TENNIS

There are 15 hard tennis courts but no floodlights. To book a court membership is required at a cost of £10/year. Courts cost £5.20/hour and at least five hours must be bought at once. Memberships forms are available from Sports Bookings, Bishop's Park Tennis Pavilion, Bishop's Avenue, London SW6 6DX, tel. 020 7736 1735 after 12.00 Monday to Friday. It is possible to play without booking if a court is free. The office has a list of licensed tennis coaches.

WALKS

The Bishop's Park Moat Trail is an easy 45-minute walk tracing the old mile-long moat around Fulham Palace. A map marks the way on a board near the All Saints Church.

Blackheath

VISITOR INFORMATION

Blackheath, SE3

Information: Greenwich Parks and Open Spaces, Shooters Hill Depot, tel. 020 8856 2232.

Bus: 54, 108, 380

Train: Blackheath (overground from Charing Cross or London Bridge)

Car: pay and display, limited availability

Blackheath is a large, flat expanse of grassland on a plateau above Greenwich Park (see p94). The Roman Road from Dover once crossed the heath. Its height and strategic position lent it its name the 'gateway to London'. This was where Henry V was welcomed home on his return from Agincourt in 1415, and where Wat Tyler led his peasant revolt in 1381. Some say the heath is named after the dark colour of the soil, others for its use as a burial ground during the Black Death. The open recreational grounds are used for many sports including football, rugby, cricket, lacrosse and gaelic football (see below). The heath is surrounded by attractive old houses and several pubs and is crisscrossed with roads. The All Saints Church spire is visible from the far end of Blackheath Avenue in Greenwich Park.

HIGHLIGHTS

- Views of London
- Fine Georgian architecture, including the Paragon
- Kite flying

Facilities

- Cricket
- Football
- Gaelic football
- Lacrosse
- Rugby
- Tennis

SPORTS: RUGBY, CRICKET AND TENNIS

The Blackheath Rugby Football Club is the oldest open rugby club in the world, formed by the Old Boys of Blackheath Proprietary School in 1858. They have men's, women's, juniors and mini sections and new members of all standards are welcome. The club is based at the Rectory Field, Charlton Road, Blackheath (just across the road from Greenwich Park), tel. 020 8293 0853, website www.blackheathrugby.co.uk.

The Blackheath Cricket Club is also based at the Rectory Field (see above). They run six Saturday teams and two Sunday teams and have an active junior section. For further information contact the club on tel. 020 8858 1578 or visit the website www.blackheathcc.com.

The Blackheath Lawn Tennis Club is also based at the Rectory Field, Charlton Road. They have four grass courts and seven hard courts, several of which are flood-lit.

Brockwell Park

VISITOR INFORMATION

Norwood Road, SE24

Bus: 37

Train: Herne Hill (from Blackfriars, King's Cross, Victoria)

Tube: Brixton (20 minute walk)

Car: pay and display only

The 128-acre Brockwell Park is Lambeth's largest open space. It is a hilly park with views to the centre of London and the East End. Its lack of trees leaves it looking rather bleak in winter but it really comes into its own in the spring. The famous Brixton Lido was voted in the top 50 lidos around the world in 2000. There is a beautiful walled English garden with yew hedging, an Italian hilltop café, a 19th century clock tower, a BMX track, tennis courts, yoga classes, a bowling green and football pitches.

HIGHLIGHTS

- Café
- Lido
- Shakespearian Garden

CAFÉ

The Park Café
The café is housed in Brockwell Hall, a 19th century villa built for the glass

Facilities

- Café
- BMX track
- Bowling green
- Football pitches
- Gardens
- Lido
- One O'Clock Club
- Paddling pool
- Tennis courts

merchant John Blades by D.R. Roper. It is situated on the crest of the hill and commands views across the park and over London. The high ceilings and lack of radiators can leave it feeling rather chilly in the winter. For the warmer weather there is an outdoor terrace. Cappuccino £1.20, tea 50p, cake £1.20, cooked breakfast £3.00, other hot meals, ciabatta sandwiches and 'specials'.

Open 09.00–park closing every day.

LIDO

The Brixton Lido was opened in 1937 and has remained popular ever since. It is large, square, distinctly 1930s with a beach atmosphere. There are even summertime barbeques. At the time of writing the lido had changed ownership to a non-profit community based company called Fusion, with the aim of restoring the buildings, developing a new health and fitness centre and renovating the café.

Open Monday to Friday 06.45–10.00 and 12.00–19.00, weekends May to September 12.00–18.00, tel. 020 7274 3088 www.thelido.co.uk.

ONE O'CLOCK CLUB

This is one of the friendliest and cosiest One O'Clock Clubs in London. There is tea, coffee and snacks served from a small bar, story telling, games and gossip. It is near the children's playground, by Arlingford Road. Open 13.00–16.00 weekdays (closed one day of the week, phone for details). Admission is free. Tel. 020 8671 4883.

SHAKESPEARIAN GARDEN

The walled Shakespearian Garden is one of the park's highlights, an unexpected treat hidden within wisteria-covered walls. There are clipped yew hedges among the geometric flower bedding, roses, tulips, irises, poppies and lilies, secluded benches, and a circular wooden pergola. This was the first

London park garden to be laid out in this way, displaying the plants mentioned in Shakespeare's plays. J.J. Sexby designed the garden in 1892. The Ada Salter Garden in Southwark Park (p233) (1936) was planted in a similar style, which became known as a 'Sexby Garden'.

TENNIS

There are six tennis courts. Booking is in person at the hut within the bowling green club (next to the courts). Courts cost £4 per hour or £2 for under-16 year olds. Coaching is available at competitive rates, £45 for six sessions, contact Derek Isaac tel. 07967 357760, email derek-isaac@hotmail.com or Quang Ngo tel. 07944 566778.

WHIPPERSNAPPERS

There is a series of 'Whippersnappers' music workshops run at the lido for babies, toddlers and 3–5 year olds, including some drop-in classes. Prices start at £5.50 per class (£3.75 concessions). Contact 020 7738 6633 or the lido (020 7274 3088) for further information.

YOGA

The lido is home to a full programme of yoga and meditation classes, cost £7 (£5 concessions). Phone the lido on 020 7274 3088 for more details.

Brompton Cemetery

VISITOR INFORMATION

South Lodge, Fulham Road, SW10

Tel. 020 7351 1689 (Friends of Brompton Cemetery)

Bus: 14, 31, 74, 190, 211, C1, C3

Tube: West Brompton and Earls Court

Train: West Brompton

This mystical bramble-filled cemetery is a peaceful haven linking the Fulham and the Old Brompton Roads. The 39 acres are actively managed for nature conservation and are crowded with hundreds of graves. It was consecrated in 1840 and was the first state run cemetery. Benjamin Baud won the competition to design and built the pretty domed chapel and the surrounding catacombs. The Chapel with its domed roof is closed to the public; the rangers will allow people to look inside but its outside is far prettier.

FAMOUS GRAVES

There are many famous people buried in the Cemetery, including Benjamin Golding (1863) who founded the Charing Cross Hospital, Francis Fowke (1865) who designed the Albert Hall and Emmeline Pankhurst, the Suffragette who died under the King's horse in 1928.

FRIENDS OF THE CEMETERY

The Friends of the Cemetery are active in promoting and preserving the cemetery. They have an annual open day and AGM. Membership costs £5/year and includes three newsletters. The Friends office sells leaflets and books, including a guidebook to the cemetery (£5), postcards (50p) and an excellent tree-walk leaflet (50p). There is a guided walk of the cemetery on the second and fourth Sunday of each month at 2pm. It costs £3/person and leaves from the South Lodge, Fulham Road. Tel. 020 7351 1689.

TREES

There are over 50 species of rare and beautiful trees in the Cemetery. A free leaflet is available from the Friends office that includes interesting tree facts, for example, the Scots pine near the Old Brompton Road entrance is one of the species of trees used for telegraph poles. It was also the first tree to re-colonise Britain after the last ice age. The silver birch is used by witches to make the bushy part of their broomsticks. The false acacia is so spikey that it was reputedly used to make the crown for Christ to wear on the cross. The weeping silver lime was probably planted in 1862 to commemorate Queen Victoria's Silver Jubilee. Its flowers are so sugary that bumble bees cannot digest their nectar and often die in consequence. The common ash was used by Cupid to make his arrows, and sycamores to make violins.

Burgess Park

VISITOR INFORMATION

Walworth Road/Old Kent Road, SE5

Tube: Elephant and Castle

Bus: 12, 21, 35, 40, 42, 45, 53, 63, 68, 171, 172, 176, 343, 468

Car: parking is available in Albany Road

After World War II the Greater London Council proposed a new 'green lung' for London. Whole streets were knocked down and the Grand Surrey Canal was filled in to make the 135 acres of Burgess Park. It is the largest park in Europe to be formed from a previously built up area and has more than 4,000 newly planted trees. Some of the older terraces still remain. The almshouses of 1821 were originally a women's asylum but are now surrounded by the pretty Chumleigh Multicultural Gardens and café. At the moment the park is in need of the major development plan that has just started. Six flood-lit tennis courts have been built and a new cricket pavilion, sports pitches and a toddlers' playground are planned: a breath of fresh air in a rather bleak area of London.

HIGHLIGHTS

- Art classes
- Adventure playground
- Chumleigh Multicultural Gardens

Facilities

- Art classes
- Café
- Adventure playground
- Football and basketball
- Gardens
- Go-karting

ADVENTURE PLAYGROUND

There is a fantastic carved wooden giraffe's head over the main entrance of this adventure playground which is a welcome contrast to the surrounding architecture. The playground is popular and well equipped. Adventure Playground, 285 Albany Road, tel. 020 7277 1371. Open in term time Tuesday to Friday 15.30–19.30, Saturdays 11.30–17.00 and during holidays Monday to Friday 10.30–18.00.

ART

Art in the Park is a non-profit-making scheme which is devoted to making art for city parks and gardens. They run a variety of activities including art, dance, music, tree and flower planting, training days and much more. They are based at Chumleigh Gardens, Chumleigh Street, Burgess Park, website www.artinthepark.co.uk, tel. 020 7277 4297.

BUTTERFLIES

The emblem of the park, the Camberwell Beauty butterfly, was first recorded in Britain in Burgess Park. It arrived here on the barges transporting imported wood on the Grand Canal. The gates at the Old Kent Road entrance bear this butterfly emblem.

CAFÉ

Chumleigh Gardens Café

There is a small café in Chumleigh Gardens serving good value food. The cakes are a little soggy. Cappuccino £1, tea 40p, English breakfast £4, jacket potato and beans £1.50 and egg on toast £1. Open Monday to Friday 08.30–18.00 and weekends 10.00–18.00. Tel. 020 7525 1070.

CHUMLEIGH GARDENS

Chumleigh Gardens is a free manicured green oasis in a rather bleak area of the park. It is divided into five sections: African/Caribbean, English Cottage, Islamic, Mediterranean and Oriental. There is also a café (see above). The tropical African/Caribbean Garden has red hot poker plants, arum lilies, cacti and succulents. The English Cottage Garden is full of lavender, rosemary, brightly planted flower-beds and neatly clipped lawns. The Islamic Garden has a bright blue mosaic tiled pond with a *butia capitata* (jelly palm) in the middle. The Mediterranean Garden has drought resistant plants many of which are aromatic. The stone pine produces the pine-nuts used in pesto sauce. There is a small olive tree that was grown from a cutting from the Chelsea Physic Garden. The Oriental Garden uses rocks to represent mountains and has a small pond and even a rice paper plant.

FARMERS' MARKET

There is a weekly farmers' market in Peckham Town Square on Sundays (09.30–13.30) which includes several French traders and many local specialities. Tel. 020 7704 9659, website www.farmersmarkets.net.

FISHING

The large fishing pond near the Old Kent Road entrance is available for fishing throughout the year. Permits cost £52/year or £26 for children. A day pass costs £2.60.

Application forms are obtainable from the Park Rangers, Chumleigh Gardens, tel. 020 7525 1066.

GO-KARTING

The popular go-karting track is next to the adventure playground. It is available for pre-booked groups only and is ideal for 8–16 year olds, as the track is quite small. For further information contact the track, tel. 020 7525 1101, 285 Albany Road.

INFORMATION

The Park Rangers in the Chumleigh Gardens have a few free leaflets. The office is open Monday to Friday 08.00–16.30.

KILN

Next to the old filled-in Grand Canal is a relic of the past, a 19th century kiln. It was used until the 1960s to turn limestone into quicklime for use in mortar for building works. The limestone would be unloaded from barges on the Canal.

SPORTS

At the time of writing the park was involved a major redevelopment. There are currently six flood-lit tennis courts. A new cricket pavilion and sports pitches including football, five-a-side and basketball are still under development.

Bushy Park

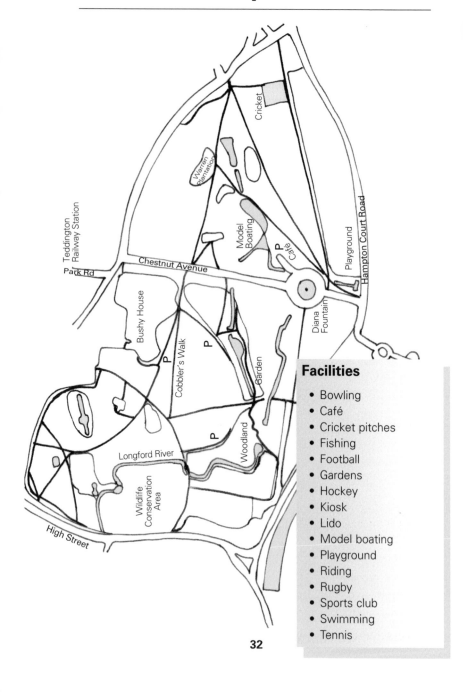

Facilities

- Bowling
- Café
- Cricket pitches
- Fishing
- Football
- Gardens
- Hockey
- Kiosk
- Lido
- Model boating
- Playground
- Riding
- Rugby
- Sports club
- Swimming
- Tennis

VISITOR INFORMATION

Hampton Court Road, Hampton, Middlesex, TW12

*Tel. 020 8979 1586. Website: www.royalparks.org.uk
email: sgedwards@royalparks.gsi.gov.uk*

*Train: every hour from Waterloo to Teddington, Hampton Wick and
Hampton Court*

Bus: 33, 111, 216, 411, 416, 461, 465, 481, 513, 726

*Car: Car parks are located near the Model Boating Pond, on Cobbler's
Walk, near the Woodland Garden and off Hampton Court Road*

Bushy Park near Hampton Court Palace, covering 1,099 acres, is famous for Christopher Wren's mile long Chestnut Avenue, the Diana Fountain, Deer Park, ponds and the 60 hectare 1950s Woodland Gardens. The park was called Bushy due to the fact that it had a large number of hawthorn bushes. Henry VIII allowed Cardinal Wolsey to enclose the park's land from farmland into three separate parks between 1500 and 1537. King Charles I in 1639 decided to create a 12-mile artificial waterway to bring fresh water to Bushy Park and Hampton Court Palace because they were always short of water. The scheme cost £4,000 and took nine months to build.

The park also offers free summer jazz concerts and a playground. It is flat and has a rural feel with a network of paths that are ideal for walking or cycling. The Chestnut Mile is beautiful, leading down to the Diana Fountain with its large round pond. Unfortunately, it is spoilt by the traffic.

HIGHLIGHTS

- Deer
- Rhododendrons and azaleas in May in the Woodland Gardens
- Feeding the birds on Duck Bridge

BEETLES

The Wildlife for All Team leads regular free walks for beetle enthusiasts and other wildlife lovers. Tel. 020 7935 7430.

BOWLING

The park's bowling green is licensed to the NPL Sports Club (see below) and is available for use in the summer.

BIRDS

All three types of woodpecker – green and the great and lesser spotted – can be seen in the Woodland Gardens. Crested grebes, coots, ducks and moorhens can be fed on Duck Bridge in the Woodland Gardens. Herons, kingfishers and snipes can also be seen. Mary's Glade (named after a park supervisor's daughter) is a nesting site for sparrow hawks, blue, coal and great tits, and tawny owls.

CAFÉ

There is a small refreshment kiosk in the car park between the Diana Fountain and the Model Boating Pond.

CHILDREN

There is a newly renovated playground near the Diana Fountain. It has a good variety of rides for children from toddlers to 12 years of age.

COBBLERS WAY

The Second Earl of Halifax was forced by a local cobbler in 1752 to re-open a right of way across the park which had been closed, resulting in a drop in passing business to the cobbler's shop. The Cobblers Way has remained in existence to the present day, running 1.75 miles across the park.

CRICKET

There are four main cricket clubs using the park. All of the clubs welcome new membership and have their own pavilion.

Hampton Wick Royal Cricket Club (1855), Park Road/Sandy Lane, website www.hwrcc.co.uk, email thehwrcc@ntlworld.com, tel. 020 8977 2378. This club has three Saturday teams in the Middlesex County League and social cricket on Sundays. They have nets practice on Tuesdays at 18.00.

Teddington Cricket Club (1891). Middlesex League Champions in 2002. This is a very active club with teams at all levels and ages, playing hundreds of matches throughout the summer. It has a smart clubhouse with a large window box on its roof. Contact Phil Eastland on 020 7957 3956, 020 8977 4437 or visit the website http://teddington.play-cricket.com, email phil.eastland@davyprotech.com.

Teddington Town Cricket Club (1870s). This club is a relaxed social club where all are welcome. The clubhouse has a cosy bar and regular events. Tel. 020 8997 4989 or 07963 614509, website www.ttcc.org.uk.

NPL Sports Club Cricket: see Sports Club below.

DEER

There are 125 red deer (*cervus elaphus*) and 200 fallow deer (*dama dama*). The red deer is the largest indigenous land mammal in Britain. Its name comes from the colour of its coat, a dappled reddish-brown, which is perfect for camouflaging the vulnerable young calves. The smaller fallow deer is the only type of deer to have a range of colours from black to brown with white spots to completely white. Both types of deer have antlers that drop out in March/April and re-grow in time for September/November when they are needed for fighting. The new antlers are covered in a soft velvet-like covering, which dries out, becoming itchy when the antlers are fully grown.

DIANA FOUNTAIN

The statue in the centre of this large circular pond is actually not Diana but Arethusa. Ovid's *Metamorphoses* explains how Arethusa was followed by a river god and later rescued by Diana who turned her into a stream. The statue is by Francesco Fanelli and was given to Henrietta Maria by her lover Charles I. It was originally in Somerset House but was moved to Hampton Court in 1656 and then into Bushy Park in 1713.

FISHING AND PONDS

Diana Fountain, Heron Pond, Leg of Mutton Pond (gets its name from its shape) and the Long Water in Home Park all have excellent fishing opportunities. Application forms for season tickets are available from the Ticket Office at Hampton Court Palace, on the website www.hrp.org.uk or by telephoning 0870 751 5175. Application forms must be accompanied by two passport photographs and a cheque for £18.

FOOTBALL

There are two football pitches where regular club meetings are held for all ages. The Hampton Cardinals FC and the NPL FC have recently merged and can be contacted via the NPL Sports Club (see below) or on 020 8287 9155. For pitch hire contact the parks office on 020 8979 1586.

FRIENDS OF BUSHY PARK

The Friends aim to support and conserve the park. A programme of walks and talks is announced in a quarterly newsletter. Membership costs £6/year. For further information contact Julie Coe, 31 Sutherland Grove, Teddington, Middlesex TW11 8RP.

GARDENS

The Woodland Gardens orginated in a woodland walk first created in 1925 from two plantations. In 1948-9 the park superintendent developed the gardens into a pretty network of paths amongst the waterways and trees.

HOCKEY

Bushy Park is home to one of the world's oldest hockey clubs, Teddington HC. The club was founded in 1871 and has had its clubhouse in the park since 1893. There are men's, ladies', mixed and junior sections. The men's team plays in the national league premier division (the only team to have done so ever since the league's formation) and has included several top international stars. The club also has fun 'recreational' hockey sides, social events and tours. They use three grass pitches in the park and astro-pitches at Teddington Sports Centre. For further information contact the Teddington HC Clubhouse, Bushy Park, Teddington, tel. 020 8977 4437, website www.teddingtonhc.com. The NPL Sports Centre uses the park's grass pitches or contact the NPL Sports Club (see below). For information about pitch hire contact the Parks Office on 020 8979 1586.

INFORMATION

Bushy Park Office, The Stockyard, Hampton Court Road, tel. 020 8979 1586. Open Monday to Friday 08.00–16.00.

PLANTATIONS

There are four plantations: Warren, Oval, Canal and the Rounds Plantations.

The Warren Plantation is so called because the rabbits that used to live in it had formed an extensive network of tunnels.

RIDING

The Park Lane Stables are located a few minutes from the park. They offer horse riding through Bushy Park for all levels and ages from Wednesday to Sunday throughout the year. The stables are BHS approved. For further information contact the stables at Park Lane, Teddington TW11 OHY, tel. 020 8977 4951.

RUGBY

The park's rugby pitch is used by the Teddington Rugby Club. This friendly club has a wide range of men's, women's, junior and mini sides and welcomes new members of all standards. The men play in the Surrey League Division 2, the ladies are part of the National Challenge 2 and the excellent mini section is one of only three mini clubs to be affiliated to NEC Harlequins.

For further information see Teddington RFC website, www.teddingtonrfc.co.uk, email chairman@teddingtonfrc.co.uk or tel. Vince Ryle (chairman) on 020 8614 6859 or 0797 409 0851 or Simon Cartmell (mini) 020 8979 8316. For information about pitch hire and prices contact the Parks Office, 020 8979 1586.

SPORTS CLUB

The NPL Sports Club (National Physical Laboratory) is an independent club located on the edge of Bushy Park near the gate at Queens Road. There are two cricket pitches, a hockey pitch, three all-weather tennis courts, four grass tennis courts (summer only), a bowling green (summer only), a football pitch (winter), volleyball, five-a-side football and archery. The clubhouse has a bar, changing rooms, snooker, pool and organises regular social events. For further information contact the Sports Pavilion, NPL, Queens Road, Teddington TW11, tel. 020 8943 6314, website www.nplsc.co.uk, email sportsclub@npl.co.uk.

SWIMMING

The Hampton Heated Open Air Pool is open every day of the year and has a café, gym and paddling pool. It was built in 1922 and is 36.5m long and 14.5m wide. The *Independent* quoted this pool in the top ten in Britain. The pool is on the western boundary of the park. Hampton Heated Open Air Pool, High Street, Hampton, Middlesex TW12, tel. 020 8255 1116, website www.hamptonpool.co.uk. Open Monday, Wednesday and Fridays 06.00–09.00 and 16.00–20.30, weekends 08.00–14.00, Tuesday and Thursdays 06.00–09.00 and 12.00–14.00. The cost for swimming is £5 for adults, £3 for children, £260/six months. The gym costs £25/month, £200/year and there is a free sauna. A joint ticket for swimming and the gym costs £360/year.

TENNIS

There are several 'turn up and play' courts on the King's Field. Contact the sports development team on 020 8831 6132. The NPL Sports Centre (see above) has three all-weather and six grass courts. The NPL Tennis Club offers a range of training, teams, events and coaching. Contact NPL Tennis Club, Queens Road, Teddington, www.nplsc.org.uk, tel. Robert Clayton 020 8287 2979.

TREES

A free tree leaflet is available from the information desk. There are also guided tree walks.

WILDLIFE CONSERVATION AND VOLUNTEERING

There is a range of activities for all interests including educational days, guided walks, practical conservation and companion cycling. Contact the Education and Community Officer, tel. 020 8979 1586.

Chiswick Park

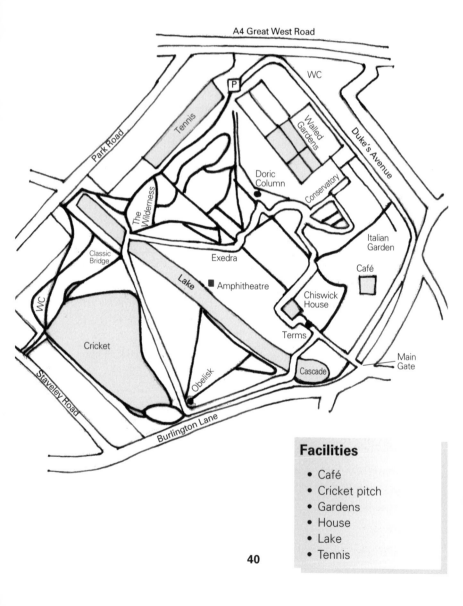

Facilities

- Café
- Cricket pitch
- Gardens
- House
- Lake
- Tennis

40

VISITOR INFORMATION

Burlington Lane, W4

Tel. 020 8995 0508, website www.english-heritage.org.uk

Tube: Turnham Green then E3 bus to Edensor

Train: Chiswick Station (overland from Waterloo via Clapham junction)

Car: there is a free car park off the Great West Road

Park open: 08.30–dusk. Free admission to the park, charge for the house.

House open: April–September 10.00–18.00 daily, October 10.00–17.00, November, December and March pre-booked appointments: £3.50 including audio guide, £3 concessions, £2 for 5–16 year olds.

Chiswick House and Park is London's life-affirming slice of Renaissance Italy. It was built by the Palladian-obsessed third Earl of Burlington in the 18th century. He had recently completed a Grand Tour of Italy and become passionate about classical architecture: in particular that of the famous Italian architect Andrea Palladio and Englishman Inigo Jones. Burlington's own villa was modelled on Palladio's 16th century Villa Rotonda at Vicenza and housed his collection of Italian antiques and art. The gardens, designed by his friend William Kent, were the first in England to break with the formal Dutch tradition. The park boasts one of the best (and most eccentric) cafés in London, tennis courts, a cricket pitch, statues, an obelisk, a large conservatory, a lake and even a temple. Vicenza really is just a tube ride away.

HIGHLIGHTS

* The Burlington Café
* Doric column
* Italian Garden
* Temple

CAFÉ

Burlington Café

The park's Burlington Café is open daily in the summer from 10.00–17.00 and in the winter Thursday to Sunday from 10.00–16.00 (closed Monday–Wednesday in winter). It is one of the most eccentric and best of any London park cafés, situated close to the house, but enclosed by trees into its own secluded garden overlooking a small lawn. It is like stepping through the looking glass, out of Renaissance Italy and into the mad hatter's tea party: sunflower painted walls, salmon pink and bottle green ceilings and giant cakes served in magnified slices. On a summer Sunday expect children and wagging tails just about everywhere. The food is homemade and fabulous. Cappuccino £1.20, tea £1.00, BLT £2.50, breakfast feast £5, roast lamb £6.75, ice-cream £1.20, enormous cakes £2.50. Tel. 020 8987 9431.

CHISWICK HOUSE

Chiswick House is owned by English Heritage and has been magnificently restored. There is a very good short film of the restoration and history of the house inside. The upper floor has an austere domed great hall, or tribunal, hung with large paintings. It was here that Queen Victoria and Prince Albert were welcomed in 1842 and the Tsar of Russia was welcomed in 1844. In the same year the sixth Duke (1811–1858) had a collection of exotic animals running around the gardens, including an elephant, giraffe, elks, emus, kangaroos, an Indian bull and cow, goats and a Neapolitan pig. Not to be missed are the three velvet rooms, like walking into inkpots: red velvet, green velvet and, the cosiest of all, the blue velvet room complete with a small desk – a blue grotto for Burlington's studies.

CRICKET

The Chiswick and Latymer Cricket Club is based in the park. The pitch and clubhouse is in the southeast corner. For further details of fixtures and membership contact Steve Rushworth, tel. 07932 173833, website www.chiswickandlatymercc.co.uk.

DORIC COLUMN

The Doric Column was placed in the gardens around 1728. It was once topped by a copy of Venus de Medici.

EXEDRA

An 'exedra' is a semicircular garden screen typical of Roman villas. At Chiswick the Exedra consists of clipped yew and it forms a striking backdrop to some of the garden's sculptures. Three of the statues are said to have come from Hadrian's villa at Tivoli, Italy (these are copies; the originals are inside the house). There are also two 'terms' (one representing Socrates), two lions and several large stone urns.

GOOSE FOOT AVENUES

The Goose Foot (Patte d'Oie) Avenues consist of three straight avenues of trees and yew hedges radiating out in the shape of a foot, and each ending with a building or ornamental feature. There are two such 'foot prints' at Chiswick. The oldest has its 'heel' between the Doric Column and the Exedra and is one of the earliest surviving features of the garden. The other starts at the obelisk near the Burlington Lane gate with the paths leading to a bridge, a temple and the villa.

INIGO JONES GATEWAY

The Inigo Jones Gateway at the south-western end of the Italian Garden was designed by Jones for Beauford House in Chelsea in 1621 and brought to Chiswick House in 1738. Inigo Jones (1573–1652), like Burlington after him, became captivated by Andrea Palladio's work while travelling in Italy. He went on to become England's formative Classical style architect and worked on many royal projects including the Queen's House at Greenwich (see p101). His statue sits opposite that of Palladio, either side of the steps to the main door of the house.

ITALIAN GARDEN

The pretty 19th century Italian Garden is located in the western corner of the park. The garden is laid out in front of Samuel Ware's impressive conservatory (1813) with its large central dome and cast iron columns. The conservatory pre-dates both the conservatory at Syon (p245) and the palm house at Kew. It may have been an influence for Joseph Paxton's Crystal Palace (p62) as he worked here as a young gardener. The sixth Duke established an important collection of camellias here which are an amazing sight in spring.

LAKE

The long lake in the park was an example of William Kent's 'natural' landscape gardening, having adjusted the garden's original straight canal into this river-like form. Kent was among the first garden designers to break from the formal traditions of English gardens, followed later by Lancelot 'Capability' Brown at the southern end and an 18th century bridge designed by James Brown and Humphry Repton. The lake runs diagonally across the park with a cascade at the northern end.

OBELISKS

Just inside the Burlington Gate, at the heel of the Goose Foot Avenue, is the park's best known obelisk. The base incorporates a 2nd century AD Roman tombstone showing a carved relief of a man and woman (a copy, the original removed for safekeeping).

SPHINXES

The entrance to the house was originally flanked by two lead sphinxes, later donated to the entrance to The Green Park (p90). The house still has one of the original lead sphinxes and there are two stone sphinxes in the garden. These creatures were used to protect and guard. In classical mythology the sphinx also signified wisdom, strangling visitors at the entrance to Thebes who were unable to solve her riddle.

STATUES

Burlington's favourite architects, Andrea Palladio and Inigo Jones, can be seen on either side of the main portico. These statues are thought to have been sculpted by John Rysbrack (1729). The forecourt of the house is flanked by Romanesque 'terms' (see below), the boundary markers peering silently out of the yew hedging. In the Exedra (see above) there are a whole collection of statues including Roman figures, more terms, lions and urns. Inside the house there is Richard James Wyatt's marble of a 'nymph preparing for the bath' (circa 1841), and the original 18th century lead sphinx.

TEMPLE

The small Orange Tree Garden lies midway along the river, almost hidden behind hedging. The grass terracing falls like a green amphitheatre to a circular pond with an obelisk at the centre. A small Ionic temple sits behind, like a scene from Italy. In summer orange bushes are placed along the curves of the terrace.

TENNIS

Will to Win Tennis Centre, Chiswick House Grounds (A4 entrance), website www.tennis-uk.com, email willtowin@btopenworld.com, tel. 020 8994 1466. The tennis courts are next to the car park. The club also organises tournaments, coaching and a large programme of activities including group lessons and drills, social tennis and women's mornings. Court hire costs £4.75 per hour, or £2.75 for under 16 year olds. Various membership schemes are available which allow seven day advanced booking and include two hours of courts per day in the price. These range from £50 for the season for Silver Cards, to £220 per season for family membership and £30 per season for junior membership. The season runs from 1 May to 30 April. There are 'social tennis' sessions on Sundays from 14.00–17.00 and Wednesdays from 18.30–dusk, where partners are arranged for players. The small pavilion sells soft drinks and snacks and there is a shower costing £1 for non-cardholders.

TERMS

The main forecourt of the house is flanked by stone figures set, almost hidden, into the yew hedges, like silent watchful guards. They look like giant chess pieces about to advance towards one another. They are a Roman design, known as 'terms' after the Roman god Terminus, used to mark estate boundaries.

TREES

The park has many beautiful trees including great cedars of Lebanon (*cedrus libani*), mediterranean oaks, lime trees and a narrow-leaved ash.

NEAR THE PARK

Hogarth's House

William Hogarth's tiny cottage is next to the park and includes engravings of his most famous paintings. Tel. 020 8994 6757, open Tuesday–Friday 13.00–17.00 (13.00–16.00 in winter) and weekends 13.00–18.00. Closed in January. Free admission.

The River Thames

Via Church Street and then along the Chiswick Mall.

Clapham Common

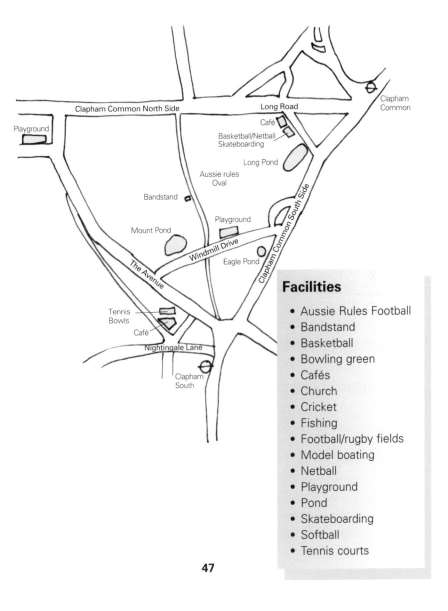

Facilities

- Aussie Rules Football
- Bandstand
- Basketball
- Bowling green
- Cafés
- Church
- Cricket
- Fishing
- Football/rugby fields
- Model boating
- Netball
- Playground
- Pond
- Skateboarding
- Softball
- Tennis courts

Long Road, Clapham, SW4

Bus: 37, 137, 155, 345, 355

Car: pay and display parking only

Tube: Clapham Common

The Common is 220 acres and although flat, is surprisingly windy, making it an excellent place for kite flying. It was a marshy area full of vermin until Christopher Baldwin arranged to have the area drained in 1722. After the vermin had been cleared it was prized for its clean air and health giving springs. It was here that the Duke of Cumberland's army camped in 1745 during the Jacobite Rebellion. The Common is a flat grassy space with a bandstand, two bowls pitches, cricket, football, softball and rugby pitches, three cafés, a model boating pond, tennis courts and two playgrounds.

HIGHLIGHTS

- Choice of three cafés
- Church activities
- Tennis and bowls

AUSTRALIAN RULES FOOTBALL

The Wandsworth Demons ARFC is based at Clapham Common. The club was one of the founders of the British Australian Rules Football League (BARFL) in 1990 and has been one of the top three teams in the league ever since. The season is played in the summer, starting in May and ending in September. Pre-season training usually starts in March on Sunday afternoons and then moves to Tuesday and Thursday evenings. Everyone is welcome, all nationalities and levels.

The club's second team is called the Clapham Demons. The oval (and changing rooms) is near the bandstand. For further details contact the club website www.wandsworthdemons.com or the BARFL website www.barfl.co.uk.

BANDSTAND

The bandstand was transferred from the Great Exhibition in Hyde Park. It is a pretty landmark in the centre of the Common next to the La Baita Italian café.

BASKETBALL AND NETBALL

There is a free but rather rundown pitch next to Cicero's Café.

BOWLING

There are two bowling greens with a small clubhouse and shelter for spectators.

Bookings must be made on the day in person from the sports manager's office next to the bowling greens. Cost £3.50/hour/person including the balls. Open every day except Christmas Day from 08.00.

CAFÉS

There are three cafés of different types to suit all moods and people.

La Baita

The Italian La Baita café by the bandstand in the centre of the common serves proper Italian cappuccinos made in the traditional Neapolitan way, with cocoa on top of the espresso before the foamed milk is added. There are live Italian football matches on the television at the weekends *con cucina casalinga* (with homemade food). Cappuccino £1.50, tea £1.20, hot toasted sandwiches £1.95, slice of cake 75p, pasta £4, Italian ice-cream £1.20, English breakfast £4 and fruit platter £1.50.

Tel. 020 7924 2429. Open every day 09.30–17.00.

The Bowling Green Café

This café by the tennis courts and bowling greens is small, cosy and child friendly with a Wendy house and other toys shaded by a large horse chestnut tree. There are magazines, newspapers and a notice board for local events. The food is cheap and homemade and service is friendly. Tea 90p, coffee 90p, homemade cakes £1.80, hotdog £1.74, flapjacks £1.20. There is also a children's menu including egg and soldiers £2. Open every day 09.30–17.00ish.

Cicero's Café

Cicero's Café is a vegetarian/vegan café near Rookery Road. It is decorated with brightly coloured lights and often has candles and incense burning. Vegetarian English breakfast £5.50, hot ciabatta sandwiches £3.75, soup of the day £2.75 and generous slices of homemade cake £2.50. Children's portions are half price and there are vegan options. Seating is both indoors and outside and there are toys and newspapers to keep everyone amused. Open every day 11.00–16.30 or 18.00 in summer. Tel. 020 7498 0770.

CHURCH

The parish church of the Holy Trinity Clapham Common is near the tube station end of the Common. It holds regular services (tel. 020 7627 0941). Website, www.holytrinityclapham.org.

There is also a range of meetings in the next-door Wilberforce Centre including yoga, a slimming group and a toddler group. Tel. 020 7720 7095. Toddler group tel. 020 7652 5756/7627 8518.

CRICKET

There are three cricket nets that can be booked in advance (only in person) from the sports manager's office next to the bowling greens.

FISHING

There are two well stocked fishing ponds, the Mount and the Eagle, managed by the Clapham Angling Preservation Society. Fishing is free but anyone over 12 must have a rod licence available from the Post Office. The Mount Pond is three acres and has carp, eels, gudgeon and roach. The Eagle Pond is only one acre with an island. It has a bigger range of fish including bream, carp, chub, gudgeon, perch, roach, rudd and tench. Check www.claphamangling.co.uk for more details.

FOUNTAIN

The 'Woman of Samaria' fountain was designed by Sir Charles Barry in 1894. It has a statue of a woman giving water to an older man with a crutch. It used to have four lions' heads from which you could drink.

INFORMATION

There is no information office but the council has a telephone line for sports and recreation on the common, tel. 020 7926 6212.

MODEL BOATING

The Long Pond on the common is home to one of the oldest model boating clubs in London, the Clapham Model Yacht Club. This friendly club is based in its own building overlooking the pond. There are races every two weeks during the season (on the first and third Sunday of the month from March to October/ November depending on conditions), and competitions including trophies. One metre yachts are raced on the first Sunday of the month and six metre yachts on the third. Membership is open to everyone and costs £20 per year. For further information either turn up at the pond or telephone the club secretary, Jack Sanday, on 020 8646 1806, website www.myc.org.uk.

PLAYGROUNDS

There are two playgrounds, a small one for two- to eight-year-olds near Clapham Common West Side and the other for under tens between the Mount and Eagle ponds. The latter is newly refurbished and has a good range of brightly coloured rides.

SKATEBOARDING

There is a free skateboarding rink behind Cicero's Café.

SOFTBALL

The common is home to the Odd Sox and Sumatra Panthers softball clubs. Both of these clubs are members of the London Softball Federation, and play in the largest league of its kind in the county. The clubs welcome new members and can be contacted direct via the London Softball Federation website www.londonsoftball.com or at the Sumatra Panthers website www.sumatrapanthers.co.uk, email dave@ecisubtitling.com.

TENNIS

There are eight courts, five of which are flood-lit from Monday to Thursday. They can only be booked on the day in person from 08.00 every day. Courts cost £4/hour. Rackets and balls are available to hire from £1/hour. Courses of tennis coaching either in a group or individually are available throughout the year for all ages. For example, six hours of group lessons for an adult beginner costs £54. The sports manager has the current programme of courses and private coaches.

Clissold Park

VISITOR INFORMATION

Greenway Close, N4

Tel. 020 7923 3644, website www.clissoldpark.com

Bus: 67, 73, 106, 141, 341, 476

Tube: Finsbury Park (15 min. walk or bus 106),
Manor House (15 min. walk or bus 141, 341), Arsenal

Train: Stoke Newington, Finsbury Park Rail

Open 07.30 until dusk

Clissold Park is a pretty 54 acre park with facilities to match. Although little known outside the area, it is a treat. The park was a private estate for many years and still surrounds Jonathan Hoare's 18th century manor house, Clissold House, now an excellent café. There are wide expanses of playing fields, tennis courts, a bowling green, and a mini zoo complete with fallow deer, pygmy goats, an aviary and a butterfly tunnel. There are lakes, fountains, a rose garden, large children's playground, bandstand, paddling pool, and the nearby Abney Park Cemetery and Nature Reserve. Stoke Newington has a green heart.

BIRDS AND BUTTERFLIES

The park's aviary has quails, lovebirds, diamond doves and zebra finches. The butterfly tunnel is open on Tuesday and Thursday from 12.30–14.30, weather

Facilities

- Aviary
- Bandstand
- Butterfly tunnel
- Café
- Cricket
- Deer enclosure
- Football
- Nature reserve
- One O'Clock Club
- Paddling pool
- Ponds
- Playground
- Tennis
- Softball

permitting. The animal enclosure has pygmy goats and fallow deer.

CAFÉ

The Manor Café

The Manor Café is housed in the original 18th century brick villa at the centre of the park. This is the heart of park life, and is near the playground, tennis courts, bandstand and zoo. The villa was originally home to Jonathan Hoare, from the banking family. The café was recently refurbished and serves excellent food and drinks. The villa has a Doric columned terrace and a raised lawn overlooking the deer enclosure and water. Tea 50p, cappuccino £1.50, breakfasts including beans on toast £1.00, omelette £2.50, child portion meals £1.95. The café is open from 09.00 until 19.00 in the summer and about 17.00 in the winter.

CRICKET

The park is home to the Church Street Nomads Cricket Club. The club was founded in 1997 and plays around 30 friendly fixtures throughout the summer. The club's 'Stoke Newington Cricket School' offers coaching to young players of all standards and meets at 10.30 on Saturday mornings at the park. For further information contact David Blundell, 16 Geldeston Road, London N16.

FESTIVAL

The annual Stoke Newington Festival takes place every summer (usually in June). There are bands, entertainments, children's competitions, and stalls.

FOOTBALL

The park has an all-weather football pitch and a grass pitch. The grounds can be used free of charge without booking. There are currently no formal clubs using the park. For further information contact the Park Ranger's Office, tel. 020 7923 3660.

FRIENDS OF THE PARK

The Clissold Park User Group has regular meetings and events to encourage feedback and change in the park. For further information email the chairman at usergroup@clissoldpark.com, website www.clissoldpark.com, or speak to the Park Ranger's Office, tel. 020 7923 3660.

ONE O'CLOCK CLUB

The park's One O'Clock Club for under fives runs on weekdays in the building at the top of the grass football pitch, opposite the tennis courts. Tel. 020 8809 6700.

PLAYGROUND

There is a large playground near the café and tennis courts with swings, slides, climbing frames and a sand pit. There is also a large paddling pool which is open in the summer, near the aviary (see above) and animal enclosure.

PONDS

There are two large ponds in the park which attract a wide variety of waterfowl.

SOFTBALL

The Tecumsehs softball club is based in Stoke Newington, and often has its season at Clissold Park. The club is part of the London Softball Federation, the largest league of its kind in the country, and plays mixed slowpitch games in the Greater London Softball Mixed League (GLSML). There are midweek evening games at the home venue and away games at other parks in London. The club welcomes new members of all standards. For further information contact the club direct on www.tecumsehs.org.uk or visit the London Softball Federation at www.londonsoftball.com.

TENNIS

There are eight high quality tennis courts near the café. Advance booking is possible either in person at the Park Ranger's Office (tel. 020 7923 3660) or by phoning the Sports Booking Line, tel. 020 7254 4235 or 020 7923 3644 (Monday–Friday 09.00–15.30), credit cards are accepted. A court costs £5/hour for adults. Discounts are available for under 16s off peak and for Hackney Leisure Card holders (£2.50 per hour). Coaching is available for adults and children, tel. 020 8318 4856, email clissoldparkjtc@excite.com, and there are numerous competitions and holiday courses.

TREES

There are tree walks every Thursday in August, meeting at the Park Ranger's Office. The park has many chestnut trees.

NEAR THE PARK

The Abney Park Cemetery and Nature Reserve is an interesting ancient cemetery and derelict church at the back of the Manor House. The grounds are overgrown and have interesting statues and wildlife. The reserve has a visitor centre and shop as well as guided walks among statues and graves. Tel. 020 7275 7557.

Coram's Fields

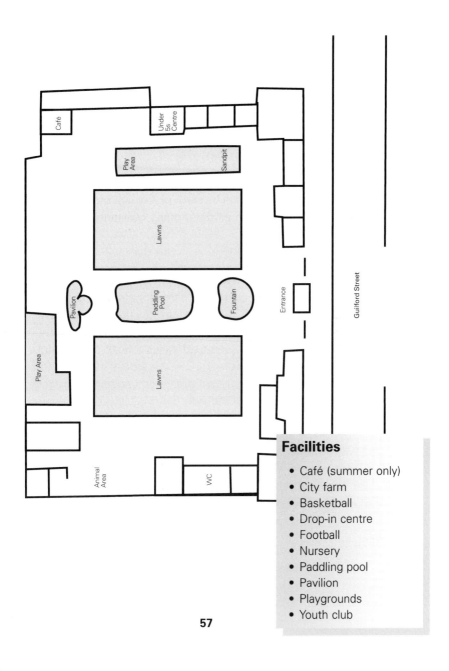

Café

Under 5s Centre

Play Area

Sandpit

Lawns

Pavilion

Paddling Pool

Fountain

Entrance

Guilford Street

Play Area

Lawns

Animal Area

WC

Facilities

- Café (summer only)
- City farm
- Basketball
- Drop-in centre
- Football
- Nursery
- Paddling pool
- Pavilion
- Playgrounds
- Youth club

VISITOR INFORMATION

93 Guilford Street, WC1N 1DN

Information number: tel. 020 7837 6138

Open 09.00–20.00 May to August and
09.00–17.00 September to April

Buses: 59, 68, 91, 168, 188 (Southampton Row), 17, 45, 46 (Gray's
Inn Road) or 8, 25, 242 (High Holborn).

Tube: Russell Square

Coram's Fields is a seven-acre children's playground near Russell Square. It occupies the site of the former Foundling Hospital, established in 1739 by Thomas Coram as a 'hospital for the maintenance and education of exposed and deserted children'. The hospital provided a safe haven for unwanted children, who were left anonymously in a wicker basket in the Guilford Street gateway. When the hospital relocated in the 1920s a vigorous campaign saved the site from development. A playground was established around the original single-storey colonnaded Georgian buildings and opened by the late Queen Elizabeth the Queen Mother in July 1936.

The area continues to be a safe place for children to play in central London and adults are only allowed into the park if a child accompanies them. There are lawns, giant sandpits, paddling pools, an adventure playground with commando ropes and helter-skelter slides, a small city farm, new flood-lit sports facilities, a nursery, drop in centres, a summer café and a youth club. The Guilford Street gateway still exists but the wicker basket is long gone. The Coram Foundation Museum gives a history of the hospital and houses work by one of the patrons, William Hogarth (see below).

HIGHLIGHTS

- City farm
- Seven acres just for children
- Excellent sports facilities (available for adults and children to hire, see below)
- The art collection and museum at the nearby Coram Foundation Museum (see below).

ANIMALS

The small city farm in the park has a friendly collection of farm animals and birds, including three sheep from Spitalfields (Tegan, Shaune and Sharon), some loud bantam chickens, rabbits and goats. The Green Fingers scheme (see below) includes a 'meet the animals' session when it is possible to feed them. Contact the information line 020 7837 6138 for more details.

ART

In 1745 the artist William Hogarth persuaded his artist friends to raise funds for the new hospital by donating paintings. The friends included Gainsborough, Reynolds and Richard Wilson. The scheme was such a success that the hospital became known as a venue for new talent spotting. Many of these paintings are on display at the Thomas Coram Foundation Offices at 40 Brunswick Square. The collection includes Hogarth's famous 'The March of the Guards to Finchley', depicting the army preparing to march to Finchley on their way to suppress the Jacobite Rebellion.

CAFÉ

There is a small café open from Easter until the end of summer which sells tasty hot and cold drinks and snacks through a hatch in the colonnade buildings.

COLONNADES

Although the main part of the Foundling Hospital was demolished, the original Georgian colonnades survive. These are the single storey buildings around the edge of the park, which house the city farm on one side and the café, nursery and play groups on the other.

GREEN FINGERS SCHEME

The Green Fingers groups include 'meeting the animals', gardening for children and parents, lessons in creating butterfly and bee gardens and opportunities to help water and plant bulbs. For more details phone the main information line, 020 7837 6138.

MUSEUM

The Thomas Coram Foundation Museum is located at 40 Brunswick Square, WC1, tel. 020 7841 3600. The museum has just been completely renovated. It houses the Court Room and the oak staircase from the original Foundling Hospital, Handel's copy of the *Messiah* (first performed at the hospital), uniforms worn by the children, mementos left with them at the hospital gates, and some of the paintings by the hospital's patron artists, including Hogarth, Rysbrack, Gainsborough and Reynolds.

MUSIC

As part of the early fundraising for the Foundling Hospital, Handel gave several concerts at the hospital's chapel. His concerts included the first performance of the *Messiah* on 1 May 1750. He gave a copy of the score of the *Messiah* to the Thomas Coram Foundation and it is on display at their offices and museum at 40 Brunswick Square. There are drop in music sessions for under fours on a Wednesday between 11.15 and 12.15.

PLAYGROUPS

There are several free playgroups for under fives. The 'Colonnades Drop In' meets Monday to Friday from 13.00–16.00 in the Colonnades. There is 'messy play' on Mondays and Thursdays, 'bouncy play' on Tuesdays and Fridays and songs on Wednesdays. The 'Colonnades Peacocks' for under threes meets Monday to Friday from 10.00–12.00. More information can be obtained from the under fives coordinator, Mary Christodoulou, on 020 7837 6611.

The Coram's Fields Community Nursery has 18 full-time and six part-time places for three- to five-year-olds living in the London Borough of Camden. Tel. 020 7833 0198 for more details.

SPORT

There are flood-lit pitches for football, basketball, netball, cricket and athletics. After-school sports sessions include free coaching for 6–16 year olds in basketball, football and netball. These run from Monday to Friday from 16.00–18.00. For further information contact 020 7837 2609, email sports@coramsfieldsyouthcentre.org. Adults can use the pitches during weekday lunchtimes and evenings from 17.00–21.00, tel. 020 7833 2393 for more details and bookings.

SUMMER EVENTS

During the summer there are picnic days, music festivals and circuses.

TREES

The park is ringed with giant London plane trees.

Crystal Palace Park

Facilities

- Athletics
- Boating lake
- Café
- Concerts
- Dinosaur Park
- Farmyard
- Fishing pond
- Information centre
- Maze
- Museum
- Pétanque
- Playground
- Sports centre
- Swimming
- Tennis

VISITOR INFORMATION

Thicket Road, Penge, SE20

Tel. 020 8778 9496 website www.crystalpalacefoundation.org.uk

Train: Crystal Palace Station (next to the park), Penge West Station (10 minute walk): both have regular services from Victoria and Charing Cross

Bus: 2, 3, 63, 108B, 122, 157, 194, 202, 227, 306, 312, 322, 358

Car: pay and display parking off Thicket Road and opposite Sydenham Avenue

Crystal Palace Park covers 200 acres in Sydenham, south London. Joseph Paxton's 1600ft by 282ft glasshouse for the 1851 Great Exhibition was moved here from Hyde Park in 1854 (and tragically burned down in 1936). The Exhibition was the world's first and possibly most successful international trade fair with 15,000 exhibitors. In the six months that it was open six million people visited it. Crystal Palace Park was supposed to offer 'refined recreation to elevate the intellect and instruct the mind' in all weathers. In its heyday it contained fountains that were 77m high with 11,000 jets of water.

Crystal Palace is a living memorial to the Great Exhibition whose remains are clearly visible and kept alive by the museum and wonderful photographs. The Palace had concert halls, aviaries, an aquarium, museums, study centres and an organ with 4,568 pipes! The sports stadium, built in 1964, can accommodate 17,000 spectators and has almost every sport including four swimming pools. There is an outdoor Concert Bowl made in special steel that rusts in a uniform colour. Crystal Palace is also home to the world's first ever Dinosaur Park. The 29 prehistoric monsters made of stucco-covered brick and iron were built in 1854 by Waterhouse Hawkins. They have been magnificently restored. There is an adventure playground, café, playing fields, maze, avenues of trees and wide grassy spaces.

The park is benefiting from a £3.6m restoration project that is returning some of its former Victorian splendour.

HIGHLIGHTS OF THE PARK

- Dinosaur Park with its prehistoric monsters
- Maze
- Museum
- National Sports Centre

ATHLETICS

Crystal Palace is the traditional home of British athletics. The National Sports Centre (see below) has magnificent facilities including Europe's first 400m outdoor track and an indoor six lane straight track. The stadium has full field event facilities and is home to the South London Harriers. The stadium is open Monday to Friday 08.00–22.00, Saturday 08.00–20.00, Sunday 08.00–18.00. (See Sports centre, below.)

BRASS BAND

The Crystal Palace Band is one of the few remaining traditional brass bands in London. They formed in 1901 and were closely associated with the park until the fire in 1936. The band still has a formidable reputation as one of the best in the region and they play at a variety of events including the traditional open air concerts in the park. Rehearsals take place on Wednesdays from 20.00–22.00 at St John the Evangelist Parish Church, High Street, Penge. Website www.crystalpalaceband.fsnet.co.uk, tel. 020 8776 2520.

CAFÉS

Park Café

The Park Café has plastic chairs and smells of burgers but prices are low. There is indoor and outdoor seating. Tea 60p, coffee 80p, burgers £1, fish and chips £3.80, English breakfast £3.80, crisps and ice creams £1. Open every day 09.00–18.00.

St. Germain

The French café, St. Germain, at 16 Crystal Place Parade (just outside the park) has an outdoor shaded terrace and indoor tables with an atmosphere reminiscent of a cosy ski chalet. Caffe latte £1.40, fresh warm pastries £1.40, pasta £3.50 or soup £2.95. Open every day 09.00–17.00.

CLASSIC CARS

The Historic Commercial Vehicle Society organises a run from the park to Brighton every year.

CRICKET

The London County Cricket Club was based at Crystal Palace and was home to one of the world's most famous cricketers, W.G. Grace (1848–1915). He lived on Crystal Palace Park Road and would walk over to play his matches. Unfortunately there is no longer any cricket in the park.

DINOSAUR PARK

Crystal Palace is home to the world's first ever Dinosaur Park. The 29 prehistoric monsters were made in 1854 by Waterhouse Hawkins, under the guidance of Professor Richard Owen, who had coined the word 'dinosaur'. Hawkins was a geologist with an interest in extinct animals and he based many of the constructions on fossils from the British Museum. The display caused a sensation when it opened. The animals were made of stucco-covered brick and iron, and have recently been magnificently restored. This is the Jurassic Park of the capital.

FARMYARD

A fantastic new steel and wooden farmyard brings a little of the countryside into the city.

FISHING

The Crystal Palace Angling Association controls the fishing rights to the park's pretty 1.5 acre lake near the Concert Bowl. Unfortunately the club's waiting list is full, and likely to be for several years to come. Juniors (14–16 year olds) may have more success. Application enquiries for the club can be made via the wardens at the Ranger's Office (central information number). There are, however, excellent facilities at the nearby South Norwood Lake, Croydon, which has a turn up and pay policy (£3 per rod per day). This 28 acre lake has recently been re-stocked, there are fishing platforms and an on-site warden to give help and advice. South Norwood Lake, Auckland Road, Woodvale Avenue and Sylvan Road.

FRIENDS OF CRYSTAL PALACE PARK

The Crystal Palace Foundation supports the museum and aims to keep alive the memory of the Crystal Palace and its role in the social development of Victorian and Edwardian England. It publishes a range of books and leaflets that bring the park to life. Membership costs £8/year or £12/year/family. Website www.crystalpalacefoundation.org.uk.

INFORMATION

The information centre has photographs of the recent restoration project as well as leaflets about Crystal Palace. Information Centre, off Thicket Road, tel. 020 8778 9496/8778 7148, open every day 09.00–16.30.

MAZE

The original maze was planted in 1870 and was the largest in London, occupying 2,000 square yards. It was replanted with 4,000 hornbeams to look identical to the original.

MEMORIAL

Two fish in a small roofed memorial near the playground support the bell from *HMS Crystal Palace*.

MUSEUM

The park's small museum is housed in the former Crystal Palace School of Engineering, the only building left after the devastating fire of 1936. This was where John Baird invented television. It has a remarkable collection of photographs and memorabilia of the Great Exhibition, including a 3D lightbox of pictures showing the Palace (the machine requires a 20p). Anerley Hill, tel. 020 8676 0700, open Sundays and bank holidays 11.00–17.00, entrance free.

PLAYGROUND

There is a large playground with a range of swings and rides in the centre of the park. Nearby is a One O'Clock Club for parents to relax together while their children play.

SPORTS CENTRE

The park's huge National Sports Centre has superb facilities including an athletics stadium (see above under Athletics), two flood-lit synthetic pitches, a grass pitch, four tennis courts, badminton courts, squash courts, a boxing hall, a climbing wall, a dance studio, four swimming pools, basketball, trampolining, volleyball and a fully equipped gym. There are classes in just about everything: aerobics, diving, football, karate, netball, yoga, summer camps for children and antenatal exercise classes to name a few. The crèche is open 10.00–12.00 Monday to Friday and costs £1.60/ child/hour. There is also a sports injuries clinic (tel. 020 8778 9050).

Crystal Palace National Sports Centre, Ledrington Road. Tel. 020 8778 0131 (reception) or 020 8659 4561 (gym). Open Monday to Friday 08.00–22.00 and weekends 08.00–18.00. Website www.crystalpalacensc.co.uk.

STATUES

'Paxton's Bust' (1869) by W. F. Woodington once looked up towards the Palace, but after the fire it was turned around to face the Sports Centre.

'The Two Sphinxes' marked the entrance to the Palace and remain with the balustrading and grand flights of steps to the park. The sphinxes are copies of the ancient Egyptian originals in the Louvre in Paris.

WALKS

The Crystal Palace Foundation runs regular historical walks around the park, including the terraces and sphinxes, the water towers and much more. The walks are led by expert guides, last one to two hours and take place at least once a month (on a Sunday) throughout the year. Walks start from inside the Crystal Palace Museum at 12.00 or 14.30 and cost £2.50/person (children free) (no booking required). For further details contact the museum (enquiries Sundays and bank holidays 11.00–17.00) and ask about the Crystal Palace Walkabouts, tel. 020 8676 0700 or 07889 338812 (anytime), website www.crystalpalacefoundation.org.uk.

Green Chain Walk is a 40-mile network of paths running from Crystal Place to the Thames Barrier, tel. 020 8921 5028, website www.greenchain.com, email info@greenchain.com.

There are three excellent trails – Trees, Paxton's Heritage and Geological Time Trail – each with its own leaflet and map which can be bought for 30p from the museum or information office.

Dulwich Park

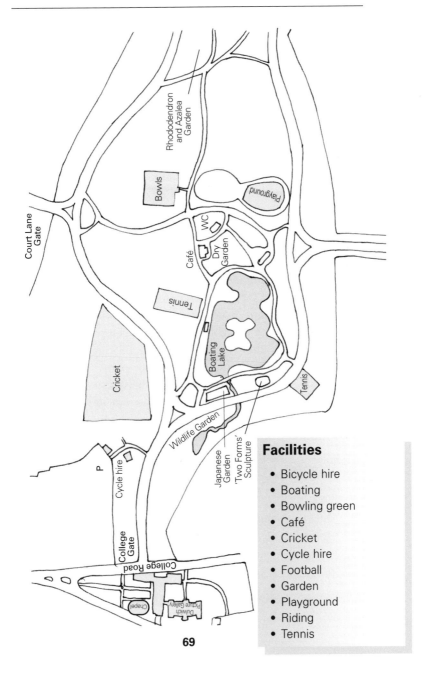

Facilities

- Bicycle hire
- Boating
- Bowling green
- Café
- Cricket
- Cycle hire
- Football
- Garden
- Playground
- Riding
- Tennis

69

VISITOR INFORMATION

College Road, Dulwich Common, Court Lane,
Dulwich Village, SE21

Bus: P4, 12, 40, 176, 185, 321

Car: there is a new car park by the visitors centre near College Gate

Train: North Dulwich (nearest), West Dulwich

Dulwich Park was created in 1890 and occupies 72 acres of land around one of London's prettiest neighbourhoods. The park was originally part of the Manor of Dulwich, once owned by Shakespeare's friend the actor Edward Alleyn. He donated the land to the newly formed Dulwich College in 1619. They in turn presented it to the public in 1890. The park became one of Queen Mary's favourite gardens and she visited every year to see the famous rhododendrons and azaleas. The gate through which she entered the park was named after her. Paths wind in and out of the many different gates and gardens like a giant maze. There is an excellent café in a restored pavilion, clipped green playing fields, tennis courts, a boating lake, formal gardens, nature trails and horse riding paths. The Dulwich Picture Gallery is across the road and the unusual and recently renovated Horniman Gardens and Museum are nearby. It is about to get better. The park has been granted, in principle, £3.89 million from the Heritage Lottery Fund.

HIGHLIGHTS OF THE PARK

- Café
- Dulwich Picture Gallery
- Horniman Garden and Museum
- Recumbent cycles for hire
- Rhododendrons and azaleas

BICYCLING

This is one of London's most bike-friendly parks. The London Recumbents have a branch here (and in Battersea Park) and have a bike of every shape and size for every mood and person, available by the hour. There are racers and recliners, trailers and tricycles, tandems and even a kind of armchair on wheels. Many look like they are straight out of one of Heath Robinson's books of invention. They also organise bike parties, special needs cycling and bike sales. Bikes cost from £5 per hour. Tel. 020 8299 6636. Open every day 10.00–16.30.

BIRDS

Bird feed is available from the Park Ranger's Office from 20p a bag. The silver birch trees are an important pit stop for migrating birds crossing the park. The lake attracts herons, kingfishers and, at dusk, bats in search of an evening snack. There are moorhens, mallards, blackheaded gulls, Canada geese, coots and tufted ducks.

BOATING

Trees and a wildlife circuit ring the pretty three-acre boating lake. The sign near the old boathouse lists pond and bird facts including 'the swift can eat, sleep and mate without landing'. The old boathouse has been demolished and a 'floating boat house' is being planned. Information about boat hire can be obtained from the visitor centre. Boats cost from £5.25 per ½ hour.

BOWLS

This is one of the oldest bowling clubs in London, founded in 1901. The Club meets from May to September every afternoon. New memberships are welcome and coaching is available for beginners. Membership costs £35/year. Tel. Michael Wise 020 8761 7690.

CAFÉ

Pavilion Café

The Pavilion Café was completely restored in July 2003. The large windows overlook the tennis courts and playing fields. The atmosphere is like a smart, warm, National Trust property. There is stylish halogen lighting, wood panelled walls, thick glass display cabinets and tasty food. Breakfasts £5.50, sandwiches £2.50, cappuccino £1.20, tea 85p, cake £1.20. Tel. 020 8299 1383 or email pavilioncafe@tiscali.co.uk. Open every day 09.00–16.00.

FOOTBALL

The grass football pitches can be booked through the booking hotline, 020 7525 1050 and cost £22 for a junior pitch, £42 for a senior pitch and £16 for small sided pitches. Jimmy Peacock organises teams and coaching for all ages from under sevens up to senior level. Tel. 020 8265 4509.

FRIENDS OF THE PARK

The Dulwich Park Friends publish a newsletter three times/year and organise events and meetings to protect and develop the park. Membership costs just £3 (single) or £5 (family). Payment is by cheque/postal order to 'Dulwich Park Friends' to Dulwich Park Friends, P.O. Box 16860, London SE21 7ZQ. Emily Montague, tel. 020 7501 9120.

GARDENS

The new drought-tolerant garden near the lake proves that even people who hate watering can have a garden. It is the first drought-resistant garden to be planted in a British park. The garden boasts plants with silver/grey leaves to reflect sunshine, and ground hugging plants to forage all available water. Leaflets are available from the visitor centre. (See also Rhododendrons, below.)

INFORMATION

Park Ranger's Lodge, College Road, London SE21 7BQ. Tel. 020 8693 5737. Email: dulwich.park@southwark.gov.uk.

The Park Ranger's Office and visitor centre is based off the College Road entrance to the park, in front of the smart new car park. Open every day 08.00–16.30 in winter (including Christmas!) and 08.00–21.00 in summer.

NATURE TRAIL

There is a small nature trail running through the park, for which a map is available at the Ranger's Office. This is particularly good for children and highlights the trees and birds found in the park.

PLAYGROUND

The park's excellent modern playground is enclosed within a figure of eight. There are slides and swings and webbed climbing frames suitable for 2–5 and 5–14 year olds.

RHODODENDRONS

Dulwich Park is famous for its rhododendrons. The American Garden has one of the largest selections in South London, which look spectacular in spring. It was one of Queen Mary's favourite gardens.

RUNNING

The Dulwich Park Runners is a small friendly club based at the Camber Tennis Clubhouse, on Dulwich Common. They meet every Tuesday and Thursday evening at 19.45 and run from three to eight miles. All levels of runners are welcome. Membership is £45/year but new members are allowed three runs for free before committing to a year's membership.

Website: www.dulwichparkrunners.com. Membership secretary, David Smith, tel. 07808 175517.

TENNIS

The park has six tennis courts. Four are in front of the café and the other two are just off the horse ride near the 'two forms' sculpture. Courts can be hired for £5.25 per hour (adults) or £3 for leisure access card holders or £1 for under 16s. In winter the courts are free of charge. Tel. 020 8693 5737.

SCULPTURE

Barbara Hepworth's 'Two Forms (Divided Circle)' (1970) is situated by the lake, and can be seen from the carriage drive.

SHELTERS

There are several tiny wooden shelters in the park with green wooden benches, white wooden walls and slate roofs. They look like out-of-place miniature bus stops on a road to nowhere. They are a good place to watch the tennis and other comings and goings in the park.

TREES

The park has some of London's finest trees. These include ashes, planes, cedars, silver birches, swamp cypress, ancient and Turkey oaks, copper beeches, a Japanese pagoda tree and even a Kentucky coffee tree. The visitors centre has a 'Tree Trail' leaflet, listing where the trees can be found.

WALKS

There are free park 'health walks' every Wednesday morning. Walkers meet at the College Gate entrance and the walks last approximately half an hour. Contact the Park Ranger's Office for more details. Tel. 020 8693 5737.

NEAR THE PARK

Chapel of Alleyn's College of God's Gift

The courtyard and chapel are well worth visiting. The regular services are open to the public and there are three chorals a year.

Dulwich Picture Gallery

This is the oldest public art gallery in England, established in 1817. It is across the road from the park and has a smart café for 'ladies who lunch' or afternoon tea. The gallery was designed by Sir John Soane in 1811 as a place to house his friend's art collection. There is a pretty garden with seats and the nearby Chapel of Alleyn's College of God's Gift (see above).

Entrance: Gallery Road. Tel. 020 8693 5254, website www.dulwichpicturegallery.org.uk.

Open Tuesday to Friday 10.00–17.00, weekends/bank holidays 11.00–17.00, closed Mondays. Admission £4 (free for students).

The Horniman Museum and Gardens

These were owned by Horniman, a tea merchant who collected during his travels. He left his house with its collection and the adjoining gardens to the people of London in 1901. The pretty 16 acre gardens are one of the area's highlights. They have views across London, an historic bandstand with regular concerts and a conservatory. The gardens are both formal and natural landscapes, with a sunken area, roses, formal bedding and a five acre nature trail and animal enclosure. The gardens have a regular programme of events, including concerts, plant sales and children's activities.

Entrance: 100 London Road, tel. 020 8699 1872, www.horniman.ac.uk. Open every day 10.30–17.30. Admission is free.

Sydenham Hill Wood

Sydenham Hill Wood is a pretty stretch of ancient woodland

which once ran from Deptford to Selhurst. It is now managed by the London Wildlife Trust. The nine hectare wood has over 200 species of trees as well as numerous plants, mushrooms, insects and animals. There are several small ponds in the woods attracting ducks, geese and frogs. The long oak avenue, Cox's Walk, is the best way to approach the nature reserve. This comes off Dulwich Common Road and leads up through the woods following an old railway line. Pissaro's painting 'A view of Lordship Lane Station' was painted from the footbridge which passes over the remains of the track. The path leads up to the top of Sydenham Hill with views across London and Surrey.

Entrances to the reserve are at Cox's Walk, off Dulwich Common Road; and Crescent Wood Road, off Sydenham Hill.

Sydenham Hill and Forest Hill railway stations offer access by train.

If you are interested in volunteering, contact the London Wildlife Trust Volunteers, tel. 020 8699 5698. Volunteers meet at 10.30 every Wednesday and the second and fourth Sunday of the month.

Finsbury Park

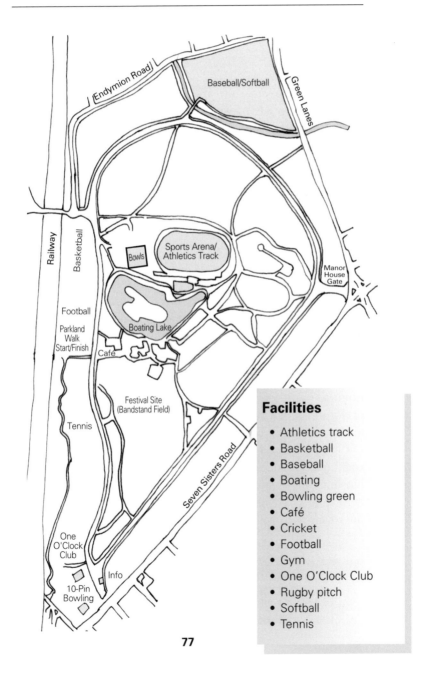

Endymion Road

Baseball/Softball

Green Lanes

Railway

Basketball

Bowls

Sports Arena/
Athletics Track

Manor
House
Gate

Football

Parkland
Walk
Start/Finish

Café

Boating Lake

Festival Site
(Bandstand Field)

Tennis

Seven Sisters Road

One
O'Clock
Club

Info

10-Pin
Bowling

Facilities

- Athletics track
- Basketball
- Baseball
- Boating
- Bowling green
- Café
- Cricket
- Football
- Gym
- One O'Clock Club
- Rugby pitch
- Softball
- Tennis

VISITOR INFORMATION

Endymion Road, N4

Tel: 020 8489 5662

Bus: 29, 106, 153, 263

Tube/train: Finsbury Park, Manor House

Car: pay and display in Endymion Road

Finsbury Park opened in 1869 to a design by Alexandra McKenzie. Its 115 acres were dubbed the 'People's Park of North London' and were a much needed breath of fresh air for the region. Unfortunately its reputation in the 1990s resulted in its omission from most recent guidebooks. This is a shame because a combination of enthusiastic management and a motivated work force are restoring the park to its former glory. The signs of renovation are everywhere: swept paths are free of litter, lawns are clipped, compost is carefully stacked, fences and gates repaired, playgrounds are tidy and safe, neat flower beds have been dug around the up-to-date information boards and helpful staff are running the well-stocked information centre.

There is an Italian café serving one of the best cappuccinos in London, a large boating lake, two excellent children's playgrounds, a One O'Clock Club and art club, an athletics track, softball, cricket, rugby, tennis courts, superb views, the five-mile parkland walk linking the park to Alexandra Palace, and London's oldest aqueduct. It is also home to the annual Finsbury Park music festival. Things are only going to get better: a £4.9 million three-year programme of further improvements has begun, funded in part by the Heritage Lottery Fund.

HIGHLIGHTS

- The cappuccinos in The Park Café
- The central boating lake/café/playground area

- The Parkland Walk to Alexandra Park
- The views across London

ARTS AND CRAFTS

There is a small arts and crafts fair on the first Sunday of every month in the park near the café, run by N4 Creative.

Tel. 0790 408 3518, email alvawilson2002@yahoo.co.uk.

ATHLETICS TRACK

The 1920s athletics track and pavilion are due for renovation with lottery fund money. It is a flood-lit 400m, six lane synthetic track with field event facilities, available to the public. The track is also home to the London Heathside Athletic Club. This enthusiastic club has road runners, track and field athletes, cross-country and casual joggers of all standards. Membership costs £25 and includes a free vest and access to the facilities as well as discounts at specialist running shops. The club trains on Tuesday and Thursday evenings and Saturday mornings (also using the Parliament Hill Athletic Track on Hampstead Heath, p115). For further details either contact the club secretary Steve Woolf, 69 Corbyn Street, London N4 3BY, website www.londonheathside.org.uk, or phone the track (see below). The pavilion has changing facilities and also a newly refurbished gym. Finsbury Park Track, tel. 020 8802 9139. Cost: £2.90/session or EasyPass £32/month including three other local gyms and pool.

BASEBALL

The London Warriors Baseball club is based at Finsbury Park. This club was formed in 1980 and was winner of the Rawlings League Championships in 2002. They can be contacted at their website www.londonwarriors.com, email info@londonwarriors.com. Pre-season training usually begins on Sunday mornings in early February.

BASKETBALL

There are several large all-weather pitches, near the staff yard, two of which are match standard.

BOATING

There is a large boating lake in the middle of the park, next to the playgrounds and Italian café. The area around the tiny boathouse and café is prettily decked and has wooden benches and tables. There is an island in the centre of the pond that is home to the park's waterfowl. Swan and duck-feed is available from the boathouse for 50p. Boat hire in summer 12.00–19.00 and in October 11.00–17.00 (closed in the winter). Tel. 07905 924282.

CAFÉ

The Park Café

An Italian couple from outside Naples run the park's café. It is a popular 'no frills' café serving good value food and drinks to the locals. They also make one of the best cappuccinos in London. Inside the walls are hung with a few slightly tatty Italian mementoes: football shirts, a flag, black and white photos and city names. The outside seating area spreads to the boating lake and overlooks the playground. The café is being modernised as part of the regeneration project. Large cappuccino £1.30, cake 80p, sandwiches £1.30. Open every day 09.00–about 16.30 (closed December–February).

FESTIVAL

The park has hosted the successful Finfest since the year 2001. This includes carnival parades, music and dance. See www.finsburypark.org.uk.

FOOTBALL

The park has a football pitch and a football club. There is Saturday coaching for 4–18 year olds, from 10.00–11.30 for

4–12 year olds and 12.00–14.00 for 13–16 year olds each Saturday. Contact Kenny Bennet, tel. 020 8442 0078.

FRIENDS OF FINSBURY PARK

The Friends of Finsbury Park acts as a forum for anyone interested in the park and runs regular events and classes as well as a quarterly newsletter. Meetings are on the last Wednesday of every month at 19.00 in the Tenants Hall, Alexander National House, 330 Seven Sisters Road. Tel. 020 8809 0039 or 020 8800 094.

INFORMATION

There is a well-stocked information centre near the Finsbury Gate. Open Monday to Friday 11.00–15.00 and weekends 13.00–17.00. Customer care telephone line 020 8489 5662, Monday to Friday 09.00–13.00 and 14.00–17.00.

The Staff Yard is opposite the Hornsey Gate, Endymion Road. Tel. 020 7263 5001. Booking hotline tel. 020 8489 5670.

Sports information: John McKinnon, Sobell Centre, tel. 020 7686 8812, www.haringey.gov.uk.

ONE O'CLOCK CLUB

The Jamboree Play Hut near the Finsbury Gate runs a free under fives drop in on weekdays and holidays. Open 10.30–12.00 and 13.30–15.00 (closed Wednesday afternoons). Tel. 020 8802 1301.

PLAY DAYS

Between July and September there are play days in the park with children's activities, face painting and games. The groups meet near the Jamboree Play Hut between 15.00–17.00 on Mondays and Wednesdays. Tel. 020 8808 0533.

RICHARD HOPE PLAY SPACE

This is a pretty, enclosed circular pit near the café. It has been landscaped with paths running between rocks and trees and in one corner are curved amphitheatre-style steps fronted with wood leading from the top of the pit to the bottom. A good place for army games or impromptu performances.

RIVER WALK

The New River Walk (see p180) runs through the bottom of the park, just above the cricket and softball pitch.

SOFTBALL

The London Meteors Softball Club has been based at the former cricket ground at Finsbury Park since 1988. They have three adult teams, a rapidly developing youth team and run both slow pitch and fast pitch games. The season runs from April to September. New members of all levels are welcome (some previous experience a bonus). For further information contact Alan Smith, tel. 020 7278 8706, website www.londonmeteors.co.uk. The club is a member of the London Softball Federation, the largest league in the country, contact www.londonsoftball.com. The pitch is available for booking through the Sports Development Officer, tel. 020 7686 8812.

TENNIS

There are four tennis courts in the park that are free but cannot be booked in advance.

TREES

Many of the park's original 19th century trees have survived. They are mostly London planes but also include willows, ancient oaks, poplars and beeches.

NEAR THE PARK

Arsenal Football Club

The club's museum in Avenell Road has Britain's largest archive of football memorabilia for a single club. Tel. 020 7704 4000, www.arsenal.com. Open Fridays and match days 09.00–16.00. Adults £4 and children £2.

Arsenal stadium tours are available on Monday, Tuesday and Fridays at 11.00 and on Wednesday and Thursdays at 11.00 and 14.00. Tours must be pre-booked. Tel. 020 7704 4504. Adults £8 and children £4.

Parkland Walk Local Nature Reserve

The Parkland Walk is a 4.5-mile nature reserve, running from Finsbury Park to Alexandra Park, through Queen's and Highgate Woods, like a secret green corridor. It follows the course of the old railway that used to run from Finsbury to Alexandra Palace. It runs over disused railway bridges, along elevated sections at the level of the surrounding rooftops, dips down into green tunnels and stretches on ahead like a parting of the seas. The unexpected views are fabulous. This is as close as it gets to feeling like a one man express train soaring over traffic, through tunnels, between back gardens, level with rooftops. Although some sections are dank and covered in graffiti the overall effect is exhilarating.

The last passenger train ran in 1954 and the tracks continued to be used for freight until 1971. It was finally opened as a nature reserve in 1984 after much campaigning. There are led walks with a natural history theme, exploring some of the 300 species of wild flower and identifying the many trees, including oaks, ash, yew and cherry. From Finsbury Park the walk is unbroken as far as Holmesdale Road (N6).

For further information and free leaflets contact the Nature Conservation Warden at the Islington Ecology Centre (191 Drayton Park), tel. 020 7354 5162.

Directions from Holmesdale Road to rejoin the Parkland Walk: turn right into Holmesdale Road, right again at the Shepherds pub and right again into Shepherds Hill. Turn immediately left in front of the library, descending a hill to reach Priory Gardens. Turn right and after a couple of hundred metres turn left into an alleyway to Queens Wood (see p136). Cross Muswell Hill Road into Highgate Wood (see p136) and rejoin the Parkway Walk on leaving the wood at the junction of Muswell Hill Road with Cranley Gardens.

Railway Fields

This is a small nature reserve on the site of a former British Rail goods depot, just off Green Lanes N4. Tel. 020 8348 6005.

Geraldine Mary Harmsworth Park

VISITOR INFORMATION

St. Georges Road, SE1

Bus: 12, 35, 40, 68, 68A, 171, 176, P3

Train: Elephant and Castle

Tube: Lambeth North, Waterloo

This small 12-acre park is next to the Imperial War Museum. It provides a welcome grassy space and includes the unusual Tibetan Peace Garden, a playground and a free play-club for under fives.

HIGHLIGHTS

* Children's playroom
* Nearby Imperial War Museum
* Tibetan Peace Garden

FIVE-A-SIDE FOOTBALL

There is a free pitch for anyone who feels like playing.

PLAYGROUND

There is a small playground with a friendly Children's Playroom for all children under five with their carers.

Facilities

* Children's playroom
* Five-a-side football
* Playground

Open Monday to Friday 12.30–16.00. Tel. 020 7820 9724.

TIBETAN PEACE GARDEN

The Tibetan Peace Garden is the highlight of the park. It was a gift from the people of Tibet and contains plants from the Himalayas. It was opened in 1999 by the Dalai Lama and Trudie Styler, the wife of the rock star Sting. The garden is a monument to the courage of the Tibetan people and their commitment to non-violence and peace.

Tel. 020 7930 6001. Website www.tibet-foundation.org.

Golders Hill Park and West Heath

VISITOR INFORMATION

Golders Hill Park Information Centre

Staff Yard, West Heath Avenue, NW11 7QR, tel. 020 8455 5183

There is disabled parking at Golders Hill Park from Monday to Friday.

Buses: 210, 268

Tube: Golders Green

Golders Hill Park is 36 acres of park adjoining Hampstead's West Heath. It was purchased in 1898 from the executors of Sir Spencer Wells. It is a gated, landscaped, child friendly park which feels a world away from the rest of the heath. There is a children's playground, a zoo, a small deer enclosure, gardens, water gardens, tennis courts (including four grass courts) and a small putting green. In the summer there are bouncy castles, children's entertainers by the bandstand, bandstand concerts on a Sunday (15.00–17.00). The zoo is currently closed for renovation but will boast enclosures for owls, otters, red squirrels and red flamingos.

The Hill Garden and Pergola is a small fenced garden in West Heath (signposted from Golders Hill Park or from Jack Straw's Castle) with a magnificent 800ft pergola. Both once belonged to Inverforth House, but are now part of the park and free to visit. The pergola was renovated in 1990 and gives views of Inverforth House and on a clear day to Harrow-on-the-Hill

Facilities

- Bandstand
- Café
- Gardens
- Golf/putting
- Horticulture clinics
- Playground
- Tennis
- Zoo

Church. It is raised on a brick base, with carved stone balustrades, columns and wooden domes. The garden can be accessed from Golders Hill Park, or from North End Way (near Jack Straw's Castle). The garden is one of the heath's best-kept secrets.

HIGHLIGHTS

- Children's zoo
- Deer enclosure
- Water gardens
- 800ft pergola

BANDSTAND

There are free Sunday bandstand concerts between the end of May until the end of August. These include brass bands, jazz and light orchestras and usually start at 15.00.

CAFÉ

Continental Café at Golders Hill Park

North End Way, NW3. Nearest tube station: Golders Green (Northern Line). Open 10.00–18.30ish (sunset) February to November.

This is a mid-priced Italian-run canteen. Both outside and indoor seating overlooks the park and highchairs are also available. The café's famous home-made ice-creams and sorbets are sold from a hatch at the far end of the building. Cappuccino costs £1.50, tea 95p, sandwiches from £2.00, croissants £1.25, bottled beer £1.85, glass of wine £1.90. There are daily specials of hot pasta and large salads costing from £4 and fresh milk shakes.

GOLF

The putting green is available on weekends and bank holidays from April to September and costs £1.70 per round (adults). Putters are available from the keeper's office with a deposit. The putting green has variable opening times (usually 13.00–19.30). Contact the Golders Hill Park Office, West Heath Avenue (off the Finchley Road), tel. 020 8455 5183.

HORTICULTURE CLINIC

The park runs a popular programme of training sessions for keen horticulturalists on some Saturdays between May and July. Admission is free and sessions last about two hours. For further information, or for any horticultural queries, contact the main office on 020 8455 5183 (the year's programme is usually available by Easter).

TENNIS

There are four asphalt courts and four grass courts at Golders Hill Park. The asphalt courts are available all year. The grass courts are available on weekends and bank holidays from April to September (turf permitting). Annual membership costs £10, and enables players to book courts by telephone three days in advance. Membership is available from the keeper's hut next to the courts. Courts cost £4.50 per hour. Open from 08.00 until park closure (dusk). Golders Hill Park (western end of West Heath Avenue gate, not far from Golders Green tube station), tel. 020 8455 5183.

Tennis coaching is available on Tuesdays and Thursdays from April to September. Tel 020 8348 9930. To reserve complete the application form and return to the information office.

ZOO

There is a children's zoo in the park, with deer, rabbits and goats on view.

The Green Park

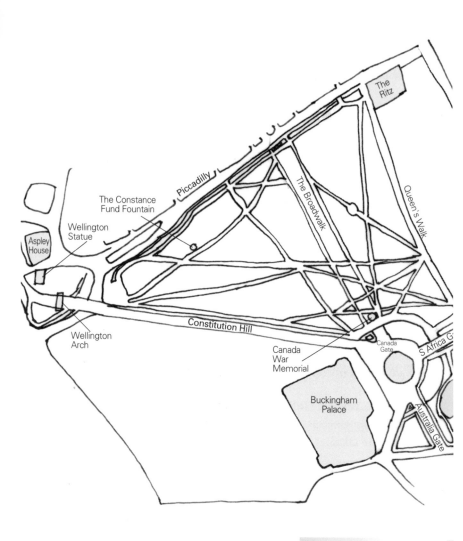

Facilities
- Gates
- Walks

VISITOR INFORMATION

The Green Park, SW1

Tel. 020 7930 1793 (also for St James's)

Tube: Green Park, Hyde Park Corner

Train: Victoria Station

Bus: 19, 14, 22, 38

Buckingham Palace, Piccadilly and Queen's Walk flank this triangular park that has been open to the public since 1826. It was once a burial ground for people who had died of leprosy but by 1749 was the site for a royal fireworks display to mark the peace treaty ending the War of Austrian Succession. Handel composed the music for the royal fireworks, which has 40 trumpets as well as 100 cannons for extra force. The Wellington Arch in the centre of Hyde Park Corner was built in 1830. The park borders Constitution Hill, named by Charles II who would take his regular constitutional walks with his King Charles spaniels in the park. The park's 53 acres (21 hectares) are quiet and covered by grassland with tall trees.

HIGHLIGHTS

- Canada War Memorial
- Devonshire Gates
- Rare trees

CONSTANCE FUND FOUNTAIN

This bronze statue (1954) on a granite pedestal is near Hyde Park Corner on the Piccadilly side of the park. It is of a young girl playing with a goat-like animal. This was a gift from the Constance Fund, a private charity commemorating the wife of Sigismund Goetze, a well known 20th century artist who also paid for the gates in Regent's Park (p208). The fountain was sculpted by E.J. Clack.

DAFFODILS

Queen's Walk was named after Queen Caroline, wife of George II, who turned the area into a fashionable strolling area. The area becomes carpeted in daffodils in spring.

FRIENDS OF THE GREEN PARK

The Friends of St James's Park and The Green Park (The Thorney Island Society) are active in preserving the heritage of old Westminster. The group was founded in 1985 and has a current membership of over 400. There are regular dinners with guest speakers, and private visits to landmarks and places of local interest, many of which are not easily accessible to the public. The society is keen to welcome new members. For information contact The Thorney Island Society, 39 Westminster Mansions, Great Smith Street, London SW1P 3BP, tel. 020 7222 2449.

GATES

Devonshire

These beautiful gilded iron gates (on the Piccadilly end of the Broad Walk) were made in 1735 for a house in Turnham Green, then moved to Chiswick House in 1837, then to Devonshire House in 1898 and finally to their current position in 1921. Portland stone Palladian pillars flank them with lead sphinxes on top (also from Chiswick House). The gates are a treat for curly iron-work lovers. The Naval and Military Club, known as the 'IN and OUT' from its traffic notices, can be seen through the gates.

Canada Gates

These gates (1908) were presented by the dominions of Canada and Australia.

MEMORIAL

Opposite the Canada Gates is the stunning Canada War Memorial carved by Pierre Granche (1994) in memory of the one million Canadians who came over to Europe to fight in the two World Wars. It is made of rose granite, with bronze maple leaves inscribed 'From dangers shared, our friendship prospers.'

TREES

Most of the trees in the park are London plane (*platanus x acerifolia*) and lime trees. The tree opposite Down Street is the cultivar of the London plane 'Augustine Henry', named after a 19th century arborist. It has vivid green leaves of at least 38cm, double the size of the London plane. There are some unusual black poplars and some silver maples with their fine silvery leaves. Near St James's Palace is a tree planted to commemorate the Coronation of George V and Queen Mary. The plaque is almost overgrown by bark.

WALKS

From Green Park tube station it is possible to walk through The Green Park past Buckingham Palace and into St James's Park to Big Ben. For a longer walk stroll through The Green Park and into Hyde Park and Kensington Gardens.

NEAR THE PARK
Buckingham Palace

Hyde Park (see p149)

St James's Park (see p236)

Spencer House

The Ritz Hotel

Greenwich Park

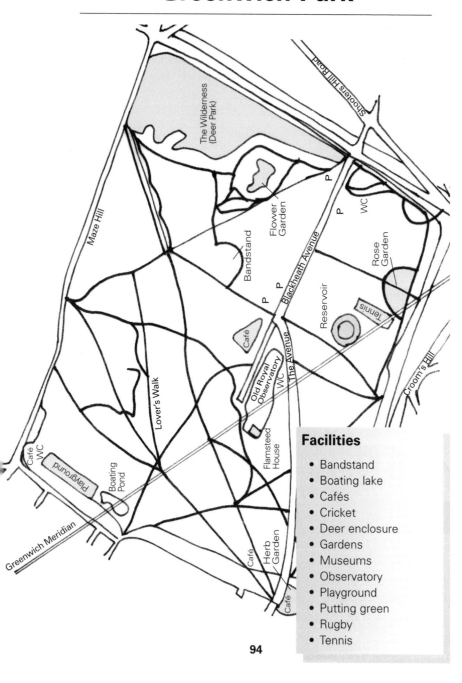

The Wilderness (Deer Park)

Shooters Hill Road

Maze Hill

Bandstand

Flower Garden

Blackheath Avenue

Rose Garden

P

WC

Reservoir

Tennis

Café

Croom's Hill

Lover's Walk

Old Royal Observatory

The Avenue

WC

Flamsteed House

Café
WC

Playground

Boating Pond

Greenwich Meridian

Café

Herb Garden

Café

Facilities

- Bandstand
- Boating lake
- Cafés
- Cricket
- Deer enclosure
- Gardens
- Museums
- Observatory
- Playground
- Putting green
- Rugby
- Tennis

VISITOR INFORMATION

Main office: Blackheath Gate, SE10 8QY.

Park Manager: Derrick Spurr

Open Monday to Friday 08.30–16.30. Tel. 020 8858 2608,
www.royalparks.org.uk.

Boat: to Greenwich Pier from Charing Cross Pier

Bus: 53, 177, 180, 286

Car: pay and display on Blackheath Avenue in the park (60p/hour,
max. stay is 4h)

Docklands Light Railway (DLR): Cutty Sark or Greenwich Island
Green (cross in the Greenwich Foot Tunnel)

Train: Maze Hill, Blackheath, London Bridge

The views and architecture of Greenwich Park are spectacular. There are over 3,000 ancient trees, flower gardens, a wilderness with a deer pen, tennis courts, cafés, a playground and a small boating lake. Greenwich Park is the oldest of the Royal Parks, dating back to 1433. It is the birthplace of Greenwich Mean Time and the Prime Meridian Line that separates the eastern and western hemispheres. Greenwich's pivotal role in mapping the stars and solving the longitude question drove Britain's extraordinary maritime achievements.

The 200 acres still have an atmosphere of past adventures and exploration. Standing on the hill by Sir Christopher Wren's Observatory (a UNESCO World Heritage Site) it is easy to imagine the great explorers setting sail from the Greenwich dock below, the ships setting their marine chronometers from the Observatory's red ball signal. The *Cutty Sark* sits in the dry dock below, the old Royal Naval Hospital fronts the river and the splendid Palladian National Maritime Museum sits at the bottom of the park. This is all combined with London's 21st century skyline including Canary Wharf flashing like a giant lighthouse. In the docks below there are river cruises and the Greenwich foot tunnel crosses to Island Green. The park is also the start of the London Marathon and borders Blackheath.

HIGHLIGHTS

- The views of London: bring your binoculars
- The Royal Observatory
- The National Maritime Museum
- The architecture of Inigo Jones and Sir Christopher Wren
- The Chestnut Avenues and flower gardens

BIRDS

There are over 70 species of bird in Greenwich Park including green and great spotted woodpeckers, jays, song thrushes, wrens, starlings, greenfinches, tawny owls and long tailed tits. Free Sunday morning bird walks are led throughout the year starting at 08.00 in summer and 08.30 in winter. Contact the Visitor Centre or check the park notice boards.

BOATING

There is a small boating lake, mainly suitable for children, next to the playground and near Queen's House. Boats cost £2 (adults) and £1 (children) for 20 minutes, available from 10.30–17.00. The lake is open from Easter to 30 October on weekends and June to August every day (weather permitting). Group bookings through Hyde Park Boat House, tel. 020 7262 1330.

BOAT TRIPS ON THE THAMES

There are regular services to Westminster and beyond which are run by a number of companies. City Cruises runs a good service. Tickets cost from £8 return. Tel. 020 7930 9033.

Travel for London has information on transport throughout London. The website is more user friendly than the telephone centre. Website www.tfl.gov.uk, tel. 020 7222 1234.

CAFÉS

The Tea House at Greenwich Park

The park's main café is opposite the Planetarium on Blackheath Avenue. It was built in 1906 and has been beautifully restored. There is a small dovecote with a weather-vane on top. The café has indoors and outdoors seating and the hot food is cooked on site. Cappuccinos £1.50, tea £1.25 per pot, sandwiches from £2.25, jacket potatoes from £2.60, sausage and mash £4.95. Tel. 020 8858 9695. Open every day except Christmas Day, 09.00–20.00 summer and 10.00–16.00 winter.

St Mary's Lodge

This small café is just inside St Mary's Gate, one of the earliest entrances to the park. The pretty white lodge is now the Visitor Centre and tearoom. They serve tasty snacks and good cappuccinos from the central octagonal room. There are informative displays and information about the park. Tel. 020 8293 0703. Open 09.00–20.00 summer and weekends, 10.00–15.00 only in winter.

Island Gardens Café

This café is on the opposite side of river, facing the park. When Wren was designing the Greenwich Observatory he would cross the river to view the park from this small garden. It was said to be his favourite view and is worth the trip through the splendid Greenwich Foot Tunnel to enjoy. An added enticement to visit these gardens, which was not available to Wren, is the Island Gardens Café. This tiny chirpy café serves tasty English and Caribbean food with a smile. It is located in the riverside gardens near the entrance to the foot tunnel. The outside seating gives the best views of the park: the old Royal Naval Hospital, the lonely statue of Woolf on the hill and the Royal

Observatory's famous red signalling ball. A mug of coffee never tasted so good. Coffee 70p, tea 60p, breakfast menu, soups, fish cakes, Caribbean curries. Open Tuesday to Sundays from about 09.30–17.00.

CHESTNUTS

In the 1660s the park was laid out in the French style with hundreds of sweet (edible) chestnut trees being planted in formal avenues. Some of the original trees have survived, including one in the Flower Garden with a girth of more than 10 metres. In autumn people compete with the squirrels to collect the delicious chestnuts.

CRICKET

There are regular cricket matches played on the Ranger's Field close to Blackheath Gate. There is a pavilion on the field with changing facilities. The Blackheath Cricket Club play here and can be contacted at www.blackheathcc.com, tel. 020 8858 4250. For details of pitch hire and prices contact the park office on 020 8858 2608.

DEER

The deer enclosure is hidden within a 'wilderness area' near the flower garden. This was planted in the 1660s, just before the Chestnut Avenues, and has a network of secluded paths running through the undergrowth. There are red and fallow deer that can be viewed from vantage points through the fencing.

DOLPHIN SUNDIAL

This pretty sculpture by Edwin Russell sits in the small Titanic Memorial Garden, in front of the Maritime Museum. The two dolphins hold a curved dial plate in their mouths, with the hours and minutes indicated by thick and thin lines. The shadow cast by the dolphins' tails tells the time. Edith Haisman, who survived the sinking of the *Titanic*, opened the garden in 1995.

There is a small wooden galleon for children next to the garden. Another bigger sundial is next to the boating lake.

FRIENDS OF GREENWICH PARK

There are many benefits of becoming a Friend of Greenwich Park, including a 25% discount at the cafés, a regular newsletter and invitations to Friends events. There are regular special interest walks including spiders, birds, bats and ecology.

Membership costs £5/year. Contact the Membership Secretary, Fran Tyler, 51 Lock Chase, Blackheath SA3 9HB.

GARDENS

The Flower Garden forms a large triangle in the southeast corner of the park. There are over 30 brightly planted flowerbeds, a lake filled with waterfowl, and some unusual trees including the prickly castor-oil tree (*kalopanax pictus*). The Rose Garden lies within yew hedging in front of the Ranger's House. There are over one hundred species of rose, listed on a board nearby. The Dell is a small enclosed sunken garden filled with rhododendrons and azaleas. It overlooks the Ranger's Field and is a haven for birds and butterflies. Near to St Mary's Gate there is a pretty herb garden that has six types of mint.

NATIONAL MARITIME MUSEUM

The National Maritime Museum in Park Row was built in the early 19th century as a school for naval orphans. It was recently reopened following a £20 million redevelopment. Its 20 galleries chart the history of Britain and the sea and it is the largest museum of its kind in the world. Admission is free. Tel. 020 8858 4422. Open every day 10.00–17.00, www.nmm.ac.uk.

OBSERVATORY

The Royal Greenwich Observatory, now a UNESCO world

heritage site, was built in the 17th century on the orders of Charles II. It was to solve the 'problem of longitude', that is, how to measure longitude at sea. This problem was one of the greatest challenges of the 17th century. Until it was solved the world's greatest adventures and explorers often sailed blind, without knowing how far east or west they were from land. It happened here, in the magnificent observatory designed by Christopher Wren. All around you can see the telescopes, clocks, maps and instruments used by the royal astronomers. The collection of Harrison's clocks H1–H4 is worth a trip on its own: they are some of the most important and beautiful timepieces in the world. The office of the Astronomer Royal has continued since 1675.

Greenwich Mean Time

In the 19th century Greenwich began a service of 'distributed time' to all of the main chronometer makers in London. They set up a new timekeeping system called Greenwich Mean Time, GMT: the time measured from the stars in relation to the Greenwich Meridian. Each Monday the Observatory staff would set their large chronometer to the calculated GMT, and take it down the hill to the clock makers of London. Eventually an electrical 'master' clock, designed by Charles Shepherd, was installed on the Observatory wall.

Longitude

Greenwich Park is home to the Prime Meridian of the World, Longitude 000° 00' 00", relative to which all space and time is measured. When Charles II appointed John Flamsteed (1646–1719) as the first Astronomer Royal in order to map the sky and solve the problem of calculating longitude at sea, he drew a line in the earth and established this small cluster of buildings as the centre of the world. The meridian line, separating east from west, is set into the ground in the courtyard of the Observatory.

Tel. 020 8858 4422. Open 10.00–17.00 (closed 24–26 December). Admission free. www.nmm.ac.uk

PLAYGROUND

There is a children's playground next to the boating lake. This has a small café open in the summer.

PUTTING

There is a small putting green next to the tennis centre. Putters and balls are available for hire when the tennis centre is open (currently from April to September). For further information contact the Hyde Park office on 020 7262 3474.

QUEEN'S HOUSE

The Queen's House was England's first Palladian villa. It was designed by Inigo Jones for Queen Anne, wife of James I. The house was only completed after her death and on the orders of Charles I for the use of his wife Henrietta Maria. It is a fine example of Palladio's classic style (see also p41) and is now an art gallery for the National Maritime Museum's collection of paintings. The house is linked to the wings of the National Maritime Museum by long colonnades built to commemorate the battle of Trafalgar.

Tel. 020 8858 4422. Open every day 10.00–17.00 (closed Dec. 24–26). Admission free. www.nmm.ac.uk

RANGER'S HOUSE

The 18th century red brick Ranger's House has recently been restored and is now a museum with a collection of 17th and 18th century portraits.

Open Wednesday to Saturday and bank holidays 10.00–16.00 (closed 22 December–2 March). Admission adults £4.50 and children £2.50 (English Heritage members free). Tel. 020 8853 0035.

RED BALL

The famous red 'time ball' above the clock on the eastern turret of the Observatory drops each day at 1pm. It was designed in 1833 to enable ships in the Thames to set their marine chronometers accurately before setting sail. In 1855 it was blown down in a gale. The original ball, which had been covered in leather, was replaced by the current aluminium one in 1919.

ROYAL NAVAL HOSPITAL

This building was intended by Charles II to replace the Tudor Greenwich Palace built by Henry VII and which was subsequently home to Henry VIII and his daughter Elizabeth I. Charles II commissioned John Webb (a pupil of Inigo Jones) to design the new palace but money soon ran out and it was not completed. It was eventually opened as a Royal Hospital for Seamen during the reign of William and Mary. Sir Christopher Wren helped to complete the building. Its painted hall ceiling took James Thornhill 19 years to paint. The building became the Royal Naval College in 1873 and is now part of Greenwich University. Several parts are open to the public, including the painted hall and the chapel.

King William Walk, London SE10, tel. 020 8269 4793, website www.greenwichfoundation.org.uk. Open every day 10.00–17.00 (closed 24–26 December). Admission free.

RUGBY

There are two rugby pitches on the Ranger's Field at the north end of the park, near Blackheath Gates, with a pavilion and changing facilities. The pitches are used by the Blackheath Rugby Club. This club was formed by the Old Boys of Blackheath Proprietary School in 1858 and is the oldest open rugby club in the world. They have men's, women's, juniors and mini sections and new members of all standards are welcome. The club is based at the Rectory Field, Charlton Road, Blackheath (just across the road from Greenwich Park), tel. 020 8293 0853, website www.blackheathrugby.co.uk. For details about hiring pitches contact the Parks Office on 020 8858 2608.

SPORTS FIELD

The Ranger's Field in front of the house is used for cricket and rugby. Contact the Park Rangers for the latest clubs and prices for using the field, tel. 020 8858 2608.

STATUES

The most prominent statue in the park is that of General James Woolf (1727–1759). He stands at the highest point in the park, at the end of Blackheath Avenue, surveying the stunning views across London with a telescope in his hand. The statue commemorates his 1759 victory at Quebec. Henry Moore's 'Large Standing Figure: Knife Edge' also commands a good view from its hill on the southwest side of Flamsteed House. The statue of the 'sailor King' William IV stands in a less prominent position, just inside St Mary's Gate.

TENNIS

There are six tennis courts, near the Ranger's House. At the time of writing the management was due to change hands to the 'Will to Win' tennis club that also runs the clubs at Hyde Park and Regent's Park. This excellent club runs an extensive tennis programme at the other clubs and is likely to do so here as well. For the latest information contact the Will to Win tennis centre at Hyde Park on 020 7262 3474 or visit the website www.tennis-uk.com, email willtowin@btopenworld.com.

TREES

André le Notre designed the park's original formal avenues of trees in the 1660s. He was a famous French garden designer, who worked on the Palace of Versailles outside Paris. Hundreds of trees were planted, some of which still survive. The most impressive trees are the park's ancient sweet chestnuts, particularly on the Great Cross Avenue, in the Ranger's field and in the Flower Garden. There is a huge ancient common beech tree in the rose garden of the Ranger's House. Elsewhere there are red oaks, scarlet oaks, elms, sycamores, pines and even an Indian bean tree. Blackheath Avenue is the start of the London Marathon and is planted with horse chestnuts.

VOLUNTEERING

The Living History project allows local schools to get involved in the park. Volunteers are needed to help expand the project. Wildlife volunteers are also in demand for Wildlife for All. There are opportunities for practical conservation work as well as educational projects. Tel. 020 7935 7430, wildlifeforall@royalparks.gsi.gov.

WALKS

There are walks in the park throughout the year, including fungi foraging (over 50 species are found in the park), tree identifying, rose pruning, plant propagation and bird watching. The walks usually meet by the notice board outside the parks office at Blackheath Gate at 10.30. Many of the walks are free of charge. Contact the visitor centre for further information.

NEAR THE PARK

The *Cutty Sark*

This is the only surviving tea clipper in the world. It was built in 1869 and is in a dry dock in the Cutty Sark Gardens by the Greenwich Pier.

Open every day 10.00–17.00 (closed December 24–26). Admission: Adults £3.95, children £2.95, family ticket £9.80.

Greenwich Foot Tunnel

The Greenwich Foot Tunnel was built in 1902 for the dockers working in the West India Docks. It is 1,217 feet long and is lined by 200,000 glazed tiles. It is like walking through a large tiled drainpipe. There are beautiful wood panelled lifts to whisk you down and up again at either end. This is open (and manned) from Monday to Saturday

07.00–19.00 and Sunday 10.00–17.30, tel. 020 8921 5472. Access is free. It runs under the River Thames from Greenwich Pier to Island Gardens, near the DLR.

Gunnersbury Park

This 185-acre Ealing park was opened to the public in May 1926 by the then Minister for Health, Neville Chamberlain. It was once a splendid park with the Rothschild's stucco-fronted Regency mansions (Gunnersbury Park and Gunnersbury House), a Japanese garden, a bathhouse, stables, cafés and numerous sports pitches. The larger mansion, Gunnersbury Park, was designed by Sydney Smirke, whose brother designed the reading room of the British Museum. It is now a free museum of local history and transport.

Daniel Defoe wrote that a tour through the park was like a tour through the whole of the British Isles. Although the park has seen better days it retains some of its old charm

Facilities

- Art classes
- Café
- Cricket
- Cycling
- Fishing
- Football
- Golf: pitch and putt
- Museum
- Netball (at sports club)
- Rugby
- Playground
- Sports club
- Table tennis (at club)
- Tennis

106

as a secret spacious park bounded by the North Circular and the M4, with high brick walls and open grassy spaces. The excellent Old Actonians Sports Club offers a wide range of sports including cycling, cricket, badminton, football, netball, rugby and table tennis.

ART

There are regular art classes run from the Small Mansion with its pretty views over the park. Tel. 020 8932 0993/8993 8312.

BADMINTON

There is a badminton club based at the Old Actonians Sport Club on Gunnersbury Drive (see below, Sports Club). They have one court in the Pavilion and play during winter months. New members are welcome. Contact the Sports Club for more details, or visit www.oldactonians.co.uk.

BATHHOUSE

The salmon coloured bathhouse was built for Princess Amelia, who was George II's daughter. It dates from 1761 and originally had a plunge pool with a cascade of ferns. It contained statues, candles and shells rather like a modern luxury spa.

BICYCLING

The Old Actonians Cycling Club is based at the Sports Club on Gunnersbury Drive (see below). They have events for serious and social cyclists of all standards. Rides leave from the club on Wednesday evenings at 18.30 (20–40 miles) with a hot meal provided after; and on Sunday mornings, throughout the year. Contact the Old Actonians Sports Club for further information (see below).

BOWLING

The bowling green is run by Hounslow Leisure Services, and is home to the Gunnersbury Bowling Club. It is on the edge of a huge expanse of grass, dotted with football and rugby pitches. To play at the club costs £1.90/hour or £1 for older people. Woods hire costs £1.20. The club plays during summer months only.

CAFÉ

The Pavilion Café

The Pavilion Café has been serving park-goers since 1958. It is located near the museum at the Popes Lane entrance to the park and has a range of tasty food and drinks. It is open every day from 10.00–16.00 (winter) and later in the summer. Tel. 020 8992 0543.

CRICKET

The Old Actonians Cricket Club is based at the Sports Club on Gunnersbury Drive (see below). The club runs three Saturday sides and two on Sundays. Outdoor nets practice is held on Tuesday and Thursday evenings. There is an active Colts section with coaching on Saturday mornings. For further information visit the Sports Club website, www.oldactonians.co.uk, or contact the club (see below).

FISHING

Fishing is available in the Potomac Pond in Gunnersbury Park. This is a 2.5 acre pretty, round pond opposite the Temple. It is well stocked with carp, pike, tench, perch, roach and eel. The fishing is on a 'turn up and fish' basis, where an attendant will come round to collect the ticket fee. A rod licence is required.

FOOTBALL

There are six grass football pitches that are free for whoever feels like a game. The playing fields on Gunnersbury Drive are home to the Old Actonians Football Club. This club was founded in 1925 and is one of the largest and most successful amateur football clubs in London. Membership to the club is open to everyone. Matches are played on Saturday afternoons and training is on Wednesday evenings from 18.30 at the park. Contact the club via the Old Actonians Sports Club, www.oldactonians.co.uk (see below).

GOLF

There is an 18 hole pitch-and-putt course and a putting green in the park, near the tennis courts. This is run by the Golfwise Group (who also run the tennis booking). Bookings are not necessary. For further details contact tel. 07956 624355, turn up at the course or contact the Golfwise Head Office, West Park Golf Centre, Waterhouse Lane, Chelmsford, Essex, CM1, tel. 01245 257682, www.golfwiseltd.co.uk.

MUSEUM

The Rothschild family mansion (the Large Mansion) is now a museum of local history and transport. The collection includes costume, archaeology, coaches, a chariot, a hansom cab and dolls' houses. Guided tours of the fully equipped Victorian kitchens are run on Saturdays and Sundays from the first weekend in April. The museum is open every day from 13.00–16.00, free entrance, tel. 020 8992 1612. The museum is near the Popes Lane entrance to the park.

NETBALL

The Old Actonians Netball Club is based at the Sports Club on Gunnersbury Drive. They often run up to five teams and have training every Tuesday evening from 19.30–21.00. The court is flood-lit and fenced and the club plays in winter and summer. Contact the Sports Club (see below) for further details or visit their website: www.oldactonians.co.uk.

PONDS

The pretty round Potomac Pond with its neighbouring temple is a good place for fishing (see Fishing, above). The larger nearby boating lake is home to a wide variety of waterfowl. It is not currently used for either boating or fishing.

RUGBY

There is a rugby pitch in the park next to the football pitches (near the bowling green). There are further playing fields in Gunnersbury Drive, home to the Old Actonian Sports Club. This club includes the Old Actonian Rugby Football Club, formed in 1972. The rugby club runs five sides and welcomes new members of all standards. There are touch rugby tournaments, 15-a-side and sevens. Pre-season training starts in July. For further information visit their website www.oldactonianrfc.com or contact the Sports Club (see below).

SPORTS CLUB

The superb Old Actonians Sports Club is based in Gunnersbury Drive, just off the North Circular and at the north end of the park. The club was founded in 1964 and has a six acre site, with over 1,000 members, 200 of which are juniors. The club has badminton, cricket, cycling, football, netball, rugby, squash, and table tennis (see separate entries). New members of all standards are welcomed, including social members. The clubhouse was completely refurbished in 1999 and has good facilities, including a bar and a wide-screen TV.

Old Actonians Sports Club, Gunnersbury Drive, London W5 4LL, tel. 020 8567 4556, website www.oldactonians.co.uk, email info@oldactonians.co.uk.

SQUASH CLUB

The Old Actonians Squash Club was formed in 1976 and plays in good facilities at the Sports Club (see above).

TABLE TENNIS

The Oaks Table Tennis Club has been based at the Old Actonians Sports Club in Gunnersbury Drive since 1998 (see above). They welcome new members of all ages and abilities and have matches and practice on Monday and Thursday evenings at 19.30. There are coaching sessions on Saturday mornings and regular social events. Contact the club for more details or visit the website www.oldactonians.co.uk.

TENNIS

The tennis courts are near the stables, in the centre of the Park. There are seven tarmac courts; at the time of writing the courts were free of charge and could not be booked in advance. There are also courts at the Old Actonians Sports Club in Gunnersbury Drive (see above). The tennis club runs regular tournaments and coaching sessions and plays throughout the year.

NEAR THE PARK

Kew Gardens, tel. 020 8332 5000, www.kew.org.uk, entrance £7.50, under 16s free.

Kids Cookery School, 107 Gunnersbury Lane, tel. 020 8992 8882.

Gunnersbury Triangle Nature Reserve, Bollo Lane, tel. 020 8747 3881, website www.wildlondon.org.uk for free events.

Hampstead Heath

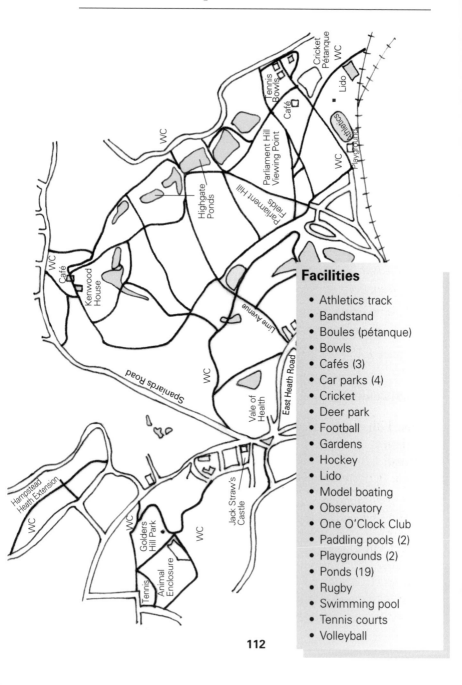

Facilities

- Athletics track
- Bandstand
- Boules (pétanque)
- Bowls
- Cafés (3)
- Car parks (4)
- Cricket
- Deer park
- Football
- Gardens
- Hockey
- Lido
- Model boating
- Observatory
- One O'Clock Club
- Paddling pools (2)
- Playgrounds (2)
- Ponds (19)
- Rugby
- Swimming pool
- Tennis courts
- Volleyball

VISITOR INFORMATION

Hampstead Heath, NW3

Tel. 020 7485 4491 (Parliament Hill Office) or 020 8455 5183 (Golders Hill Office)

Website: www.cityoflondon.gov.uk

Tube/train: Gospel Oak, Kentish Town, Hampstead (all about a 20-minute walk).

Bus: 24, 46, 168, 214, C2, C11

Car: There are four car parks on the heath which close before dusk:

1. East Heath Road (near Hampstead Heath station) Open every day from 11am.

2. Kenwood (West Lodge, just off Hampstead Lane). There are also a few disabled parking spaces here, and outside the Brew House Restaurant. Access to the disabled spaces at the Brew House Restaurant is via an intercom at East Lodge (off Hampstead Lane).

3. Parliament Hill Lido (next to the Lido Swimming Pool, off Gordon House Road), open every day from 07.15 until dark.

4. Heath Car Park (behind Jack Straw's Castle), open every day 10.00–18.00..

In the 17th century Hampstead Village was a spa town where Londoners would go to enjoy the fresh air, spring water and views of London. Artists and writers such as Betjeman, Blake, Byron, Constable, Keats, Lamb and Shelley all found inspiration here and little has changed since their time. The Heath covers 320 hectares (800 acres) of land and includes Golders Hill Park (containing fine English gardens), the estate of Kenwood House (with its summertime concerts) and Parliament Hill (famous for kite flying). It provides some of the most spectacular scenery anywhere in the country. There are grassy hills, woods, wild areas and landscaped parkland. The Corporation of London manages the Heath to ensure conservation with maximum recreation at no cost to the local taxpayers.

There is a wealth of opportunities for all interests including athletics, bat and bird watching, bowls, cricket, cross-country running, a deer park, fishing, football, gardens, golf, hockey, horticulture, model boating, concerts, petanque, photography, rugby, swimming, tennis, volleyball, walking and wildlife events. Golders Hill Park, less well known than other parts of the heath, includes a small deer enclosure and zoo (currently being renovated), a café and the beautiful but rarely visited Hill Garden with its 800ft pergola. Golders Hill Park is covered separately on p87.

HIGHLIGHTS

- The evening light along Lime Avenue (leading to Wells Walk)
- Swimming in the 60m lido and in the bathing ponds
- Hampstead Village for shopping, espresso or the Everyman cinema
- The free picture collection at Kenwood House
- Kite flying and the views on Parliament Hill
- Open grassy spaces that feel like the countryside
- A drink at the Parliament Hill Café
- Playground and huge paddling pool
- Sunset by the model boating pond
- Views over the City of London

ATHLETICS

There is a 400m eight-lane flood-lit synthetic track at Parliament Hill Fields. The track is fully certified and includes full field event facilities, a water jump and changing rooms in a trackside pavilion. The facilities are open to the public and are used by the Highgate Harriers, London Heathside Runners

Athletic Club and University College London Athletic and Cross Country Club. See also 'Duathlon' (below). There is an excellent fenced, outdoor circuit for fitness training next to the athletics track, available for over 13s free of charge. There is also a 90-metre, six-lane grass running track available during the summer, at Hampstead Heath Extension (in the far north of the heath).

Highgate Harriers

The Highgate Harriers have regular meetings and training sessions for cross-country running and track and field events. They were founded in 1879 and are based at the Parliament Hill Athletics Track. The club welcomes new members of all standards. Enquiries to Richard Dawson, tel. 020 7281 6183, website www.highgateharriers.co.uk.

London Heathside Athletic Club

The London Heathside Athletic Club uses the track for some training sessions. They are based at Finsbury Park Athletic Club, see p79. www.londonheathside.org.uk.

Parliament Hill Fields Athletics Track

Tel. 020 7284 3648 (office) or 020 8348 9930 (bookings).

Open Monday to Saturday 07.45–dusk, Sundays and bank holidays 07.45–16.00. There are flood-lit sessions on Tuesdays and Thursdays until 20.40. Cost: £2.20/day (£1.10 concessionary) or £35/season ticket (£15 concessionary). Track meetings Monday to Friday £58, weekends and bank holidays £85.

BANDSTAND

The Parliament Hill Fields Bandstand (next to the café near the athletics track) has Sunday concerts from the end of May until the end of August. These usually run from 15.00–17.00 and include brass bands, jazz and light orchestras.

BICYCLING

There are four cycle routes on the heath, marked with a yellow cycle. These are from Nassington Road to Highgate Road, East Heath Road car park to Millfield Lane, Spaniards Road to Millfield Lane, and West Heath Road to North End Way.

BIRD WATCHING

Marylebone Bird Watching Society organises bird watching walks on the heath on Tuesdays. They start at 10.00 at the Parliament Hill café. They also organise local outings and talks. For further information contact Judy Powell, tel. 020 7485 0863, website www.geocities.com/birdsmbs. The Hampstead Heath information centre also runs a series of walks throughout the year including 'Dawn Chorus' walks, starting at 4am. See below under 'Walks', or tel. 020 7485 3873.

BOULES (PÉTANQUE)

The French version of bowls, pétanque, is now available on the heath. Payment and equipment hire is available from the tennis hut (Parliament Hill Fields). No booking is required, just turn up on the hour to play. Boules costs £1.80 per hour and a £10 deposit for the boules themselves.

BOWLS

There is a bowling green next to the café at Parliament Hill open between late April and the end of September. The rinks are open to the public from 13.00, apart from bank holidays and weekends. A season ticket costs £49 (£15 pensioners), or pay £2.20 per hour. Lessons are available. For further information contact the Parliament Hill Fields Staff Yard on 020 7284 3648. The Parliament Hill Bowling Club is also based at the ground and welcomes new members of all standards. Further information about the club is available at the bowling green or from the membership secretary, Robert Atherton, 85 Cressfield Close, Grafton Road, London NW5 4BN, tel. 020 7482 6608.

CAFÉS

The D'Auria Brothers Parliament Hill Fields Café

This cheap canteen-style café is on the south end of the heath near the bandstand, tennis courts, lido, paddling pool and athletics track. It is a purpose built, one storey red brick building with inside and outdoor seating. The café recently featured in the film 'Enduring Love'. Hot dishes range from a baked potato with cheese (£2.70) to chicken Milanese (£6), cappuccino (£1.15), tea (60p), hot bacon sandwich (£1.80), crisps (35p), bottled beer (£1.20), half-litre of water 80p. There is also a children's menu including sausage and chips (£2) and pasta bolognaise (£2.60). Tel. 020 7485 6606. Open daily in July and August from 09.30–21.00 and Tuesday to Sunday from September to June 09.00–16.00. Nearest stations: Gospel Oak, Hampstead Heath.

Kenwood House, Steward's Room

Open daily 10.00–17.00. This small café has outdoor seating only. Italian ice-creams are sold from a hatch from £1.40 in all the usual flavours as well as Caribbean coconut and mango sorbet. Simple snacks such as cake and sandwiches are available. Prices start at 90p for teas, cappuccino £1.25 and crisps £1.25.

Kenwood House, The Brew House Café

Open daily 09.00–18.00, October to March 09.00–16.00, tel. 020 8341 5384. This smart self-service café uses top-quality free-range eggs, bacon and sausages as well as organic flour. It is more expensive with sandwiches starting at £2.95, cappuccino £1.50, tea £1.15, cakes £1.60, bottled beer £2.75, crisps 75p and biscuits 65p. Tap water is free. The treacle tart has the perfect ratio of syrup to buttery pastry to lemon zest (£1.50). There is indoor and outdoor seating as well as a dog walkers seating area.

CRICKET

The cricket pitch and practice nets are available at Parliament Hill and the Hampstead Heath Extension between the end of April and end of August. A senior pitch costs £50, junior £9.50 and practice nets £5 per hour.

DUATHLON

There is an annual Hampstead Heath Duathlon (running and swimming). This includes individual and team competitions with the emphasis on 'taking part and having a go'. For further details contact Paul Maskell (sports and entertainment manager, Hampstead Heath) tel. 020 7485 4491 or Mark Spilsbury tel. 020 8347 7178.

FAIRS

Funfairs are held on the late Spring bank holiday and the late Summer bank holiday.

FISHING

Fishing is allowed in six ponds on the heath. These include the Highgate Men's Pond, the Model Boating Pond, Hampstead No. 3 and No. 4 ponds, the Viaduct Pond and the Vale of Health Pond. Anglers must be in possession of an Environment Agency annual licence (available from Post Offices and angling shops) and a free permit to fish (provided by the Corporation). There are free 'learn to fish' days held from 12.00–16.00 during summer. For further information contact the Parliament Hill Staff Yard on tel. 020 7485 4491.

FOOTBALL

There are football pitches at Parliament Hill and Hampstead Heath Extension and rugby pitches at the Extension available between early September and the end of March. A pitch with goal posts costs £50, goal nets cost £11 and private changing rooms £29. Football coaching is available from Football

Association approved instructors. The courses are for 7–14 year olds and are based at the Parliament Hill pitches. They run between mid September and the end of October and each lasts for six consecutive Saturday mornings at 09.30. Booking is essential, tel. 020 8348 9930.

FRIENDS OF HAMPSTEAD HEATH AND KENWOOD TREES

The Friends of Hampstead Heath and Kenwood Trees group was set up to preserve the natural aspects of the heath and represent its users. Contact the secretary Peter Appleby on 020 7435 3154 or email the chairman, Anna Farlow on afarlow@lineone.net.

GARDENS

The bare remains of 'Pitts Garden' are a short walk from the famous Bull and Bush pub on North End Way. This was once a walled garden which formed part of Pitts estate. All that remains now are the ruined classical arch and the flat rectangular shape of the plot. It is all being reclaimed by nature and unfortunately nearby developments. There are still some spring flowers that presumably had their origins in this garden as well as ancient rhododendrons. The English Garden at nearby Golders Hill Park and the Pergola at the Hill Garden, in contrast, remain pristine (see Golders Hill Park, p87).

GETTING AROUND THE HEATH

The Heath Mobile Loan Service has battery-powered cars for less mobile people. Contact tel. 020 7485 5757 for further information.

HOCKEY

Fun, informal, mixed matches are played on Sunday afternoons from October to May on the pitch near the radio mast at the southwest corner of the Kenwood estate. Games start at 15.00

and everyone is welcome. The tradition of informal hockey matches at this pitch pre-dates World War II. In the words of a club member it is 'London's answer to beach volleyball'. Early members included Professor Joad, of the Brains Trust fame. Current members range from an Oxford Blue to complete beginners. To join in either turn up at the pitch on a match day or contact Nick Prag, email nprag@europe.com,tel. 020 8830 1211, website www.hampstead-heath-hockey.org.uk. Spare sticks are usually available. The pitch is just off Spaniards Road, halfway between Jack Straw's Castle and the Spaniard's Inn, near the radio mast on the Kenwood estate, but check for possible changes in location on the website. Post-match drinks are at the Spaniard's Inn.

INFORMATION

The main information office is based next to the Parliament Hill Lido (near the Gospel Oak entrance to the park). Information Centre, Staff Yard, Highgate Road, NW5, open Wednesday to Friday 13.00–17.00, Saturdays and Sundays 10.30–12.30 and 13.00–17.00.

The information offices close one hour earlier from November to February. Tel. 020 7482 7073, www.cityoflondon.gov.uk, email hampstead.heath@corpoflondon.gov.uk

KENWOOD HOUSE

This 18th century neo-classical villa was designed by the architect Robert Adam and contains a collection of paintings by Gainsborough, Rembrandt, Reynolds, Turner, Van Dyck, Vermeer and others. It is located at the top of Hampstead Heath, a 30-minute walk from the shops of Hampstead Village and Hampstead tube station. It is surrounded by parkland with a sculpture by Henry Moore and another by Barbara Hepworth. There are stunning views across the rolling lawns to the lake and the rest of the heath. In spring there are swathes of daffodils and rhododendrons and in summer there are lakeside classical concerts. The villa is open every day and is free. There are two cafés serving a range of snacks as well as hot meals, toilets for wheelchair users and baby changing facilities (see above under Cafés).

Kenwood House, Hampstead Lane, NW3, tel. 020 8348 1286, website www.english-heritage.org.uk. Opening times 1 April to 30 September 10.00–17.30, October 10.00–17.00, November to March 10.00–16.00. The house is open every day except 24–26 December and 1 January. On Wednesdays and Fridays the house opens at 10.30. The Suffolk Collection is open Thursday to Sunday 11.00–15.00.

Visitor Centre, Mansion Cottage, open Monday to Sunday 11.00–15.00, tel. 020 7973 3891. Kenwood House Lakeside Concerts tel. 020 8233 7435. Ticket sales 0870 8900146, website www.picnicconcerts.com, Saturdays 19.30 from July to August and August Bank Holiday Sunday.

KITE FLYING

Parliament Hill is the best place for kite flying in London. It has the added attraction of one of London's best panoramic views.

MODEL BOATING

Model boats can be used on Highgate No. 3 pond from Monday to Friday 14.00–16.30 and at weekends from 12.00–16.30. Boat runners need to have insurance.

OBSERVATORY

The Hampstead Scientific Society has an observatory near Whitestone Pond, the highest natural point in London. They have a superb six-inch Cooke refracting telescope which was built in 1899, with modern modifications including remote controlled guidance. The telescope gives excellent views of the planets and the moon. A demonstrator and members of the society are on hand during public opening times to help out and answer questions. Entrance is free (donations welcome) and the observatory is open to non-members on Friday and Saturday

20.00–22.00 and Sunday 11.00–13.00 September to April
(weather permitting). The observatory is also open for eclipses,
comets and other special occasions. The society has regular
lectures in St John's Church Crypt, Hampstead, and even runs a
telescope-making class. For further details contact the society's
website www.hampsteadscience.ac.uk or visit the observatory
(located on a grass-covered underground reservoir surrounded
by railings, off Hampstead Grove, near the corner of Heath
Street and Hampstead Grove close to Whitestone Pond)
(Hampstead tube, parking on Hampstead Grove after 20.00).

ONE O'CLOCK CLUB

The Parliament Hill Fields Drop In One O'Clock Club is based
at the Peggy Jay Centre just behind the lido (Gordon House
Road entrance). Sessions run from Monday to Friday
10.00–12.00 with a small charge and from 13.00–16.00 free of
charge. Tel. 020 7485 6907 or 020 7435 6178, or contact the
main information number on 020 8348 0024.

ORIENTEERING

The London Orienteering Klubb (*sic*) was founded in 1971.
The club has a current membership of about 100 which ranges
from complete beginners to international standard. There are a
number of competitions, regular training sessions, meetings
and dinners. Training sessions take place every Thursday
evening on Hampstead Heath and start at 18.30 outside the
Royal Free Hospital Recreation Club (Fleet Road). The club is
open to all ages. For further information contact the
Membership Secretary, Julie Cleary, 9 Lydia Mews,
Welham Green, Herts, AL9 7PZ, tel. 01707 275934,
website www.londonorienteering.co.uk,
email membership@londonorienteering.co.uk.

PLAYGROUND AND PADDLING POOL

There is a fantastic children's playground and giant paddling
pool next to the athletic track at Parliament Hill Fields. This is

supervised and includes several types of swing, roundabouts and a sand pit. In summer an ice-cream van usually parks outside, but otherwise the Parliament Hill Café is nearby. The vast grassy slopes facing the track and playground are a popular spot for sunbathing, picnics and football. The paddling pool is open 11.00–17.00 from May to September.

RUGBY

Hampstead Rugby Football Club has teams for all abilities. The club is one of the oldest rugby clubs in the world and is one of the most active clubs in London. There are currently six teams playing weekly matches during the season (September to May). Training takes place on Tuesdays and Thursdays from July until April at 19.00 at the Parliament Hill Athletic Track (see Athletics).

Further information is available from the club secretary Mark Spilsbury, 39 Langbourne Avenue, Holly Lodge, Highgate, tel. 020 8347 7178, website www.hampsteadrugbyclub.co.uk, email newplayers@hampsteadrugbyclub.co.uk.

RUNNING

The heath is an excellent environment for cross-country running. There are several annual races held there including the Southern Counties Cross Country Championships (in January) and the Greater London Cross Country Championships in November. The Highgate Harriers have regular meetings and training sessions for cross-country running, track and field and road running. They were founded in 1879 and are based at the Parliament Hill Athletic Track. The club welcomes new members of all standards. Enquiries to Richard Dawson, tel. 020 7281 6183, website www.highgateharriers.co.uk.

SCHOOLS EVENTS

There are events and teaching for schools and children organised on the heath. A teacher's pack is available from the Parliament Hill information centre, tel. 020 7482 7073.

SWIMMING

There are many opportunities for swimming including the 60m lido and three ponds.

Parliament Hill Lido

This huge open-air pool is 60m by 28m with a depth of 2.7m at the deep end for diving. The pool is not heated but people swim all year round. There is a small paddling pool for the under fives and a café next to the pool. The baby changing facilities are a small shelf next to a basin. A renovation project is underway to improve both the quality of the pool and accessibility. The pool is free between 07.00–09.00. Children under eight must be accompanied by an over-16-year-old.

Parliament Hill Fields, Gordon House Road, NW5, website www.lidos.org.uk, tel. 020 7485 3873 (summer time recorded message) or 020 7485 4491 (staff yard). Summer (first Saturday in May to the third Sunday in September) daily 07.00–18.00. Winter daily 07.30–10.00 (depending on demand and staffing availability). Swimming is free between 07.00–09.00. After 09.00 £3.60 (adults), £10 (family ticket), adult season ticket £40, concessions season ticket £18. Documents needed for concession include UB40, student card, pension book or income support book. Café open daily from 10.00.

Kenwood Ladies' Bathing Pond

(East of South Meadow, near Fitzroy Park Road) Entry free, over-eights only. Open December and January 07.30–15.30, November and February 07.00–15.00 and from March to October 07.00 until sunset. The Kenwood Ladies Pond Association represents the pond users and membership costs £2 per year, contact Margaret Hepburn, tel. 020 7435 4382.

Highgate Men's Bathing Pond

(Off Millfield Lane, east of Parliament Hill Fields) Entry free, over-eights only. Open December and January 07.30–15.30, November and February 07.00–15.00 and from March to October 06.00 until sunset.

Mixed Bathing Pond

(North of the fairground and car park in the Hampstead Heath train station/South End Green end of the park.) Entry free, over-eights only. Open from 07.00–19.00 for the summer season only.

The United Swimmers Association of Hampstead Heath represents the interests and concerns of swimmers in all the heath's ponds and holds regular meetings. Contact Peter Cuming, tel. 020 7485 5476, 56 Talacre Road, London NW5 4LX.

TENNIS

There are ten hard courts available at Parliament Hill Fields, not far from the lido and athletics track. Annual registration cards cost £10 and allow players to book courts three days in advance. The registration cards are available from the Tennis Courts Hut by the courts. Bookings are taken every day from 08.30–10.00 and cost £4.20 per hour (£2.10 for concessions). Tel. 020 7485 4491 (office) or 020 7284 3779 (bookings).

Tennis coaching is available April to September, tel. 020 7485 4491. Golders Hill Park: Tuesdays and Thursdays. Parliament Hill: Mondays, Wednesdays and Fridays. To book complete the application form and return to the information office.

VALE OF HEALTH AND THE PRYORS

The Vale of Health was part of Sir Thomas Maryon Wilson's estate in the 19th century. He began property development on the land in the mid 19th century, which was quickly halted by local protests. The estate therefore remained small and exclusive and includes its own fishing pond. The walk from Jack Straw's Castle, through the Vale of Health to the beautiful Pryors Field, is worth considering. The Pryors Field is a tall-grass covered hill next to ponds with views over London. On Sundays it is often used for kick boxing and tai chi lessons, while others bring chairs to read the papers and admire the views.

VOLLEYBALL

Grass volleyball courts can be laid out on request during the summer months on the field next to the lido. Pitches cost £31 each, including a net. Tel. 020 8348 9930 for bookings or 020 7284 3648 for the office.

VOLUNTEERING

Heath Hands is a volunteer group open to everyone over 16. The supervised work sessions seven days a week include planting, weeding, litter picking and maintaining paths and benches. Heath Hands has its base at West Lodge, Kenwood, Hampstead Lane (Monday to Friday 9.30–1.30), tel. 020 8458 9102, website www.heath-hands.org.uk or email info@heath-hands.org.uk.

WALKS

The heath information centre, the Heath and Hampstead Society and the Kenwood Estate run walks throughout the year. These take place on the first Sunday of every month except January. The walks include ancient trees, bat and bird walks, mushroom treats, festive December walks, autumn treasure hunts, October conker championships and foraging in September. The walks usually last under two hours and are free of charge. The yearly timetable is available from tel. 020 7482 7073 or the main office.

The Camden and Islington Health Walks in association with the London Borough of Camden and the Corporation of London also run weekly walks on Hampstead Heath (Mondays at 10.00) and Regents Park (Tuesdays and Wednesdays). The walks last about two hours, are led by qualified walk leaders and are suitable for all levels of fitness (older people especially welcome). For further details contact Emma Charlton on 020 7527 2626 or Trish Tenn on 020 7974 4186.

WILDLIFE

All three species of woodpecker as well as kingfishers can be seen on the heath. There is a Wildlife WATCH club for over eights and other wildlife activities for children (information from the Parliament Hill information office, tel. 020 7482 7073).

WORKSHOPS

The information centre runs in-depth Saturday workshops at the lido classroom throughout the year. These include nature photography, tree identification, gardening, mushrooms and bats. Booking and information is available from the Parliament Hill information centre, tel. 020 7482 7073.

NEAR THE HEATH

Everyman Cinema Club, 5 Hollybush Vale, tel. 0870 066 4777, website www.everymancinema.com.

Fenton House and Gardens, Hampstead Grove, tel. 020 7435 3471.

Golders Hill Park, the Hill Garden and Pergola.

Hampstead and **Highgate Villages**.

Hollybush pub, 22 Holly Mount, tel. 020 7435 2892.

The Wells restaurant for a smart meal.

Keats' House, Keats Grove, tel. 020 7435 2062.

Hampton Court Gardens

VISITOR INFORMATION

East Molesey, Surrey, KT8 9AU

Tel. 020 8781 9500 or 0870 752 7777 (24 hour recorded) or 0870 753 7777 (tickets). Website www.hrp.org.uk

Summer (April–October) opening times:

Garden 10.00–17.30, Palace 10.15–18.00 Mondays and 09.30–18.00 Tuesday–Sunday

Winter (November–March) opening times:

Garden 10.00–16.00, Palace 10.15–16.30 Mondays and 09.30–16.30 Tuesday–Sunday

Entry to the gardens and park is free, palace entry £11.30, £8.25 (concessions)

Train: Hampton Court Station (overground from Waterloo and Clapham junction)

Bus: 111, 216, 411, 416, 451, 461, 513, 726

River: boat from Westminster Pier

Car: the car park in the grounds costs £3.50 for the day. Alternatively park for free in nearby Bushy Park (see p32)

Hampton Court and Bushy Park form almost 1810 acres of Royal Park on either side of the Thames. The palace was built by Cardinal Wolsey in 1514, with later additions by Henry VIII and Sir Christopher Wren. It is one of the finest Tudor palaces in the country and is set

Facilities

- Cafés
- Flower Show
- Maze
- Model boating
- Picnic areas
- Ponds
- Winter ice skating

128

within 60 acres of gardens, including court yards and flower gardens, fountains, canals, giant clipped yew trees in the shape of toadstools, extravagant wrought iron screens, the famous maze and Great Vine. The recently restored Privy Gardens alone justify a trip. The gardens are free of charge and are just opposite Bushy Park (p32).

HIGHLIGHTS

- Privy Garden
- Topiary

CAFÉS

The Tiltyard Tea Rooms

These are located in the area once used by Henry VIII for jousting. The bright white building has large windows with views of the grounds and outdoor seating. The food is bland and overpriced with coffee fresh from a vending machine (and tasting like it). Cappuccinos £1.50, tea £1.10, soup £3.50, cake £1.80, sandwiches £3.00. Open Monday to Friday 10.00–16.00 and weekends 10.00–16.30. Tel. 020 8977 2295.

Privy Kitchen Coffee Shop

This is located within the palace (not accessible without a ticket), near the Chapel Royal.

CHAPEL ROYAL

The Chapel Royal is open to the public from 12.45–13.15. Visitors can attend Sunday services, with the choir, at 11.00 and 15.30.

FLOWER SHOW

Hampton Court Palace is host to the world's largest annual horticultural show. The show is run by the Royal Horticultural

Society and features hundreds of specialist nursery displays and show gardens. The show is usually in early July. For further details visit the RHS site www.rhs.org.uk.

FRIENDS OF HAMPTON COURT PALACE

The recently formed Friends of Hampton Court Palace benefit from a range of perks including free entry to the palace and gardens, behind the scenes tours, walking tours of the gardens, a newsletter, a friends room for relaxing, previews of talks, a half price ticket for an accompanying family member per visit, and the opportunity to participate in a volunteer programme. Membership costs £39.50 (single), £72 (joint), £87 (family) and £35 (concessions). Contact Friends of Hampton Court Palace, Admissions, Hampton Court Palace, Surrey KT8 9AU, tel. 0870 751 5174, website www.hrp.org.uk.

GARDENS

North Gardens: the Wilderness and the Maze

The gardens to the north of the palace, dominated by the Lion Gate, include an area called the Wilderness. In Tudor times this referred to an area of evergreen hedges divided by straight paths to form geometric patterns. In the 18th century the style went out of fashion and the area was planted with trees including cherry, crab apples, chestnuts and beech. The area is at its best in spring when the daffodils, bluebells and azaleas are in flower. To one side of the Lion Gate lies a pretty pergola walk and to the other, the gardens, famous maze and the 17th century brick 'Wilderness House'. Capability Brown, the palace's master gardener, lived here from 1764.

East Gardens: Broad Walk and the Great Fountain Garden

The magnificent East Gardens are one of the most spectacular sights in London. They consist of the Broad Walk and the Great Fountain Garden. The Broad Walk runs for almost half a mile from the Thames in the south along the front of the palace and past King Henry's Royal (Real) Tennis Court in the north. It has a wide and brightly planted herbaceous border running its length. The Great Fountain Garden sits halfway along the Broad Walk, in front of the palace. It is an enormous semi-circle of grass, flower beds and clipped yew trees in the shape of giant toadstools, surrounding a central fountain. A 'patte d'oie' (goosefoot) design of lime tree avenues dissects the semi-circle (see also Chiswick Park, p43) and the central avenue ends at the Long Water canal. This three-quarters of a mile long canal stretches into the distance, in Home Park, with occasional views of the fallow and red deer and the many waterfowl.

South Gardens: Privy Garden, Sunken Garden and the Great Vine

The gardens to the south of the palace consist of the Privy Garden, the Sunken Garden and the Great Vine. The Privy Garden was the King's private (privy) gardens, the most intimate area of the palace. It was meticulously reconstructed and restored in the early 1990s following painstaking research into the original plantings and arrangements, even down to the same species of grass seed used in the original garden. The restoration required over 30,000 box plants. The garden was re-opened by the Prince of Wales in 1995 and is one of London's prettiest gardens. Halfway along the pergola is a secluded bench, with the best view of the gardens in the park. The Tijou screen at the river end of the garden consists of 12 panels of intricate wrought iron work. This was made for William III by Jean Tijou.

The Sunken Garden to the west of the Privy Garden is located in the old Tudor fish ponds which supplied the palace's kitchens. In the corner of the garden is the entrance to the Great Vine, planted in 1768 by Lancelot Capability Brown. It is the oldest known vine in the world and still produces around 500 bunches of grapes a year.

ICE-SKATING

There is a (very) small outdoor ice skating rink at Hampton Court for about six weeks from December to mid January. Sessions cost £8.50 (adult), £6.50 (under 16s), £26 (family ticket), see the website www.hamptoncourticerink.com.

MAZE

The Hampton Court Maze is one of the most famous mazes in Britain with over half a mile of paths. It was originally planted in 1690 for William III and covers one third of an acre. It is located in a corner of the Wilderness, near the Lion Gate. Entry costs £3.50 for adults and £2.50 for children.

MODEL BOATING

The Hampton Court Model Yacht Club is based at Rick Pond in Hampton Court Park (otherwise known as Home Park). The club meets most Wednesdays and Sundays at 11.00. To join the club either turn up at the lake on a Sunday or Wednesday (usually at 11.00), or contact John Mayhew on tel. 01372 843 180 or visit www.radiosailing.org.uk and click on the Hampton Court link.

PICNICS

There are picnic tables in the Wilderness and on the lawn in front of the Tiltyard Tea Rooms.

SHOPS AND INFORMATION

There are four souvenir shops at Hampton Court, two inside the palace and two outside. Of the two outside, the Barrack Block shop and ticket office is just inside the main entrance gate and the Garden Shop is by the East Front Gardens. This also has a video room which has an excellent free film about the restoration of the Privy Garden.

Highbury Fields

VISITOR INFORMATION

Highbury Crescent, N5

Tube: Highbury and Islington

Bus: 4, 19, 30, 43, 236, 271, 277

Open 24 hours

Highbury Fields is a pretty park that forms a tranquil green oasis near the busy Holloway Road in north London. It is the borough's largest open space. Giant ancient sycamores and pristine 18th century terraces ring the sloping green park. It is a cocoon of untouched Georgian splendour, Islington's Smith's Square. The park has an excellent children's playground, football pitches, tennis courts, a small café, an award-winning leisure centre and of course the fields. Film buffs will recognise its location from *Four Weddings and a Funeral*.

HIGHLIGHTS

- Highbury Pool and gym
- Flood-lit tennis courts
- Excellent children's playground
- Elegant Georgian terraces
- Ancient sycamore trees

Facilities

- Café
- Football
- Leisure centre
- Playground
- Tennis
- Two O'Clock Club

PLAYGROUND

There is one of London's best playgrounds in Highbury Fields, particularly for older children. This includes a strikingly long, steep silver slide into soft cork chips, a large helter skelter, climbing nets, commando slides, as well as younger children's sandpit, mini slides, tubes and a paddling pool. The playground is open on weekdays from 08.00, Saturdays from 09.00 and Sundays from 10.00 until dusk. The paddling pool is open from 26 May–30 September (there is always the cosy indoor shallow pool listed above if it is closed). The playground gets very busy on holidays and summer weekends.

SWIMMING POOL AND LEISURE CENTRE

The Highbury Pool (tel. 020 7704 2312) is a superb 25m indoor pool and 10m shallow pool. It is situated at the south end of Highbury Fields. In addition to the pool there is a modern, well equipped gym, steam room, sauna, sunbathing patio and outdoor paddling pool. This is run by Islington's friendly, multi-award-winning Aquaterra Leisure (www.aquaterra.org) – a non-profit organisation that ploughs earnings back into the facilities. They run numerous courses, swimming lessons, and a discount Izz card scheme, all priced very competitively

TENNIS

The Highbury Tennis Centre is at the north end of Highbury Fields. There are eight very good all-weather courts, seven of which are flood-lit (open 08.00–21.00). Non-members can book in advance or turn up to play on the day. Courts cost £8 for adults (or £6 with an Izz card) and £4 for children. Bookings are taken at the tennis hut by the courts, tel. 020 7226 2334 (the phone is usually available from ten minutes to the hour until ten minutes past the hour). Tennis coaching is also available. Viren is one of the chirpy coaches; lessons cost £25 per hour plus the court fee (£6), tel. 07973 179 580.

The Highbury City Tennis Club is also based at the park and runs a wide range of courses and matches for juniors. For further information contact Rob Achille on 020 7697 1206, website http://citytennisclubs.lta.org.uk.

The Izz card scheme gives many benefits of reduced court fees, and access to the Aquaterra Leisure centre (see above).

TWO O'CLOCK CLUB

The Highbury Fields Two O'Clock Club is a friendly drop in centre for under fives. The club is based in the bandstand in Highbury fields (in front of the Oasis Café). The club is open weekdays from 14.00–16.00 and costs just £1 per carer (50p for low income). For further information contact Roy Squibbs (playleader) on 020 7704 9337.

NEAR THE PARK

Upper Street: Islington's trendy road full of restaurants and cafés.

Freightliners City Farm: Paradise Park, Sheringham Road, N7 (see above).

Highgate Wood and Queen's Wood

VISITOR INFORMATION

Muswell Hill Road, NW6

Tel. 020 8444 6129

Bus: 34, 43, 263

Tube: Highgate

Queen's Wood (52 acres) and Highgate Wood (70 acres) are descendants of the original 'wildwood' which covered Britain until 4,000 years ago. They are two of London's gems: part of its last remaining ancient woodland. The area was once a source of wood for the ships which sailed with the Spanish Armada. Stepping into such pretty woodland from Highgate tube is as unexpected as finding a beach on your doorstep. Bluebells cluster around closely packed oaks and hornbeams, holly and hawthorn.

Although the two woods are only separated by a road they each have their own character. Highgate Wood, owned and managed by the Corporation of London, is the smarter of the two, with an award-winning adventure playground, a large sports field, information centre, a team of keepers, a cricket pavilion café and well tended paths. Queen's Wood is an undeveloped oasis; left to run wild with the exception of its cosy vegetarian café. The wood was named after Queen Victoria and became a public space in 1898.

Facilities

- Cafés
- Cricket pitch
- Information hut
- Playground
- Sports fields

HIGHLIGHTS

- Adventure playground
- Cafés
- Ancient woodland trees
- Wildlife

ANIMALS AND INSECTS

The wood is home to foxes, 80 species of spider, more than 20 species of butterfly, and an impressive 400 species of beetle. Five species of bat have also been recorded, perhaps encouraged by the Corporation of London's bat boxes.

BIRDS

The woods have a large number of rare species of birds including the sparrowhawk and the golden oriole.

CAFÉS

Oshobasho Café (Highgate Wood)

Highgate Wood's café is housed in the old cricket pavilion, in the middle of the woods, overlooking the sports fields. There are large cosy radiators, terracotta walls and long slit windows facing the outside terrace and gardens. The wisteria-covered terrace leads into a wooden fenced herb garden with outdoor seating surrounded by the scent of sage, rosemary, thyme and lavender. The café serves homemade vegetarian meals, including fresh foccacia, pasta bakes (£6.30), soups (£3), as well as tasty tea and coffee and cakes (cappuccino £1.40, tea 90p, cake £2.30).

Open: Monday 10.30–15.00 and Tuesday to Sunday 08.30–wood closing. The café will be reopening under new management. Contact the main parks number for further information.

Queen's Wood Café

The Queen's Wood Café is like a rosy glow in the middle of the Hansel and Gretel forest. It is (unfortunately) open only at the weekends. It is housed in an ancient lodge dating from 1898, which has recently been restored. There is a huge comfy sofa and armchair, under a window looking out into the woods. The tables have candles and velvet tablecloths, in dark reds and light blues. The café serves a tasty Green and Black's hot chocolate, teas (£1.00) and coffees (£1.50), homemade cakes (£2.60), and homemade vegetarian food: bean burgers £4.90, pitta breads, soups £3.50 and Jamaican curries. It is also available to hire for private parties and children's events.

Queen's Lodge, 42 Muswell Hill Road, London N10 3JP. Open weekends only: 10.00–18.00. Tel. 020 8444 2604.

CRICKET AND FOOTBALL

Highgate Wood's sports ground is a giant green oasis in the middle of the woods. There are cricket and football pitches, both in regular use in the summer.

DRINKING FOUNTAIN

There is a 19th century, red granite drinking fountain, complete with dog bowl, at a crossroads in Highgate Wood near the café.

FUNGI

The woods are a fungi *festa* with rarities like the blusher and the clouded agaric.

INFORMATION

Highgate Wood's information hut is located near the café and sports ground. It has leaflets and details of events. Further information can be obtained from the Corporation of London's website: www.cityoflondon.gov.uk/openspaces or from the manager on tel. 020 8444 6129.

Information on Queen's Wood is available from the Haringey

Parks customer care line 020 8489 5662 or email parkscustomercare@haringey.gov.uk.

PLAYGROUND

The large, award-winning adventure playground in Highgate Wood has a giant map in Braille, explaining all of the rides. There are climbing frames, swings, helter skelters and rope tunnels, a Pisa tower, a pyramid and an under fives' area with a rocking elephant, Wendy house, sand pit and special needs swing.

VOLUNTEERING AND THE FRIENDS OF QUEEN'S WOOD

The Friends of Queen's Wood organise volunteer groups on the last Sunday of each month to help with the wood management. There are also regular organic gardening volunteering days. Membership costs £5 for individuals, £10 for a household and £3 for concessions. Contact Lucy Roots (020 8883 8875) or Alison Watson (020 8883 0734), 13 Wood Vale, N10 3DJ.

Haringey's Nature Conservation Team at Railway Fields Nature Reserve also organises mid-week volunteer groups all over Haringey. Contact Jan Wilson on 020 8348 6005.

WALKS AND TALKS

There are regular guided walks in the woods, including bat walks, bird walks, mushroom foraging, seasonal excursions and even a beetle safari. Contact the manager, Highgate Wood, tel. 020 8444 6129 or email parks.gardens@ms.corpoflondon.gov.uk.

NEAR THE WOODS

Highgate Village for shopping, exploring, or eating.

Highgate Cemetery see (p271).

Waterlow Park see (p268).

Holland Park

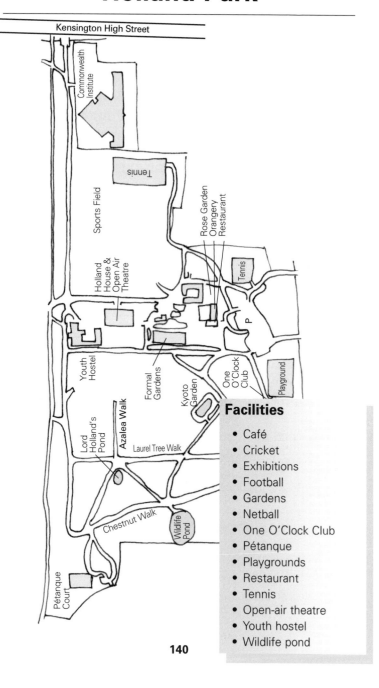

Facilities

- Café
- Cricket
- Exhibitions
- Football
- Gardens
- Netball
- One O'Clock Club
- Pétanque
- Playgrounds
- Restaurant
- Tennis
- Open-air theatre
- Youth hostel
- Wildlife pond

VISITOR INFORMATION

Holland Park Avenue W11 / Kensington High Street, W8

Tel. 020 7602 2226

Tube: Holland Park, Kensington High Street/Notting Hill Gate

Bus: Kennington High Street 9, 10, 27, 28, 31 and 49, Holland Park Avenue 12 and 88

Car: pay and display off Abbotsbury Road

In the 17th century, Holland Park was part of a beautiful country estate built for Sir Walter Cope. The park surrounds a huge Jacobean mansion that was named Holland House after a subsequent owner, the Earl of Holland. In the 18th century, Lady Holland became the first person in England to successfully grow dahlias, and they have been grown in the park ever since. In the 19th century, the park became a centre of literary and political life and was visited by Byron, Dickens, Disraeli and Sir Walter Scott. In 1939 King George VI held a grand ball in the house and soon after, a bomb almost completely destroyed it. Parts were restored and now form a backdrop for the superb Holland Park Opera. The east wing has been incorporated into one of London's best youth hostels.

The park is packed with facilities. Within its 55 acres (22 hectares) are woodland walks, exhibitions, tennis, football, netball, cricket, adventure playgrounds, outdoor opera, a new café and even a Marco Pierre White restaurant. The gardens include the Kyoto Gardens, created by a team of Japanese gardeners. The park gives easy access to Kensington High Street and Notting Hill.

HIGHLIGHTS

* Azalea Walk in spring
* Holland Park Opera and outdoor theatre
* Japanese Kyoto Garden

- New café
- White peacocks

CAFÉ

The new modern café has exposed brick walls, granite flooring, trendy up lighting and big windows with views of the garden. The prices are low and there is a proper Gaggia coffee machine. Most of the food comes out of a plastic wrapping... Cappuccino £1.15, tea 60p, sandwiches from £2.70, soup £1.85, pizza slice 90p, pasta from £2.75, jacket potato from £1.60, cans of coke 75p and crisps 40p.

Open every day 10.00–16.00. Tel. 020 7602 6156.

CHILDREN

There are several play areas for children. These include an under fives', an under eights' with a pre-school and an adventure playground. The under fives' toddlers play area is near the Ilchester Place entrance and has a large sand pit in which to get really messy. The larger adventure playground for 5–15 year olds is near the Abbotsbury Road entrance and car park. Here there are climbing frames, tubes to crawl through, ropes to commando glide down and space to run and shout. The under eights' enclosure is next door to the adventure playground. There is a pre-school nursery every weekday during school term time 09.00–15.30. Reduced rates are available for concessions and there are two free places for children with adverse financial positions. Tel. 020 7603 2838.

COMMONWEALTH INSTITUTE

The Queen opened the Commonwealth Institute in 1962. Its roof is made up of five hyperbolic pyramids covered in Zambian copper. It is now used as a conference centre.

DOGS

Dogs have their own exercise path in Holland Park. It is a pretty tree lined path running from Kensington High Street entrance up to Holland House. At both ends there is a special dog loo.

DRINKING FOUNTAIN

There is a drinking fountain near the Parks Office.

ECOLOGY CENTRE

The Holland Park Ecology Centre, in the Old Stable Yard next to the park information centre, runs a junior environmental club (one Saturday of every month), volunteer conservation work, walks, talks and children's holiday activities. There is a half term ecology programme for 5–10 year olds that includes bird watching, mini-beast hunts and tree walks. There are also bat, bird and tree walks for adults. Booking is essential. Tel. 020 7471 9802. Email ecology.centre@rbkc.gov.uk.

EXHIBITIONS

There are art exhibitions in the Orangery and the Ice House from April to October (see below).

FRIENDS OF HOLLAND PARK

The Friends of Holland Park are active in their work to protect and promote the park. There are regular meetings, guided walks, parties, talks, concerts and an annual art exhibition. Membership costs £10/year. Contact Mrs Rhoddy Wood, tel. 020 7602 0304. Website www.friendsofhollandpark.org.uk, email FriendsHollandPark@virgin.net.

GARDENS

A team of Japanese gardeners from the Kyoto Garden Association created the beautiful Kyoto Garden in 1991. There has been a Japanese Garden in this part of the park for over 100 years.

The Dry Garden next to the Abbotsbury entrance is built around a giant tortoise sundial (see below) and has benches nestled among herbs and aromatic plants.

The small Formal Garden's brightly coloured flowers run below the steps leading to the western side of Holland House. Benches line the ancient brick wall among the plants and creepers and there is a covered grotto at one end to take shelter during storms. The gardens lead to the Belvedere Restaurant in the former Garden Ballroom, at one end of the Orangery.

The Dahlia Garden at the far west of the formal garden is where Britain's first dahlias have been growing since 1790.

The Iris Garden surrounds a central pond and fountain within an enclosed courtyard formed by the Orangery and a covered arched walkway with its mural of a summer garden party.

GOLF

Golf nets are available from May to September for golf practice. The cost is £1.50/ hour. Players must bring their own clubs and balls. Tel. 020 7471 9813 or 020 7602 2226.

ICE HOUSE

The small circular brick ice house near the Stables was built in the 18th century to store ice for Holland House. It is now used for exhibitions.

MURALS

The large murals in the arcade near the Old Stables show one of the Earls of Ilchester's garden parties in the park in the 1870s.

NETBALL

There are two netball courts in the park. There is a fun Netball Revival Club with games, coaching, skills and rules for over 16s of all abilities 'even if you haven't touched a netball in 15 years…!'. Contact the Leisure Development Officer, tel. 020 7471 9803.

OPERA

Holland Park Theatre runs a superb outdoor summer opera season. This is set against the backdrop of the remains of Holland House. Tel. 020 7602 7856.

POND

The wildlife pond, just off the Chestnut Walk, was set up along with a smaller marsh pond to encourage water-loving plants and birds.

RUNNING

The park organises courses in spring and summer, which combine jogging and walking for beginners/improvers. These cost £2.50/session and concessions are available. Contact the Leisure Development Officer, tel. 020 7471 9803.

SCULPTURES

The small Napoleon Garden, at the western end of the formal garden, is used to exhibit a new piece of contemporary sculpture each year. Previous sculptures have included works by David Nash, Beth Cullen and Sir Anthony Caro. The statue of the third Lord Holland by G.F. Watts (1840) sits at the end of the Azalea Walk in front of a pond.

The café holds 'The Maid' by Eric Gill (1882–1940). The eccentric artist kept meticulous notes of his work; the statue in Portland stone took 285.5 hours to carve. Gill is also known for his dress-sense – he wore his own design of tunic with brightly coloured socks. His other works are in Westminster Cathedral and Broadcasting House.

SPORT

Sports Booking Office, The Stable Yard, Holland Park, Ilchester Place. Tel. 020 7602 2226. Open Monday to Sunday 08.00–19.00 (April to September) and 08.00–17.00 (October to March). The sports facilities can be booked through the Parks Office in the Stable Block. Leisure Development Officer, tel. 020 7471 9803.

Cricket nets (summer)

Cricket pitch (April to September)

Football pitch (grass) (October to April)

Golf nets (three) and bunker

Netball courts (two) (see below)

Pétanque (Boules) pitch

Tennis courts (see below)

TENNIS

There are six tennis courts, two of which are flood-lit. Only members are allowed to book courts in advance, and membership is only open to residents or people working in the Borough of Kensington and Chelsea. Non-members can turn up and play if a court is free (often possible off peak). Membership costs £10 and courts cost £5.20 an hour for adults, £2.30 for juniors. Racket hire is £3 (adults) £1 (juniors).

TORTOISES

'Tortoises with Triangle and Time' by Wendy Taylor CBE is a superb giant sundial commissioned for the Millennium celebrations. It is built on raised ground in the centre of the Dry Garden by the Abbotsbury Road entrance to the park, near the adventure playground. There are two giant tortoises, one with a large triangle on his back, telling the time.

TREES

There are ten woodland enclosures in Holland Park, situated to the west of the park. At the northwest corner is the Beech Enclosure, full of beech and holly. Close by is a 19th century avenue of horse chestnuts which leads to the Wildlife Reserve and Wildlife Pond. Other areas include the Lime Tree Walk, which was replanted after the 1987 Great Storm. The main avenue of trees from the Kensington High Street gate is of planes and chestnuts.

WALKS

There are hidden gardens, avenues of woodland, fountains, statues, lawns and ponds. The Chestnut Walk's long avenue of horse chestnut trees had to be replanted in 1997 after disease and storm damage. The Azalea Walk suffered from a sprinkler mishap in 2004, but is due to be as bright as ever in May 2005. This walk has had its problems in the past. Lady Ilchester originally planted it as a Rose Walk in the 19th century. The roses died. She had more success with dahlias. She was the first person to successfully germinate them in England, when they were planted in the arches of the formal garden.

The Park Sports team runs a series of walks including walking for health, walking for people with pushchairs, history walks and power walking. Most of the walks include a drink in the café and cost from £3. Tel. 020 7471 9803.

YOGA AND TAI CHI

Yoga and tai chi classes are led in the park in the summer. Contact the Sports Booking Office for the latest details. Tel. 020 7602 2226.

YOUTH HOSTEL

The King George VI Memorial Youth Hostel in the park is part of the original 17th century Jacobean mansion. It is one of London's bargains at £21 per night in a dormitory including breakfast. There are excellent facilities, cheap evening three course meals (£5), lockers, computers, vending machines, and lots of cheap excursions. Identification is needed to joint the National Youth Hostel Association, and membership costs £13/year. Tel. 020 7937 0748.

NEAR THE PARK

Leighton House Museum (1866): The house is known for its Victorian art and architecture and Arab Hall. There's also a collection of Pre-Raphaelite works by Burne-Jones, Millais and Watts. Tel. 020 7602 3316. Entrance at 12 Holland Park Road.

Lidgate Butchers: one of the best butchers with award-winning pies and sausages. 110 Holland Park Avenue, W11 4UA, tel. 020 7727 8243.

Notting Hill: Portobello Market, Books for Cooks, the Spice Shop.

Hyde Park

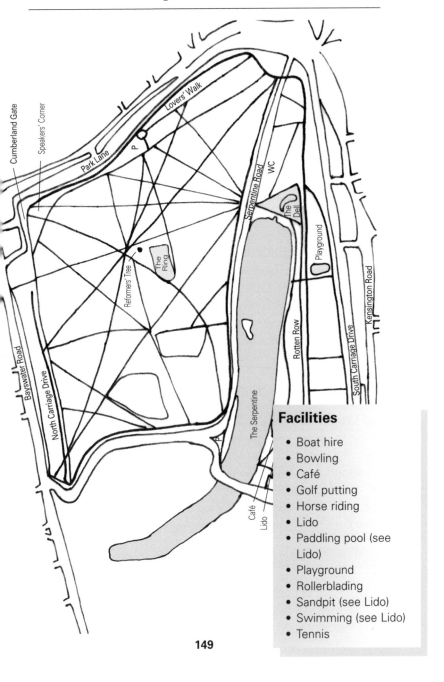

Facilities

- Boat hire
- Bowling
- Café
- Golf putting
- Horse riding
- Lido
- Paddling pool (see Lido)
- Playground
- Rollerblading
- Sandpit (see Lido)
- Swimming (see Lido)
- Tennis

VISITOR INFORMATION

Hyde Park, W2

Website: www.royalparks.org.uk, tel. 020 7298 2100

Bus: 2, 8, 9, 10, 12, 14, 16, 19, 22, 36, 38, 52, 73, 74, 82, 94, 137

Tube: Hyde Park Corner, Knightsbridge, Lancaster Gate, Marble Arch

Car: pay and display every day 08.30–18.30 along West Carriage Drive

The land for Hyde Park, Kensington Gardens and Regent's Park was acquired for hunting by Henry VIII in 1536. For the next two hundred years, the area was used for hunting and military reviews. Between the 17th and 19th century Hyde Park was gradually transformed from woods and rough pasture into a formal enclosed landscaped park. Firstly in 1690 Rotten Row was built to link Kensington and Westminster Palaces and became the first lamp-lit road in Britain. Then in 1730 the Serpentine Lake and Long Water were dug, in celebration of Queen Caroline, the wife of George II. In the early 19th century carriage drives and entrance gates were added.

Hyde Park is divided from Kensington Gardens by the West Carriage Drive road. In 1851 the Crystal Palace was built for the Great Exhibition. In 1872 Speaker's Corner was officially designated for public speaking. In 1930, after extensive cleaning work to improve the water purity, the Lido was opened for swimming. Today the park covers 340 acres with a network of well maintained paths and shady avenues of London plane trees. On the Serpentine there are boats for hire and swimming. There are sports facilities, a playground and a lakeside café.

HIGHLIGHTS

- View from the Dell Café
- Joy of Life Fountain
- Apsley House: No 1 London

- Diana Statue and Rose Gardens
- Avenue alongside the parade ground

APSLEY HOUSE

The home of the first Duke of Wellington, Arthur Wellesley, with the address No. 1 London, is on the corner of the park overlooking Hyde Park Corner. It has a sumptuous collection of paintings, porcelain, silver, sculpture, furniture, medals and memorabilia and Wellington's sword. It was designed and built by Robert Adam between 1771–78. The address derives from the fact that it lay just inside the toll gate leading into London. The first floor windows are a good place to view the arches of Hyde Park Corner and to see the Wellington statue. In the basement of the house is a small collection of caricatures of Wellington, who on becoming a statesman after the battle of Waterloo was frequently lampooned in the press. The excellent book *Wellington Caricatures* by Sir Edward du Cann is available from the shop upstairs. Before or after visiting the house be sure to see the Achilles statue and walk over to the Diana statue in the rose garden.

Tel. 020 7499 5676, website www.apsleyhouse.org.uk. Open Tuesday to Sunday, winter 10.00–16.00, from Easter 10.00–17.00. Adults £4.50 including audio guide. Free entry for under 18s and over 60s. Free tickets for all on 18 June (Waterloo Day).

BIRDS

The memorial to the author and naturalist W.H. Hudson is a bas-relief figure of 'Rima', by Jacob Epstein (1925). Rima is a character from one of Hudson's books. The setting of the memorial is a small bird sanctuary, which lies in front of the three acres of greenhouses and nursery of the park.

BOATING

The Boathouse is on the northern bank of the Serpentine, near the Dell café/restaurant.

The Serpentine is one of the prettiest lakes in London. It is also one of the best places to go boating. There are a wheelchair boat, pedal boats, a ferry boat and traditional rowing boats. Hire costs £3.50 for half an hour (£1 for children) or £5 per hour. Lessons are a rather steep £9.

BOWLING

There is a well maintained six-rink bowling green at the Tennis Centre. Woods are not available for hire. Contact the tennis centre for details about booking (season starts in April), tel. 020 7262 3474.

CAFÉS

The Dell

The Dell café and restaurant has a panoramic view of the Serpentine Lake. The huge thick glass windows face the lake. Having a cappuccino here is like sitting at the helm of a giant ship, charging up the Serpentine. There is outdoor waterside seating with views of the boating. Breakfast £5.50, vegetarian breakfast £4.95, soup £3.32, cappuccino £1.50, tea £1.10, mineral water £1.35, coke £1.40, beer £2.95, cake £2.35, sandwich £2.25. Jugs of free water are available next to the cutlery. Open 09.00–20.00 in summer and 10.00–16.00 in winter. Tel. 020 7066 0464.

The Lido Café

The Lido Café is based on the south side of the Serpentine, next to the Lido swimming area. There is indoor and outdoor seating with views across the lake. The food is the same as that at the Dell. Open 09.00–20.00 in summer and 10.00–16.00 in winter.

Hyde Park Tennis Centre Café

There is a cosy small café at the recently refurbished tennis centre (see below under Tennis) off South Carriage Drive. The centre is one of the best kept secrets in London. There is outdoor seating with views of the courts and putting green. Open 09.00–21.00 in summer and 10.00–16.00 in winter.

The Honest Sausage

There is a tiny Honest Sausage kiosk at Speakers Corner (on the northeast side of the park), serving the excellent organic 'Park Porker' as well as a range of vegetarian options. Open 09.00–20.00 in summer and 10.00–16.00 in winter.

CLASSIC CARS

The London to Brighton Veteran Car Run takes place on the first Sunday of November every year, and begins at Hyde Park Corner. This is the world's longest running motoring event (since 1896) and frequently attracts over 500 participants. All vehicles must be pre-1905. There is a *concours* of over 50 of the participating cars on the Saturday (the day before the race) and entry to watch both the run and the *concours* is free. See www.lbvcr.com for further details.

FOUNTAIN

'Joy of Life' (1963) by T.B. Huxley-Lones forms part of a beautiful fountain near a tree-lined avenue alongside Park Lane. Two central figures hold each other, surrounded by four children diving towards the water. The water from the inner stone pond overflows into the outer pond, and the noise of water drowns out the traffic from Park Lane. It is also not far from Apsley House. There are wooden benches surrounding it, making it a peaceful place to read the paper.

GOLF

The Hyde Park Tennis Centre has a very interesting putting course through the well maintained flower beds, a kind of horticulturalist's crazy golf. Putters and balls are available at the club (see Tennis for details).

INFORMATION

The Parks Office is near the Old Police Station. The information office is poorly signposted. It is called the Ranger's Lodge and is next to the Old Police Station. Tel. 020 7298 2100, open Monday to Friday 10.00–12.00 and 14.00–16.00.

KIOSKS

There are numerous kiosks around the park selling snacks and drinks. The one at Speaker's Corner includes Honest Sausage and Marine Ices ice-cream. Marine Ices has the best ice-creams in London, an Italian-run *gelateria* based in Chalk Farm. The Honest Sausage has old-fashioned traditional sausages slow cooked in a range of different flavours.

MOBILITY

There are free electric buggy rides provided by the charity Liberty Drives. Anyone with mobility problems can be collected from eight pick-up points. The buggies have seats for up to five people including wheelchair users. Tel. 07767 498 096. Open May to October from Monday to Friday 10.00–17.00.

MUSIC

On Saturday afternoons in August there are free concerts at the Hyde Park Bandstand (near the Dell Café, Queen Elizabeth Gate and Hyde Park Corner).

There are pop concerts throughout the summer, including the Party in the Park at the beginning of July. Check www.bookingsdirect.com or tel. 0870 735 5000.

The Last Night of the Proms Concert in the Albert Hall is broadcast live to the park on a big screen in September. Check www.bbc.co.uk/proms or tel: 0870 899 8100.

RIDING

Hyde Park Stables, 63 Bathurst Mews (between Sussex Square and Sussex Gardens near Lancaster Gate tube station). Tel. 020 7723 2813. Website www.hydeparkstables.com, email info@hydeparkstables.com.

The stable provides free safety helmets and boots. Anyone is welcome from the age of five upwards. There are five miles of paths in the park and an arena for riding lessons. Beginners are welcome and lessons can be booked individually or in a group. Prices start at £40/hour.

ROLLER-BLADING

Hyde Park is one of the most popular parks for roller-blading. The Serpentine Road, which runs alongside the Serpentine, is where most of the bladers hang out at weekends.

ROTTEN ROW

Rotten Row was built during the reign of William III and Mary II to link the palaces at Kensington and Westminster. The area was notorious for thieves and became the first road in the country to be artificially lit. The three hundred oil lamps were a deterrent to the thieves, but the road nevertheless acquired its nickname 'Rotten Row'.

SWIMMING AND PADDLING

The Serpentine Lido was founded in 1931 as part of the improvement of public amenities. The lido is a marked area of the Serpentine Lake used for outdoor swimming. There is also a separate area for children, including a pretty circular paddling pool with fountains, a sand pit, a small café, a play area that includes carved wooden sculptures and a lawn for sunbathing. It is raised above the bank of the pond and gives a beautiful, secluded view of the park and Serpentine. There are black and white photos on the walls of the lido showing swimmers from past generations and fashions. There is a large café on the bank with outdoor and indoor seating, serving the same food at the same prices as the other cafés. The Serpentine Swimming Club uses the lido for their famous Christmas Day dip. There is a lift for wheelchair users and a conference room for hire. Tel. 020 7706 3422, website www.serpentinelido.com. Open every day from the beginning of June until September 10.00–17.30 (note: opening dates and times may vary). Adults £3, children 60p, family ticket (two adults and three children) £6.

Membership of the Serpentine Swimming Club entitles you to swim in the Serpentine 365 days a year from 06.30–09.30. Annual membership costs £15/year. For further information visit the website www.serpentineswimmingclub.com or tel. 01344 291578.

STATUES

The statue of Achilles was completed in 1822 by Sir Richard Westmacott, in honour of the Duke of Wellington. This huge bronze is located a few metres from Apsley House (see above). It was cast from bronze cannons taken in the Napoleonic wars: Salamanca, Toulouse, Vittoria and Waterloo. It is based on a statue of a horse-tamer on the Quirinal in Rome.

The Diana Statue by Countess Feodora Gleichen is set within beautiful enclosed formal flower gardens. The pretty statue depicts a small girl drawing a bow and arrow, in a small pond and fountain. The statue and gardens are near Apsley house and not far from the Dell restaurant. The gardens include a long pergola and secluded wooden benches among the flowers. The area is well worth visiting.

TENNIS, GOLF, BOWLS AND BOULES

The Hyde Park Tennis Club is one of London's secrets. There are six courts tucked almost out of sight behind hedges and a beautiful bowling green in an enclave with its own mini formal garden which includes a nine-hole putting course. Stepping into the club is like being whisked into another world. The entrance is through a small, refurbished wooden clubhouse, which has a pro shop, a cosy café and changing rooms. The clubhouse leads out to the bowling green and the tennis courts. The courts are set among high quality teak garden furniture and the mini formal gardens. The nine-hole putting course runs through the twisting formal garden, like a horticulturist's crazy golf course. The gardens have views to the London Eye in one direction and to the Albert Memorial in the other. It is a precious secluded area to unwind after a game or to eat lunch while watching one. The club is one of the best park-clubs in London. There is a weekly programme of group lessons, group games, evening classes and junior camps. Membership is limited but there are new places available each year. Non-members can play but have fewer benefits.

Court bookings are for 45 minutes. Peak time (weekends and weekdays after 18.00) costs £7 for members and £8.50 for non-members. Off peak costs £6 members and £7.50 non-members. Members can book up to seven days in advance, non-members two days in advance. Rackets and balls can be hired for £3. Bowling and pétanque costs £2 for members and £4 for non-members. Private tennis lessons are available from £27/hour. Hyde Park Tennis Centre and Café, South Carriage Drive (at the corner of Hyde Park by Alexandra Gate), Hyde Park, London W2 2UH. Website www.tennis-uk.com, email willtowin@btopenworld.com, tel. 020 7262 3474.

WALKS

The Diana, Princess of Wales Memorial Walk is a seven-mile walk crossing St James's Park, The Green Park, Hyde Park and Kensington Gardens. (See p168.)

NEAR THE PARK
Royal Albert Hall

Victoria and Albert Museum

Harvey Nichols and the shops of **Knightsbridge**

Kennington Park

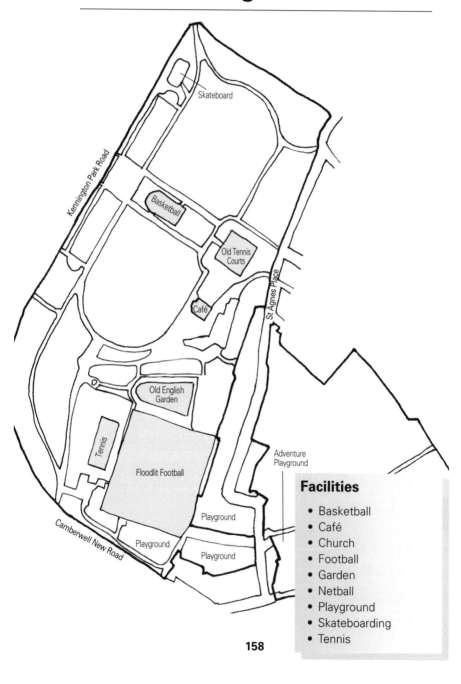

Skateboard

Kennington Park Road

Basketball

Old Tennis Courts

St Agnes Place

Café

Old English Garden

Tennis

Adventure Playground

Floodlit Football

Playground

Camberwell New Road

Playground

Playground

Facilities

- Basketball
- Café
- Church
- Football
- Garden
- Netball
- Playground
- Skateboarding
- Tennis

VISITOR INFORMATION

St Agnes Place, SE1

Tel. 020 7926 9000 (call centre) or email parks@lambeth.gov.uk

Tube: Oval tube (at the park)

Kennington Park has been a 36-acre green oasis since 1854. It was not always as pretty as it is now. It was originally part of Kennington Common, and one of the main execution sites for Surrey. In the 19th century it was described by Thomas Miller as a 'grassless square, surrounded by ... black sluggish ditches ... and poisoned by the stench of vitriol works'. The park is now full of mature trees including many ancient London planes. There is an English flower and herb garden, rose beds, a cosy lodge café serving excellent coffee, a pretty church and a modern flood-lit sports complex including basketball and tennis courts. It is also conveniently near the Oval Cricket Ground.

HIGHLIGHTS

* Excellent café
* English walled garden
* Sports complex

CAFÉ

Café in the Park

The café is housed in the tiny park lodge, designed by Henry Roberts and originally the Prince Consort's Model Lodge. It has been transformed by the current owners into one of the best cafés in the area. It is like stumbling across a cosy warm cottage among the trees. In the half light a warm glow shines through the trees from crescent shaped windows. The design is modern

Italian with frosted glass-topped tables, pretty vases and a large sofa below a low wooden ceiling. There are newspapers and magazines to read while drinking the excellent coffee. The prices are low and there are cakes, biscuits, homemade soup and sandwiches. Cappuccino £1.10, tea £1.00, sandwiches £2.50, soup £2.00. They also organise parties.

Opening hours: Monday to Friday autumn 09.00–19.00, weekends 10.00–19.00; Opening hours: winter 08.00–16.00, weekends 10.30–16.00. Tel. 020 7793 8886.

DOGS

The park has a large enclosed area for dogs to run around in.

FOUNTAIN

The park's fountain by the Kennington Park Road entrance is being restored.

FRIENDS OF KENNINGTON PARK

The Friends of Kennington Park organise regular meetings to plan the development and running of the park. Their influence can be seen everywhere, from the new up-to-date information boards, to the thoughtful touches such as the dog exercise area, to the restoration of the park's fountain. Contact Mark Rogers, tel. 020 7582 2849.

GARDEN

The old English garden is a pretty walled garden with a stone pergola, sunken beds and secluded seating.

PLAYGROUND AND ONE O'CLOCK CLUB

The park has a free open access adventure playground with disabled access and a One O'Clock Club. Tel. 020 7735 7186. Open Monday to Thursday 12.00–15.30.

SPORTS

The park has an excellent flood-lit sports area including three tennis courts, two multi-courts (basketball or netball) and a full size (or two half) synthetic football pitch. These can be booked by telephone on 020 7926 0759. The pitches are available from 09.00–22.30. Tennis courts cost £6 per hour and a half pitch costs £30/session, which includes use of the changing room and showers. There is also an open, free basketball pitch in the middle of the park, which does not require booking.

NEAR THE PARK

The Oval Cricket Ground, home of the Surrey County Cricket Club and one of London's most famous landmarks, www.surreycricket.com.

Burgess Park (see p28)

Imperial War Museum, Lambeth Road, SE1, www.iwm.org.uk, tel. 020 7416 5320.

Tate Britain Art Gallery (north side of Vauxhall Bridge), tel. 020 7887 8008, www.tate.org.uk.

Kensington Gardens

VISITOR INFORMATION

Bayswater/Kensington Grove, W2

Website: www.royalparks.org.uk

Tube: Queensway, Lancaster Gate (nearest), High Street Kensington

Bus: 9, 10, 12, 27, 28, 31, 49, 52, 70, 94

Car: NPC car park on Bayswater Road. Costs £5/2h or £11/6h, website www.npc.co.uk

Kensington Gardens' 111 hectares (275 acres) is next to Hyde Park but different in character. The garden has something for everyone: two formal water gardens, the three hectare Round Pond busy with model boats, Wren's Kensington Palace (built in the garden's clean air to soothe the asthma of William III), many interesting trees and peaceful footpaths for strolling. Queen Anne's Orangery (1704) with Gibbon's carvings serves classic English food as well as proper afternoon teas with views of perfectly rolled lawns. The gardens have been open to 'respectably dressed' people since George III moved to Buckingham Palace in 1761. For children there is the Diana Princess of Wales Memorial playground with the nearby Elfin Oak (1911) carved from an 800-year old oak tree decorated with tiny brightly coloured gnomes, birds, a fox, Snow White and an old shoe. Conveniently there is a double-fronted café, one side in the playground and the other for those wanting a quieter eating experience.

Facilities

- Bandstand
- Cafés
- Model boating
- Playground
- Pond
- Serpentine Gallery
- Guided walks

HIGHLIGHTS

- The Sunken Garden
- Tea in the Orangery
- The Diana Playground

ART

The Serpentine's delightful free gallery has a range of changing exhibitions throughout the year. On Friday evenings in July and August, there are talks, readings and film shows costing £5. The Serpentine Gallery (1908) (south of the Serpentine on West Carriage Drive, tel. 020 7298 1515/7402 6075, website www.serpentinegallery.org. Open every day 10.00–18.00, Fridays in July and August open until 22.00. Admission free.

BANDSTAND

The gardens' 1930s bandstand has better acoustics than the classic round bandstands. There are regular concerts at the bandstands during summer months. Contact the parks office or website for the latest programme, www.royalparks.org.uk.

BIRDS

Opposite the Peter Pan statue is a board with pictures of the huge number of different species of birds that live in the gardens. The bird records of the gardens go back more than 100 years and list more than 178 species. Canadian geese, coots, great crested crebes, mallards, moorhens and mute swans are easily spotted. Green woodpeckers nest in the gardens.

CAFÉ

The Orangery

Queen Anne's Green House (1704) was used for exotic plants and entertaining. It came to be known as the Orangery as it was filled with orange trees in winter to protect them from the frost. The Orangery is now a grand restaurant with a fantastic array of cakes and smiling waitresses to greet those wanting a little pomp and ceremony. Cappuccino £1.85, tea £1.75, full cream tea £6.95, homemade cakes £3.45, Chelsea buns £1.95, sandwiches £5.95 and hot dishes from £8.95. The Orangery, Kensington Palace, Kensington Gardens, W8, open every day 10.00–18.00 (17.00 in winter), tel. 020 7938 1406.

DRINKING FOUNTAINS

'Time Flies' (1909) (near the Diana Playground). The clock tower and drinking fountain were designed to evoke a feeling of passing time in Edwardian childhoods. It has a weather vane with a bird on top and the water once flowed from fishes' mouths.

'Two Bears' (1939) (near the Italian Garden). This fountain marked 80 years of the Metropolitan Drinking Fountain Association. This association built a number of drinking fountains to try to combat the scourge of cholera in the 19th century. It was also against the use of alcohol but was much less successful with this aim!

FLOWERS

The Flower Walk (1843) consists of almost 457 metres of shady exotic trees mingled with carefully chosen flowers. The weeping beech trees are like green tents where Peter Pan once spent a cold wet night…

GARDENS

The Sunken Garden (opposite the Orangery and Kensington Palace)

This hidden treasure was developed in 1908 on Queen Anne's original site. It is a water garden modelled on a Tudor design similar to one in Hampton Court, with 18th century lead cisterns with fountains. There is a 45m rectangular pond surrounded by three tiers of flowerbeds with neat clipped lawns between them.

The Italian Gardens (1860)

Queen Victoria's formal garden was designed by James Pennethorne with five octagonal ponds with marble fountains and balustrades by John Thomas. The Italian Pavilion was copied from a similar one in Versailles and originally contained a pump to bring water from the well on Duck Island in St James's Park to Long Water and the Serpentine. Its large chimney is a clue to the power needed for the job.

GATES

'Queen's Gate' (1858): the original pillars were supported by muscular athletes but were replaced in 1919 by groups of deer.

'Coalbrookdale Gates' (1851) (on the corner of Kensington Gore and West Carriage Drive): these remarkable bronze painted cast iron gates were the entrance to the Great Exhibition in 1851.

MEMORIALS

Prince Albert Memorial

Sir Gilbert Scott designed this London landmark (opposite the Albert Hall) and thought it to be his best work. It has a huge bronze statue of Prince Albert holding a catalogue of the Great Exhibition of 1851. It is easy to dismiss this enormous Victorian Gothic monument but on closer inspection it is a remarkable history lesson. On each corner of Prince Albert are two sets of four statues. The first four are the continents, America is represented as a bull with a gun-wielding man, Africa is a camel and a sphinx, Europe is a cow, Asia is an elephant with stars on its tusks. The second set of statues depicts manufacture, agriculture, commerce and engineering, which were celebrated in the Great Exhibition. Around the bottom are beautifully carved statues of leading historical figures including Barry, Gainsborough, Pugin, Reynolds, Turner and Wren. The finer points of the memorial can be learned about during the Sunday tours at 14.00 costing £3.50. Tel. 020 7495 0916.

Speke Monument

John Speke was the first European to discover Lake Victoria and its northern outlet as the source of the Nile. The memorial (1866) is a polished red granite obelisk of Aberdeen granite. The granite mine in Aberdeen was once the biggest man-made hole in Europe.

MODEL BOATING

The Round Pond is one of the oldest model boating lakes in the country. It has been home to the Model Yachting Association since 1876 and the London Model Yacht Club since 1884. These venerable clubs were amalgamated in 1972 and are more active than ever. The principal class sailed is the 10 Rater. There are races most Sunday mornings from 10.00–13.00, throughout the year. To join the club either turn up on a Sunday, visit the website www.mysa.org.uk or telephone Graham Frazer on 020 7351 5398.

PLAYGROUNDS

There are two playgrounds. The Diana Princess of Wales Playground is one of the biggest in London. It has a pirate ship in a giant sandpit, a trio of wigwams, a raised walkway with slides, swings, Wendy houses and more. The café has a children's menu with hot dinners for £3.25 as well as adult food such as Peter Pan Salad £5.95, sandwiches £3.25, tea 80p, cappuccino £1.45, Ribena 80p and fresh pastries from 90p. The playground, café, toilets and first aid centre are open daily from 10.00. Closing time depends on the weather, 19.45 in summer and 15.45 in winter. Tel. 020 7298 2000. The other playground is small and has a selection of brightly coloured slides, swings and a see-saw. It is near the Italian gardens.

THE ROUND POND

The Round Pond was originally a smaller rectangular pond for George I's turtles with a neighbouring 'snailery' and tiger's den. It now covers nearly three hectares and is home to a multitude of birds. The pond is also one of the oldest model boating lakes in the country and host to dedicated model yachting enthusiasts (see above).

SHELTERS

The Broadwalk Shelters (1919). Were presented to the gardens in memorial to the soldiers who died in World War I.

The pretty Queen Ann's alcove (1705) is, surprisingly, wood panelled.

STATUES

'Esme Percy Memorial' (1961) by Silvia Gilley. This bronze statue of a playful dog sits on top of a granite birdbath which doubles as a dog's drinking bowl.

'Edward Jenner' (1858) by William Calder-Marshall. Jenner developed the smallpox vaccine in 1796 which led to the worldwide eradication of smallpox by 1980.

'Queen Victoria' (1893) by Princess Louise, Queen Victoria's daughter. This marble statue shows Queen Victoria admiring the Round Pond in her coronation clothes and crown.

'Peter Pan' (1912) by Sir George Frampton. Frampton was commissioned by Sir James Barrie who wrote the children's play *Peter Pan*, about a boy who never grew up. The royalties still go to Great Ormond Street Hospital. The statue shows Peter Pan with pipes, surrounded by animals and fairies.

'Physical Energy' (1907) by G.F. Watts OM. This equine statue is a replica of part of the Rhodes Memorial on Table Mountain overlooking Cape Town, South Africa.

'William III' (1907) by H. Baucke. The first king to live in Kensington Place is remembered by this bronze statue standing proudly on a pedestal by Sir Aston Webb outside the palace.

WALKS

The Diana, Princess of Wales Memorial Walk is a circular seven-mile walk through Kensington Gardens, Hyde Park, The Green Park and St James's Park. Ninety plaques, each with an aluminium heraldic rose emblem, mark the route. The walk passes many of the houses associated with the princess's life including Kensington Palace, Buckingham Place, Clarence House, St James's Palace and Spencer House. The walk can be started at any point but the Broad Walk opposite Kensington Palace is a good starting point.

The Royal Parks organise free guided seasonal walks through the gardens, including bird watching, winter gardens, autumn colours and much more. Walks usually start at 14.30 and last about an hour. Booking is essential. For further information contact the Central Royal Parks Office on 020 7298 2100.

NEAR THE GARDENS

Part of the money from the six million visitors that visited the Great Exhibition of 1851 went into building the nearby museums:

The Victoria and Albert Museum, Cromwell Road, tel. 020 7942 2000, www.vam.ac.uk. Open every day 10.00–17.45. Admission free. The Pirelli Garden where the dog belonging to the creator of the museum, Sir Henry Cole, is remembered, is a tranquil spot to read or picnic.

Natural History Museum, Cromwell Road, tel. 020 7942 5000, www.nhm.ac.uk. Open every day 10.00–17.50. Admission free.

Science Museum, Exhibition Road, tel. 020 7942 4454, www.sciencemuseum.org.uk. Open every day 10.00–18.00. Admission free.

The State Apartments and the **Royal Dress Collections** in Kensington Palace (1689–1727) are worth a visit. Open every day 10.00–17.00, tel. 020 7937 9561. Adults £10.50, children £7 and family ticket £31. The shop has a range of all things royal as well as baby changing facilities.

King George's Park

Garratt Lane, SW18

Bus: 270, 44

Train: Wandsworth Town

Car: pay and display parking only

Along the banks of the Wandle river in Wandsworth is the pretty King George's Park. It is divided between open grassy space and formal park areas with a playground and sports centre. It is just 55 acres and is dominated by a huge duck pond with weeping willows and fountains.

HIGHLIGHTS

* Duck pond
* Playgrounds
* Sports centre

BOWLING

To play bowls, ask at the clubhouse for details of games and membership prices.

FOOTBALL

There are three full-size pitches and three junior pitches which cost from £38/session. Tel. 020 8876 7685.

Facilities

* Adventure playground
* Bowls
* One O'Clock Club
* Sports centre
* Tennis courts

PLAYGROUNDS

There are three playgrounds, one for under sixes, one for older children and the Kimber Adventure Playground.

The One O'Clock Club has a smart wooden building and is open to children under five with their carers. Tel. 020 8871 1865. Open Monday to Friday 13.00–15.30.

The Kimber Adventure Playground is open Tuesday to Friday 15.30–19.00 during termtime and Monday to Saturday 11.00–18.00 during school holidays. It is open to all children from age five to 16 and includes a rollerskating and skate boarding area. Children under eight must be accompanied by an adult.

ROSE GARDEN

There is a small formal rose garden with seats for picnics near the Wandle Recreation Centre.

SPORTS CENTRE

The Wandle Recreation Centre has a playzone, gym, crèche, badminton courts as well as Astroturf pitches. The gym is fully equipped and costs £40/month. There is no joining fee. Badminton courts cost £8.20/hour/court. Rackets and shuttlecocks are available for hire costing £1.20 and £1.50 respectively. The Playzone is a giant indoor climbing frame for children up to the age of seven. There is also a ball pit for further adventure. The Astroturf pitch is available for hire from £33.20/session. Tel. 020 8871 1149. Open Monday to Friday 07.30–22.00, Saturday 09.00–20.00 and Sunday 09.00–22.00.

The crèche is open Monday to Friday 10.00–12.00 and costs £2.80/child/session.

TENNIS

There are eight tennis courts. To book a court telephone David Magalhaes 0781 597 5960. The cost is from £3.50/hour.

Marble Hill Park

VISITOR INFORMATION

Richmond Road, Twickenham, TW1 2NL

The park is open daily. Tel. 020 8892 5115, website www.english-heritage.org.uk

Bus 33, 90, 290, H22, R70

Tube/train: Richmond, St Margaret's

Marble Hill in Richmond is one of London's gems, a perfect Palladian villa by the Thames set in elegant parkland. The large soft lawn sweeps down from the villa to the Thames and is framed with clusters of woodland and chestnut trees. The villa was designed by Roger Morris and built, between 1724 and 1729, for Henrietta Howard who was George II's mistress. Charles Bridgeman designed the gardens. The park includes a riverside playground and café, rugby and football pitches, tennis courts and an art gallery. The riverside walk is one of London's prettiest and is directly opposite Ham House. There is a ferry across the river, linking Ham House to Marble Hill, as well as boats for hire.

HIGHLIGHTS

- The Octagon art gallery
- River walk
- Marble Hill House

Facilities

- Art gallery
- Café
- Football/rugby
- Playground
- River walk
- Tennis

ART

The Octagon was designed in 1720 by James Gibbs, the famous architect of St Martin-in-the-Fields and St Mary-le-Strand. It was originally the garden room and is now used as a free art gallery with changing exhibitions throughout the year.

Open Tuesday to Saturday from 13.00–17.30 (16.30 October to March) and Sundays and bank holidays 14.00–17.30 (16.30 October to March). Orleans Road, tel. 020 8831 6000, website www.richmond.gov.uk.

CAFÉ

Marble Hill Café

There is a café in Marble Hill's 19th century coach house. The opening hours are the same as the house (see below). Tel. 020 8744 1118.

FERRY TO HAM HOUSE

There are regular ferries across the river to Ham House run by Jennifer Spencer. These run from 10.00–18.00 on weekdays February to October and weekends all year. The ferry costs 60p (adults) and 30p (children), tel. 020 8892 9620. There are boats to hire by the hour costing £2.50 (adults) £1.50 (children).

Ham House is a stunning baroque villa with one of the finest 17th century gardens in London, geometric and immaculate. The National Trust owns the house and gardens.

Tel. 020 8940 1950, website www.nationaltrust.org.uk.

MARBLE HILL HOUSE

Marble Hill House is owned by English Heritage and has been beautifully restored and furnished with Georgian furniture and paintings.

Tel. 020 8892 5115, website www.englishheritage.org.uk. Entrance £3.70 and under fives free. Open April to September

10.00–18.00, October 10.00–17.00, closed November to March.

TERRACE

Montpelier Row, off Orleans Road, which runs alongside the park, is well worth a visit. It is a fine example of an early Georgian terrace.

NEAR THE PARK

Ham House (across on the ferry).

Richmond and **Richmond Park** (see p216).

Horace Walpole's house 'Grotto', tel. 020 8240 4224, open May to September for guided tours on Sundays 14.00–15.30. The cost is £5/adult.

Syon Park (see p244).

Mile End Park

VISITOR INFORMATION

Locksley Street, E3

Tel. 020 7264 4660 (Victoria Park and Mile End Park),
Town Hall 020 7364 3106

Information on the facilities in Tower Hamlets: 020 7364 5000

Website: www.mileendpark.co.uk

Tube/train: Mile End (Central, District and Hammersmith lines),
Limehouse Station (DLR and BR)

Bus: 25, 277 339, D6, D7,

Mile End Park is a superb 90-acre 'green corridor' that runs from Victoria Park (see p256) to the Limehouse Basin and the Thames. The park was created in 1943 as part of the post-war County of London Plan. It has been completely transformed in the last few years with the help of a Millennium Lottery Grant.

There are flood-lit terraced gardens, a beautiful ecology park with a high-tech arts centre, a £2 million playground and children's drop-in centre, football pitches, the East London Stadium, canal-side walks, and the nearby newly developed Bows Wharf. Much of the surrounding area of Stepney remains unchanged, however, and still gives a good impression of the old East End. This was where the second of Dr Barnardo's Ragged School orphanages was set up, which is now a museum (see below). This is one of London's best modern family parks.

Facilities

- Art centre
- Athletics stadium
- Canal-side walks
- Cycle paths
- Drop in centre
- Ecology centre
- Fishing (canal)
- Football
- Go-karting
- Modern gardens
- Museum
- Playgrounds
- Stadium

HIGHLIGHTS

- The Green Bridge crossing the Mile End Road: a grassed bridge with trees
- Superb ecology centre and arts park
- Brand new playground and drop in children's centre
- Cycling paths
- Giant pools of the modern terraced garden
- Views of Canary Wharf and the classic cityscape
- Nearby Limehouse Basin
- Canal-side walks

ATHLETICS

The Victoria Park Harriers and Tower Hamlets Athletic Club (VPHTHAC) (tel. 020 8510 0869) train at the Mile End Stadium (at the southern end of the park). The two clubs were combined in 2001, bringing together well over 100 years of club history. Their aim is to provide a friendly environment for the local community to get involved in athletics, track and field and road running. Membership is open to anyone over the age of nine, regardless of ability. There are two types of members: road runners and track and field athletes. The road runners train at Victoria Park (see p262) The track and field athletes train at the Mile End Stadium. They meet at 18.30 on Tuesdays and Thursdays for sprints, hurdles, jumps (including pole vault), throws and middle distance. There are also 'introductory' hurdle sessions on Monday evenings at 18.30. For further details see the website www.vphthac.org.uk, or email info@vphthac.org.uk. Mile End Stadium, Rhodeswell Road, Poplar, London E14 7TW, tel. 020 8980 1885.

ART

The arts centre is housed in an impressive grass-covered building in the ecology park (see below). The grassy slopes behind the centre lead up to Regent's Canal and the outside terrace overlooks reflective pools of water. It is as if the area has been carved into the landscape. The centre hosts regular workshops, events and exhibitions.

BICYCLING

There is a well-maintained cycle route through the park. Regent's Canal is a superb cycle ride and runs from the Thames (at Limehouse Basin) right through London, passing through Mile End Park, Victoria Park and Regent's Park in Camden.

CANALS

Regent's Canal was the brainchild of Thomas Homer, who planned a lucrative link between Paddington (Grand Junction) and the East Docks in the early 19th century. He designed the 8.5 mile canal in collaboration with John Nash (of Regent's Park fame) and it was opened in 1820. The canal is one of the most picturesque walks and cycle routes in London, linking Maida Vale to Regent's Park and Camden, to Victoria Park, Mile End Park and then out to Limehouse Basin and the Thames. Much of the route is very well maintained, with easy access to cafés and pubs. Limehouse Basin was created in 1812 and is now a marina. It was once London's gateway to England's canal network, with branches to the Midlands leading from the Grand Junction at Paddington. The canal's office can be contacted on tel. 020 8571 8900 or 020 7286 6101. They also run guided historical walks. The London Canal Museum is based at New Wharf Road, King's Cross, tel. 020 7713 0836, open 10.00–16.30 Tuesday to Sunday.

CLIMBING

The Mile End Climbing Wall is based at Haverfield Road and is open from Monday to Friday 12.00–21.00 and at weekends 10.00–18.00. Sessions cost £6. Tel. 020 8980 0289, website www.mileendwall.org.uk.

ECOLOGY

The Art and Ecology Pavilion is on the north side of the Green Bridge. The grounds are set around reflective pools of water. The events building has six metres of dry earth and grass encasing it, like a cosy winter coat designed to trap heat in the summer and to keep the building warm in the winter. It is like a hobbit's house in the East End.

FRIENDS OF MILE END PARK

For details about the Friends of Mile End Park contact Alex Williams at 17 Haverfield Road, Bow, London E3 5BH.

GO-KARTING

The newly opened 500m go-kart track in St Paul's Way is one of the first in London to use silent electric go-karts. Practice sessions cost from £10 and various competitions are run including a mini grand prix, team racing, open racing and sprints. Revolution Karting, Arches 422-424, Mile End Park, Burdett Road, London E3 4AA, tel. 020 7538 5195, website www.revolutionkarting.com, email sales@revolutionkarting.com.

GREEN BRIDGE

The Green Bridge, designed by Piers Gough, is one of the park's highlights. It is a 25-metre-wide, yellow-bottomed pedestrian bridge and cycle path, which has been grassed and planted with trees. The bridge is built out of special lightweight polystyrene laid over concrete. It allows an uninterrupted journey across the busy Mile End Road. Its trees include Himalayan birches and pines.

MUSEUM

This museum is where Dr John Barnardo set up his second Ragged School orphanage in the 19th century. The building is one of the few remaining canal warehouses in the area. The school provided free education and meals for homeless and neglected children in the area. The Ragged School Museum,

46-50 Copperfield Road, E3 4RR, tel. 020 8980 6405. Open Wednesday and Thursday 10.00–17.00, first Sunday of the month and bank holidays 14.00–17.00. Free entrance. Café.

PLAYGROUND

The brand new £2 million playground and drop-in centre is a big hit and includes scrambling walls, web climbing frames with springy rope centres, swings and slides. The playground is open from 10.00–20.00. There is also an under fives' One O'Clock Club which runs on weekdays from 12.30–16.00.

STADIUM

The Mile End Stadium at the southern end of the park has an eight-lane all-weather athletics track, an artificial hockey and football pitch, a grass football pitch and tennis courts. There are numerous classes, clubs and training sessions including athletics, tennis, karate and football. Mile End Stadium, Rhodeswell Road, Poplar, London E14 7TW, tel. 020 8980 1885.

TREES

There are many unusual trees in the park including large multi-stemmed Himalayan birches (*betula utilis*) with graphic white trunks, evergreen black pines (*pinus nigra*) and silvery Weymoth pines (*pinus strobus*).

WIND TURBINE

Water pumps in the park's many ponds and lakes are powered by a large wind turbine that silently spins in the Ecology Park. The turbine is nine metres tall, has a normal running speed of about 200rpm and a power output of 300V (6kw).

NEAR THE PARK

Limehouse Basin: London's old gateway to the canals

Regent's Canal: quiet waterside walks and pubs

New River Walk

VISITOR INFORMATION

St Paul's Road, N1

Train: Canonbury (Silverlink), Essex Road (WAGN)

Bus: 38, 56, 73, 271, 341

Website: www.thames-water.com.

New River Action Group: tel. 020 8363 7187

The New River is London's oldest aqueduct so it is neither new nor a natural river. It was built between 1609 and 1613 to bring fresh spring water from Hertfordshire to London. Its gentle curves follow the 100ft contour line and fall just 15.5ft from the source in mid Hertfordshire to the head at the West Reservoir in Stoke Newington. It is still used by Thames Water for London's drinking water. It also forms a pretty 28 mile (45km) footpath into London.

The now redundant channel south of Stoke Newington (the aqueduct's original head was in Clerkenwell) has been developed into a long linear park (four acres). This runs along the line of the New River from St Paul's Road to Canonbury Road. This park is fringed with flowers, trees, rock pools and mini waterfalls that form popular summer paddling pools. Other areas of the walk include Finsbury Park (see p82) and the Gentleman's Walk in Enfield.

HIGHLIGHTS

- A local and long-distance footpath linking Hertford with Islington
- Nearby Clissold Park (see p53)

- River wildlife
- Rock pools and waterfalls

THE NEW RIVER PATH ROUTE MAP

Thames Water has published an excellent (free) leaflet detailing the entire 28-mile (45km) route from Hertfordshire to Islington. The leaflet includes maps and divides the walk into three sections.

The Hertfordshire section, 14 miles (22km) long, runs from New Gauge in Hertford to Theobalds Park and passes through the Lee Valley corridor. The London section, 11 miles (18km) long, continues into Stoke Newington. The final 'Heritage' section, 3 miles (5km) long, goes up to the New River Head.

The leaflet is available from Thames Water, tel. 0845 920 0800, or by writing to them at Thames Water, PO Box 286, Swindon SN38 2RA, website www.thames-water.com.

Osterley Park

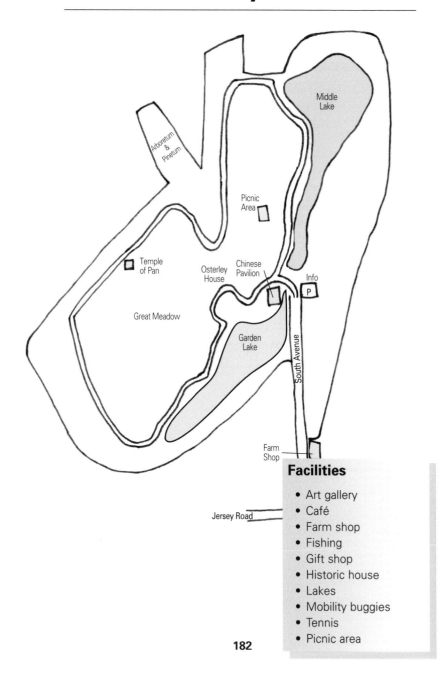

Middle Lake

Arboretum & Pinetum

Picnic Area

Temple of Pan

Osterley House

Chinese Pavilion

Info

P

Great Meadow

Garden Lake

South Avenue

Farm Shop

Jersey Road

Facilities

- Art gallery
- Café
- Farm shop
- Fishing
- Gift shop
- Historic house
- Lakes
- Mobility buggies
- Tennis
- Picnic area

Jersey Road, Isleworth, TW7 4RB

Bus: H28, H91

Car: admission £3 (National Trust members free). Free parking is available outside the park gates.

Train: Syon Lane (1.5 miles)

Tube: Osterley (20 minute walk)

Osterley Park has 350 acres of landscaped park and farmland surrounding a beautiful 18th century Robert Adam-designed house. The landscaped parkland has ornamental lakes, woodland walks, lawns, picnic spots, a café, farm shop, horse riding and a free exhibition gallery. There is a programme of events, many of which are free, throughout the year. These include jazz in the afternoon, an open-air cinema, fireworks, exhibitions, guided walks and lectures. The park has an average of 300,000 visitors a year but is spacious enough never to be crowded.

HIGHLIGHTS

* Farm shop
* Osterley House, designed by Robert Adam

ARCHITECTURE

Robert Adam (1728–92) was Britain's most famous 18th century architect and interior decorator. After training in Rome he joined forces with his brother, James, and took on some of the most important country house conversions of the century. They managed to incorporate neoclassical panache into the home: it caused a sensation. Osterley, Kenwood and Syon Houses are the most complete examples of his work.

ART

The Jersey Galleries were opened in 1995 and run exhibitions of contemporary art including painting, sculpture, photography, ceramics and videos. Website: www.nationaltrust.org.uk/osterley.

BUGGIES

Battery powered buggies are available free of charge from the Stable yard 13.30–16.30 on Wednesdays, Thursdays, Saturdays, Sundays and bank holidays. There are two outdoor and two indoor wheelchairs available and an electric courtesy bus between the car park, house and tea rooms.

CAFÉ

The tea rooms are in the old stables, which surround a pretty cobbled courtyard and are topped by a clock tower with a weathervane. There is a children's corner with small chairs, a blackboard and some small toys. The walled tea garden at the back is much prettier than the rather gloomy interior. Sandwiches are made to order from £2.60, filter coffee is £1.20, tea £1.20, homemade lemonade £1, treacle tart £2.45, slices of cake £1.50, soup £3.35 and jacket potato £4.75. Lunch is served from 12.00–14.00 only.

Open: 2 April to 2 November 11.30–17.00, Wednesday to Sunday (plus bank holidays); 5 November to 21 December 12.00–16.00 Wednesday to Sunday.

FARM SHOP

This superb farm shop sells fresh seasonal vegetables, eggs, fruit and hay from the 62 hectare (153 acre) Osterley Farm at bargain prices. Open daily 08.00–18.00, South Avenue (main drive leading to Osterley House).

FILM AND FIREWORKS

There is an annual open air film and fireworks evening with hot food stalls and a wine bar. Box Office tel. 01494 755572.

FISHING

There is a beautiful fishing lake within the grounds of Osterley Park. Season tickets are available from the Head Gardener in the Estate Office in the park either by post or in person during office hours Monday to Friday. Each permit can be paid for by cheque or cash and must be accompanied by two passport photographs. Season tickets cost £23 for two rods and there are no day tickets available. Each person must have a rod licence, available from Post Offices. Carp, pike and the usual lake species can be fished and there is good tench water. Tel. 020 8560 5421.

FRIENDS OF OSTERLEY PARK

The Friends of Osterley take an active part in the running of the park and in fund-raising. Since 1990 they have raised over £44,000 to help maintain the house and park. There are many benefits for Friends including private members' events, weekend coach trips, opportunities for voluntary work and fund-raising events. Membership costs £5/year. Membership Secretary, tel. 020 8737 0744, chairman, tel. 020 8560 8523.

GIFT SHOP

The small gift shop is open from 13.00–17.30 Wednesdays to Sundays from 2 April to 2 November and from 12.00–16.00 from 5 November to 12 December.

HOUSE

Osterley House is a stunning 18th century reconstruction of a house originally built by Sir Thomas Gresham in the 16th century. He was the founder of the Royal Exchange and Chancellor of the Exchequer to Queen Elizabeth I. The banker, Sir Francis Child, bought the house in the early 18th century, in order to store his bank's money in its vaults. He commissioned the famous neoclassical architect Robert Adam to redesign the house. The project took almost 20 years to complete but resulted in one of Britain's finest houses. It remains virtually unaltered and is one of the best preserved of Adam's interiors. The estate was given to the National Trust in 1949.

Osterley House and Galleries, Jersey Road, Isleworth, Middlesex TW7 4RB. Website www.nationaltrust.org.uk/osterley, email osterley@nationaltrust.org.uk, tel. 020 8232 5050. Open Wednesday to Sunday and bank holidays 2 April to 2 November 13.00–16.30. Admission £4.50 (adults), £2.25 (children), £11.20 (family), National Trust members free.

PINEAPPLES

A giant white pineapple tops each of the four towers of Osterley House. They were carved out of pine wood in the 19th century and were recently restored. A pineapple which was beyond repair is on display in the Information Centre.

TEMPLE

The Temple of Pan is a small summerhouse designed by Chambers in classical Greek style with Doric columns. The prettier Adam's Garden House is nearby. This is a beautiful semicircular building with curved arched windows overlooking a neat formal flower garden.

TREES

The park has beautiful trees. The main drive, South Avenue, is lined with horse chestnuts, lime trees and liquidambars. The Cedar Lawn to the south of the house has cedars of Lebanon which were planted in 1760 and there is even an ancient Mediterranean cork tree. A path running through the west woods passes ancient Hungarian and North American oaks, giving glimpses of the cattle chewing grass in the Great Meadow. It is hard to imagine that this is London.

WALKS

Themed and guided walks are available throughout the year. These include birds, trees, nuts and berries, ghosts of Osterley, winter wanders, wine tasting, conservation, wartime and Christmas walks. There are also walks and talks for children. Many of the walks include a cream tea. Booking is essential. Tel. 01494 755572. Some of the events are free, while others cost from £1.50 (children), £6 (adults).

WORKSHOPS

There are numerous workshops and adult evening and weekend classes in life drawing, watercolours and stitched textiles. There are also children's half-term courses in subjects such as fan making and sugar mice. Tel. 020 8232 5052. Website www.nationaltrust.org.uk/osterley.

Paddington Recreation Ground

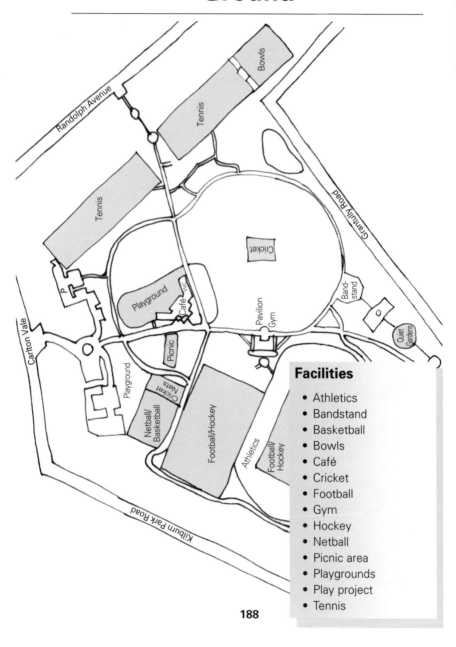

Facilities

- Athletics
- Bandstand
- Basketball
- Bowls
- Café
- Cricket
- Football
- Gym
- Hockey
- Netball
- Picnic area
- Playgrounds
- Play project
- Tennis

VISITOR INFORMATION

Randolph Avenue , Maida Vale, W9 1PD

Bus: 6, 16, 28, 31, 36, 97, 98, 187

Car: pay and display parking

Tube: Maida Vale

This 27-acre recreation ground is dominated by sports facilities but also has two quiet rose gardens, a café, three playgrounds and therapeutic massage available. There is a six-lane, 400m athletics track, bowling green, cricket pitch, ten tennis courts, an all-weather flood-lit sports pitch and a fully equipped gym. Roger Bannister trained here while studying medicine, before running the first four-minute mile in 1954.

HIGHLIGHTS

* Playgrounds for all ages
* Sports facilities for all interests
* Therapeutic massage at the therapy rooms

ART

Kevin's Art Club for Children has regular meetings for children of all ages in the studio behind the café. Prices start at £15/session and include materials. Tel. 020 7706 0056.

CAFÉ

Café Verona

Although this café is less Italian than its name suggests, it had jazz playing and was warm despite the wet cold winter day on which we visited. There is indoor and outdoor seating and large windows overlooking the grassy outside space. The studio joins on to the café and has a range of keep-fit classes (see Sports, below).

Kids menu from £1.60, *di sotto* Italian ice cream £1.20, Costa coffee £1.20, tea 80p, English breakfast £3.60, toasted sandwich £1.70, hotdog £1.50, crisps 40p. Tel. 020 7625 2632. Open Monday to Friday 09.30–17.00 and weekends 09.30–16.00.

GARDENS

There is a pretty 'quiet' garden with a many different species of rose plus a pergola. The Knot Garden, near the tennis courts, offers a small Tudor experience.

MASSAGE

Omni Therapies have a range of therapeutic massage including aromatherapy, ayurvedic massage, clothed seated massage, cranial sacral therapy, holistic massage, no-hands massage, reflexology and sports massage. The therapy rooms are next to the Café Verona. Prices start at £40/hour. Tel. 020 7328 0828, website www.omnitherapies.com.

PLAYGROUNDS

There are three playgrounds, an under fives, an under 12s and a small adventure playground including a fantastic slide. The Play Project has table tennis, pool and other games. Tel. 020 7625 7024.

SPORTS

The sports facilities have recently been refurbished and include an all-weather sports pitch, bowls, cricket, gym, running track and tennis. Keep-fit class include aerobics, boxercise, circuit training and yoga. There are three-day courses for children including mini-soccer, football and tennis. Tickets are available for individual sessions and there is a range of discount options for membership, families and children. Tel. 020 7641 3642.

Membership options:

'Ultimate' membership is unlimited use of the gym, fitness classes, running track, court booking service and swimming pool in a neighbouring centre. The cost is £41/month.

Gym membership is unlimited use of the well-equipped gym. The cost is £35/month.

TRIM-TRAIL

All around the grounds are different stations for exercising. These include two balancing beams, parallel bars, a pole climb, over and under hurdles, horizontal monkey bars, single trapeze swing and pull-up bars.

Paradise Park

Paradise Park is a small square green near Pentonville Prison. It looks unassuming but it is a small child's paradise. There is a superbly run city farm, a small children's playground with one of the best interactive fountains in London, an all-weather five-a-side pitch and an after-school club. The park is near Highbury Fields, Caledonian Park and the Islington Tennis Club.

HIGHLIGHTS

- City farm
- Interactive fountains

FARM

The Freightliners City Farm is a well-run small city farm with three cows, two pigs, four sheep, four geese, 23 ducks, numerous chickens, turkeys, rabbits and bees. Look out for the Indian runner, a duck that looks like a penguin. The new glasshouse looks like a mini Eden Project and is surrounded by plants and herbs and a nearby planted-up rail carriage on its own section of track. The small shop sells fresh vegetables, eggs, honey, straw and animal feed. The 'café corner' serves up delicious informal

Facilities

- Farm
- Football
- Playground

mugs of tea and coffee: essential energy for parents.

Open 10.00–17.00 Tuesday to Sunday (sometimes earlier closing in winter). Entrance is free but donations are always welcome. Tel. 020 7609 0467, website www.freightlinersfarm.org.uk.

Animals

It is possible to sponsor a Freightliners Farm animal for as little as £15 a year. Bargains at the time of writing were Maisie the Toggenburg goat, Mamog the black Welsh mountain ewe, Olivia the Dexter cow and Harvey the rabbit. Sponsors receive a photograph of the animal, a window sticker and four progress reports per year and are informed of anything exciting that happens to their animal.

FOOTBALL

There is an enclosed all-weather five-a-side football pitch opposite the playground.

ISLINGTON GREENSPACE AND LEISURE TEAM

The Greenspace team manages Islington's parks and green spaces extremely well. They produce a regular events leaflet. To be put on the mailing list telephone the Islington Ecology Centre on 020 7354 5162, or visit the website www.islington.gov.uk.

PLAYGROUND

The supervised playground in Paradise Park looks standard but has some interesting features. The stainless steel pole in the centre is not an outdoor gas heater but a pressure-pad activated fountain. Stamp on the innocuous rubber pad underneath and it erupts into a mushroom of water. In fact the whole area is dotted with similar pressure pads, activating jets of water from holes recessed in the ground. There are fine sprays and tall jets angled to catch passers-by unawares.

Peckham Rye Park

Peckham Rye Park is a pretty 50-acre park that joins Peckham Rye Common (64 acres), an open space dating from the 14th century. It has been a public park since 1894 and is famous for two well-known people. Elizabeth Cadbury, the wife of the chocolate manufacturer, grew up by the park. William Blake saw a vision of angels in an oak tree on the common. The park is currently being renovated, having won a Heritage Lottery Fund grant. There are several gardens, large groups of beautiful trees, sports fields, a bowling green, secluded walks, wide expanses of grassland and meadow, an adventure playground, a small lake and an information centre.

HIGHLIGHTS

- Sexby Garden
- Open grassland

ADVENTURE PLAYGROUND

The enclosed adventure playground is open from April to September from Tuesday to Friday

Facilities

- Playgound
- Information centre
- Bowling green

15.30–19.00, Saturdays (all year) 11.00–17.00 and school holidays Monday to Friday 10.30–18.00. It is just off Homestall Road, and is free of charge. Tel. 020 7635 0430.

BOWLING

The bowling green is currently being renovated. The original 1910 bowling pavilion burned down but a new one is planned. Membership costs £10/year and new members are welcome. For the latest update contact the Information Centre.

FOOTBALL

The football pitch can be reserved through the booking office. The cost is £42/game or £22 for juniors. Tel. 020 7525 1052.

FRIENDS OF PECKHAM RYE PARK

The Friends of Peckham Rye Park meet most months and are active in promoting and preserving the park. Tel. Mai-Ling Savage 020 8299 3393, website www.foprp.org.uk.

GARDENS

The newly designed Sexby Garden has a pretty pergola walk with roses and wisteria and a crazy paving path network around a central small round pond. The Japanese Garden was opened in 1908 and is being restored. There is also a Water Garden, separated by large groups of trees into discreet, secluded nooks of the park.

INFORMATION

There is a small information centre on Strakers Road, off Peckham Rye Road East, open 10.00–15.30. Tel. 020 8693 3791.

SKATEBOARDING

A conversion is planned for the old tennis courts to be made into a new skateboarding area.

Queen's Park

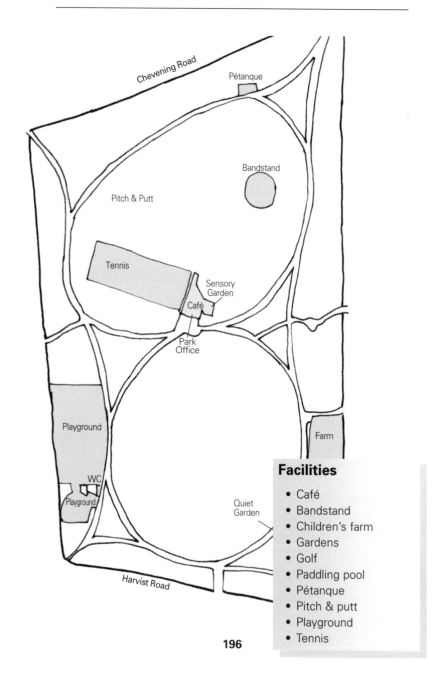

Chevening Road

Pétanque

Bandstand

Pitch & Putt

Tennis

Sensory Garden

Café

Park Office

Playground

Farm

WC

Playground

Quiet Garden

Harvist Road

Facilities

- Café
- Bandstand
- Children's farm
- Gardens
- Golf
- Paddling pool
- Pétanque
- Pitch & putt
- Playground
- Tennis

196

VISITOR INFORMATION

Harvist Road/Chevening Road, NW6

Tube/train: Queen's Park, Brondesbury Park

Bus: 6, 187, 206, 316

Car: pay and display parking only

The Lord Mayor of London opened this 32-acre park in Kilburn to the public in 1887. It was named Queen's Park in honour of Queen Victoria's Golden Jubilee. Alexander Mackenzie, who had been involved in the construction of Alexandra Palace Gardens, designed the park on a small budget. During World War II, the park had a barrage balloon and allotments were grown as part of Britain's Dig for Victory campaign.

HIGHLIGHTS

- Pitch and putt nine-hole course
- Chess boards built into some of the café tables
- Children's farm

BANDSTAND

The bandstand was added to the park in 1891. There are summertime concerts – the programme can be obtained from the hatch near the tennis courts.

BOULES

The pétanque (boules) rink is at the northern end of the park.

CAFÉ

The Park Café

The Park Café is in the centre of the park, next to the tennis courts and golf. There is outside seating, and some of the tables have chess boards built into the tabletop. Chess sets can be hired from inside for a £10 deposit. The café sells tasty snacks and hot meals. Cappuccino £1.50, cooked breakfast £4.50, crisps 50p, coke 50p, cake £2.25, fish and chips £5.95. The park's toilets (including disabled and baby changing facilities) are next to the playground, a short walk away. Open 09.00 to about 19.00. Tel. 020 8969 9553.

CHESS

Some of the café's outdoor tables have tabletop chess boards. The pieces can be obtained from the café for a £10 deposit.

CHILDREN'S FARM

The tiny children's farm is perfectly designed for small children. It is an enclosed area near the Kingwood Avenue entrance and is open daily, free of charge. There are chickens, rabbits, goats, a small duck pond, turkeys and even a scarecrow. It is then only a short run to the sandpit (see Playground and paddling pool, below).

GARDENS

The quiet garden is near the children's farm. It is an enclosed formal garden, planted to a Victorian design. There are benches and a gate shelter. The small sensory garden near the café was designed as a kind of sensory massage. There is a water feature, gentle wind chimes, fragrant plants and specially designed benches.

INFORMATION

The park's main office is above the café. Information can be obtained from the hatch by the tennis courts. Tel 020 8969 5661 or email parks.gardens@ms.corpoflondon.gov.uk. Open 08.00–16.00.

PICNICS

The nearby Salusbury Road (NW6) has several delicatessens, cafés and a Baker and Spice to stock up for a picnic in the park.

PITCH AND PUTT

There is an excellent nine-hole golf pitch and putt course next to the tennis courts. Clubs and balls can be hired from the hatch at the entrance to the course. Opening hours vary according to the season. The cost is £3.20 including clubs and balls.

PLAYGROUND AND PADDLING POOL

The playground includes an under sevens' area with a sandpit and a 7–12s' area with climbing frames and a commando slide. There are picnic tables and undercover seating. There is also a smart rectangular paddling pool with attendants on duty.

TENNIS

There are six tennis courts. Advance booking is not possible. Courts cost £4.80/hour or £2.40 for half an hour. The small hatch office by the courts also rents racquets and can provide a list of local coaches.

NEAR THE PARK

Baker and Spice on Salusbury Road sells some of the best bread and cakes in London.

Regent's Park

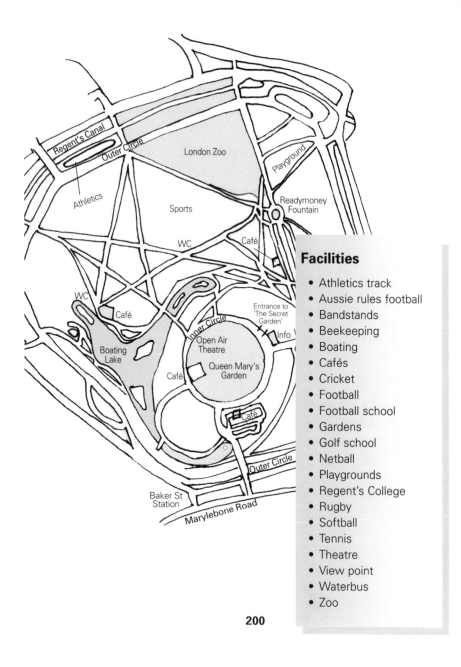

Regent's Canal
Outer Circle
London Zoo
Playground
Athletics
Sports
Readymoney Fountain
WC
Café
WC
Café
Inner Circle
Entrance to 'The Secret Garden'
Open Air Theatre
Info
Boating Lake
Café
Queen Mary's Garden
Café
Outer Circle
Baker St Station
Marylebone Road

Facilities

- Athletics track
- Aussie rules football
- Bandstands
- Beekeeping
- Boating
- Cafés
- Cricket
- Football
- Football school
- Gardens
- Golf school
- Netball
- Playgrounds
- Regent's College
- Rugby
- Softball
- Tennis
- Theatre
- View point
- Waterbus
- Zoo

VISITOR INFORMATION

Regent's Park, NW1

tel. 020 7486 7905, website www.royalparks.org.uk

Tube: Baker Street, Camden Town, Great Portland Street, Regent's Park and St. John's Wood. For the most picturesque approach take the tube to Camden and walk along Regent's Canal, or take the waterbus.

Bus: C2, 2, 13, 18, 27, 30, 74, 82, 88, 113, 115, 139, 148, 189, 274

Car: There is pay and display parking in and around the park and free parking after 18.30. The maximum stay is four hours from Monday to Saturday but there is no maximum on Sundays or bank holidays.

In 1650 more than 16,000 trees were felled in the area now known as Regent's Park to raise money to pay the cavalry troops. The Prince Regent commissioned the design of Regent's Park in 1811 to celebrate the victory at Waterloo. His favoured architect, John Nash, was in charge of the project. Nash had already designed Marble Arch, Carlton House Terrace and Regent's Street and not only landscaped the park but designed many of the surrounding Regency terraces. His original plan was a housing development for the rich: grand Regency villas set among parkland. Fortunately Parliament intervened and saved the park for public use. It finally opened in 1835.

The park covers 472 acres and includes beekeeping and boating, a secret garden and shady tree-lined avenues, playgrounds, tennis courts and sports fields, a rose scented café, an open-air theatre, large expanses of grass, Regency villas and nearby Regent's Canal, London Zoo and Primrose Hill (see p213). The tranquillity of this park is only 20 minutes' walk from Oxford Circus.

HIGHLIGHTS

- Birds: the largest public waterfowl collection in the country
- John Nash's Regency buildings within and around the park
- London Zoo: a brilliant day out for everyone since 1820
- London Central Mosque
- Open-air theatre with summer plays and concerts
- Queen Mary's Gardens with over 400 varieties of rose
- Regent's Canal and the waterbus
- The largest outdoor sports space in London (being developed)
- Secret garden – even missed by many of the locals

ART

There are regular free exhibitions in the Avenue Gardens (also known as the Italian Gardens, see Gardens, below) and in the Open Air Theatre (see below).

ATHLETICS

The athletics track is located on the north side of the Outer Circle. It is a rather eccentric 387m, six-lane, enclosed track with a grass infield. The track has been around since the early 1930s. It is in reasonable, if rather uneven, condition and is popular with joggers, and lunchtime sprinters. There are no changing facilities. Tel. 020 7486 7905 (main park office) for further information.

AUSTRALIAN RULES FOOTBALL

The park is home to the North London/Regent's Park Lions Australian Rules FC. They were one of the founding clubs of the British Australian Rules Football League (BARFL) in 1990, formed by a group of homesick Australians. The league is now huge with two-tier 13 team competitions, coaching, training and facilities. The club welcomes new players of all backgrounds and levels of experience. Pre-season training usually starts mid-February on Sundays then increases to include Tuesday and Thursday evenings as the season approaches (May to September). For further details contact the club website www.aussierules.co.uk, email info@aussierules.co.uk or check the BARFL website www.barfl.co.uk.

BEES

The Beekeepers Association holds a yearly talk in the park and runs regular courses in beekeeping (also for complete beginners). There is also a unique 'adopt a hive' scheme for those who pass the course. Membership costs £33/year, tel. 020 7624 2225 or visit the excellent website www.beekeeping.org.uk.

BIRD WATCHING

Regent's Park is so rich in bird life it has become an officially designated inland bird observatory. The Royal Waterfowl Collection (based at the pond) is the largest public collection in the country. There are more than 90 species of waterfowl, Hawaiian geese, seven species of swan and a heronry. At times the path surrounding the pond is so full of birds it is difficult to walk – the waterfowl equivalent of Trafalgar Square's pigeons. Sightings of unusual birds are printed around the lake. Free guided Sunday morning bird watching walks are led throughout August and September. Places must be booked in advance at the main information office, tel. 020 7486 7905.

BOATING

Regent's Park Boating Lake is near Hanover Gate (next to the mosque). Tel. 020 7724 4069 (Boathouse Café), or Park Boats

Mobile 07973 347078. Open April to September Monday to Friday 10.00–17.00 and weekends 09.00–19.00. Rowing boats cost £2.50/30mins for children, adults £4.00/30 minutes or £5.50/hour. Pedalos cost £3/20 minutes. There is a smaller children's boating pond with 30 pedalos opposite the four-sided clock tower and Boathouse Café. Children must be over 70cm tall – there is a measuring board next to the boat hire to check! The boating lake is one of the park's highlights. It covers nine hectares in a giant Y shape and is home to the Royal Waterfowl Collection (see above). There are weeping willows, winding lakeside paths and waterfowl nesting on the banks.

BROAD WALK

The Broad Walk was designed to be a carriageway accessing the many villas that Nash had planned for the park. When Parliament intervened to stop the housing developments the avenue became the fashionable tree-lined Broad Walk. Nesfield's Avenue Gardens at the southern end were part of the redevelopment.

CAFÉS

Queen Mary's Gardens, Inner Circle

This is the park's main café, which is located in the spectacular Queen Mary's Gardens. There is a wide selection of self-service food – including salads, pastas, sandwiches and sausages, and coffee and cakes (for the best coffee go to the nearby Honest Sausage Café, below). There is outdoor seating, baby changing facilities, a function room and a children's adventure playground.

Prices: beer £2.75, cake £2.35, cappuccino £1.40, crisps 75p, hot dishes from £6, ice cream £1.40, sandwiches £2.95, soups £3.35, tea 90p, water £1.34. Open daily 09.00–20.00 (summer) and 10.00–16.00 (winter). Tel. 020 7935 5729, website www.parkcafe.biz.

The Boathouse Café

This small café overlooks the lake. There is mainly outdoor seating and the café serves tasty stone-baked pizza slices (£2.95), burgers (£4.95) and jacket potatoes (£5.25) as well as the standard fare. Adult and children's boating is available (see 'Boating', above). Tel. 020 7724 4069.

The Honest Sausage

Located on the Broad Walk (off Chester Road), this is described as a 'Swiss-style chalet café' but looks like a cross between an English Tudor house and Swiss chalet. It is the best of the park's cafés for coffee and sausages. The Park Porker is its speciality free-range sausage (£2.75), bacon butties are also tasty (£2.95) and there is seating inside and out. No toilets. Tel. 020 7224 3872, open 09.00–20.00 (summer) and 10.00–16.00 (winter).

Park Café Kiosk

Open every day from 10.00–19.00 during the summer only. This kiosk is at Chester Gate.

Pavilion Café

At the Regent's Park Tennis Centre, York Bridge (see below under tennis), this club-house café including a 'healthy eating' option, with views of the courts. Tel. 020 7486 4216, open 09.00–21.00 (summer) and 10.00–16.00 (winter).

CIRCLES

The design of the park is circular. The Outer Circle defines the park's boundaries. The much smaller Inner Circle contains the Queen Mary's Gardens, the café and the Open-Air Theatre. John Nash had planned to build the Prince Regent's new residence within the Inner Circle. The newly built Regent's Street would have conveniently linked this to his other residence at Carlton House (now Carlton House Terrace). The Inner Circle was built according to plan but the residence never materialised. Instead the Royal Botanical Society leased the area and when the lease ran out it was developed into Queen Mary's Rose Garden.

COLLEGE

Regent's College is located at the Clarence Gate corner of the park. It was formerly Bedford College, the first university college for women. It was built in the early 20th century on the site of a villa designed by Decimus Burton (who also designed the Hyde Park Corner Screen), the gate lodge of which still exists. The college has a Business School and a renowned School of Counselling and Psychotherapy. There is a wide range of courses available. Contact: Regent's College, Inner Circle, Regent's Park, NW1 4NS, tel. 020 7487 7406.

CRICKET

The park has five club standard and one county standard cricket squares. The new sports pavilion (see below) will have changing and catering facilities and will be the base for 'Capital Kids Cricket', encouraging children to become involved in cricket. Tel. 020 7486 7905 for further information about sports.

DRINKING FOUNTAINS

Hanover Gate Drinking Fountain (near the Boathouse) was built from red Aberdeen granite in 1901 due to local concern about children drinking from the lake, as the nearest drinking fountain was over a mile away.

Readymoney Fountain (Broad Walk near the Gloucester Gate) – this 22-foot high drinking fountain is made of Sicilian marble and polished red Aberdeen granite. The man who paid for it was an Indian money-lender from Bombay, hence the fountain's name. It was commissioned and erected by the Cattle Trough and Drinking Fountain Association in 1868. Laser beams inside the water pipes (just put your finger in to trigger them) now work the fountain. There are two water bowls at foot-level for dogs on the side of the clock.

FOOTBALL

The park has superb football facilities. These include 16 mini-pitches for children and small games, eight mid size and 15 full size. The popular QPR Saturday Morning Soccer School runs in the park, every week from 09.00–12.00 from January to the end of April. The sessions are suitable for boys and girls aged 6-12 years old and cost £1.50. Places should be booked in advance, tel. 020 8743 0262. The QPR School also runs intensive week-long courses, from 10.30–15.30, that cost £7 per day and are suitable for 6–15 year olds.

FOUNTAINS

'Boy and Frog Fountain' (Begonia Garden): this bronze statue was bought with the leftover money from the Jubilee Gates in 1936. The pedestal is made of Finnish granite, which was carved in Aberdeen.

'Hylas and the Nymph' (Secret Garden of St John's Lodge): this 1930s bronze statue on a plinth of Portland stone is set in the middle of the pond in the Secret Garden. The legendary Hylas was so beautiful that the nymphs were compelled to pull him into the ground. His cries are said to be heard today in the form of echoes around the ponds.

'Triton Fountain' (opposite the Jubilee Gates in Queen Mary's Gardens): this pretty 1930s fountain is set in a large round pond full of well-fed carp. Triton was the son of Poseidon, god of the sea. He was half human and half fish and rode sea horses, calling to his father with a shell. The fountain is by William McMillan.

GARDENS

Avenue Gardens and the English Gardens

(Between Chester Road and the Outer Circle) The Avenue Gardens, also known as the 'Italian Gardens', were designed in the mid 19th century by the Victorian garden designer Andrew

Nesfield, who also designed the Palm House in Kew. His son, Markham Nesfield, landscaped the adjacent English Gardens. Both were restored in the 1990s with the addition of fountains. The simple layout of the garden consists of four avenues of trees, long gravel paths and colourful flower beds among stonework and evergreen hedging. The huge Lion Tazza urn overflows with flowers in the centre of the garden. This is the original Nesfield bowl, supported by four winged lions.

Queen Mary's Gardens (Inner Circle)

In the Silver Jubilee year of 1935 the Inner Circle Gardens were renamed Queen Mary's Gardens by George V, as she often visited them. Her gardens include the spectacular Rose Garden, formed in 1930 following a donation of bushes from the British Rose Growers Association. This garden includes more than 400 types of rose, the scent of which reaches the furthest boundaries of the park. The gardens' recently restored black and gold Jubilee Gates show the date 6 May 1935, under the King's initials. These gates, along with the Chester Road gates, were a gift from the painter Sigismund Goetze to commemorate the Jubilee.

The Secret Garden

This small, secluded garden is one of the park's hidden highlights. It was designed in 1891 for the third Marquis of Bute, who wanted a garden 'fit for meditation'. The entrance is through unmarked green iron gates, off the Inner Circle, near Chester Road. The garden has statues of Hylas and the Nymph set in a stone pool, the topless Goatherd's daughter and the Awakening, two faces within a split seed. There are elegant high-backed wooden benches, numerous nooks of clipped yew and lavender and a sunken lawn rolled out like an exotic rug from the gently curved stone steps facing St John's Lodge, the first villa to be built in the park.

GOLF

The Regent's Park Golf (and tennis) School is located on the north side of the park, on the Outer Circle close to London Zoo. The facility consists of golf nets that can be used for practice or for lessons and three flood-lit tennis courts. Golf lessons include video analysis of the swing and cost £25 for half an hour. Net practice costs £2.50 for 45 balls. Membership costs from £75 per year and gold membership (which includes golf and tennis hire) £250 per year. The school is open from 08.00–21.00, tel. 020 7724 0643.

INFORMATION

The Royal Parks Office, Storeyard, Inner Circle (near the junction with Chester Road) has free leaflets, and a map of the park. There are also excellent books for sale on the history and wildlife of the park. Open Monday to Friday 08.30–16.00, tel. 020 7486 7905.

MOSQUE

The London Central Mosque's 195ft tower and gold dome can be seen for miles around. The mosque was finished in 1978 and is the site of the London Islamic Centre. It is located just outside Hanover Gate and is open to respectful visitors. Once you are inside the mosque, London feels a world away. The carpeted area beneath the dome is filled with shoeless worshippers; prayers resound through corridor speakers, people in gowns throng the stairways leading to the library. On the ground floor there is a shop selling books and other religious items, and a free guide to Discovering Islam is available from the porter's lodge.

MUSIC

There are free concerts by musicians from the Royal Academy of Music in the Rose Garden Café, Queen Mary's Gardens on Tuesdays in June and July at 18.15.

The Bandstand was moved from Richmond Park in the 1970s. It is located between Regent's College and the Boating Lake. It is possible to see the damage around its top from the bomb that killed seven people in 1982. From June to August during the weekends, there are free concerts by musicians from around the world.

NETBALL

There are three courts marked out for netball at the Regent's Park Tennis Centre, near York Bridge (see below). These are available for booking, tel. 020 7486 4216.

RUGBY

The park has one full-size rugby pitch. There will be changing facilities in the new pavilion (see below under Sports Development). Tel. 020 7486 7905 for further information.

SCULPTURE

'Goatherd's Daughter', 1932 (Secret Garden)

'Awakening', 2002 (Secret Garden)

'Japanese Eagle', 19th century (in the lake in Queen Mary's Gardens)

SOFTBALL

The park has 19 grass softball pitches, which can be booked on 020 7486 7905. The park is home to many clubs from the London Softball Federation, the largest softball league in the country, and has matches on weekday evenings. The Softball Federation's website lists all of the London clubs and contact numbers, www.londonsoftball.com. Clubs based at the park include the Cheetahs and the Mighty Muppets. The Cheetahs can be contacted at their website www.cheetahssoftball.co.uk, email captain@cheetahssoftball.co.uk. They are using the pitch at Clapham Common South until the Regent's Park pitches reopen. The Mighty Muppets can be contacted at www.mightymuppets.com and are temporarily using

Paddington Recreation Ground.

SPORTS DEVELOPMENT

Regent's Park is the largest single outdoor sports venue in central London. Currently £5.5 million is being spent improving the sports pitches and facilities, including building a new Bernhard Baron Pavilion (due to open 2005). This will be the base for 'Capital Kids Cricket', encouraging children to become involved in cricket. It will also serve the new rugby pitch and the football pitches.

TENNIS

The Tennis Centre has 12 outdoor courts and a club running events, matches and coaching for all ages and abilities. There is a cosy clubroom with satellite TV and a sofa, a small tennis shop including a re-stringing service (from £22) and changing rooms with showers and baby changing facilities. The adjacent licensed bar has indoor and outdoor seating. A seasonal 'booking card' costs from £30 per season and gives discounts on court bookings. Cardholders can book up to seven days in advance and pay £7 peak time (Monday to Friday from 16:00 and all weekend) and £5 off peak (07:00–16–00). Non-cardholders can book a court one day in advance at £9 per hour in peak time and £7 off peak. Student and OAP cardholders pay £6 peak time and £4 off peak. Juniors can play for free during quiet periods of the day. There are three further flood-lit courts at the Regent's Park Golf and Tennis School (see Golf, below) on the Outer Circle near the Zoo.

The Tennis Centre (near York Bridge), tel. 020 7486 4216 or answer-phone/fax 020 7224 1625, website www.tennis-uk.com, email willtowin@btopenworld.com.

THEATRE

The superb Open Air Theatre (Inner Circle near the Queen Mary's Gardens) has a full programme of concerts, comedies, musicals, plays and children's shows from the beginning of June until mid September. The programme includes late night concerts (starting at 23:00) and weekday matinees. The theatre opens at 18.45 for eating and drinking before the performance. Tickets start at £9 and there is a full range of hot dishes from the theatre café as well as a barbecue. Picnic suppers can be booked at the box office for £8.50 per person. Tickets sell out up to three months in advance. Tel. 020 7935 5756 (administration) or 0870 0601811 (booking). Box office open: 31 March–31 May Monday to Saturday 10.00–18.00, from 2 June Monday to Saturday 10.00–20.00 and Sundays 12.00 until the start of the performance. Website: www.openairtheatre.org (£1 booking fee per ticket), email info@openairtheatre.org.

WALKS

A stroll around the borders of the park is an easy three-mile walk. One of the nicest ways to walk either to or from the park is via Regent's Canal, either to Camden Lock or on to Maida Vale. The canal-side path leads up to the entrance to London Zoo.

ZOO

Regent's Park lays claim to the world's oldest zoo, London Zoo, laid out by Decimus Burton in 1827. It is still one of the best days out in London. Tel. 020 7722 3333, website www.londonzoo.co.uk. Open every day 10.00–16.00 (last in 15.00). Adults £12, children £9, family £38.

NEAR THE PARK

Camden Market

John Nash Regency terraces

Madame Tussaud's

Primrose Hill (see below)

Regent's Canal

PRIMROSE HILL

The view of London from Primrose Hill is the best in London. The 112 acres have been a public space since 1841. The hill was given its name after the flowers that have grown there for more than 600 years. Before the reign of Elizabeth I, the hill was a forest full of 'game, stags, buck, boars and wild bulls' and was a popular place for duels.

Nowadays, the rolling grassy hill above Regent's Park and London Zoo is a trendy place for picnics, kite flying and the annual November fireworks that draw people from near and far. Primrose Hill was the setting for *101 Dalmatians*; Pongo began the twilight barking from the top of the hill. At the bottom of the hill are a fantastic adventure playground, two boules pitches, public lavatories and an exercise trail.

The neighbouring Regent's Park Road has smart shops to suit all tastes including designer clothes, restaurants, delis, a health food shop, bathroom shop, Triyoga yoga studio, kitchen shop, fabric shop, hardware store, bookshop, opticians, Post Office, mini-market and two pubs.

The nearest tube station is Chalk Farm.

Richmond Old Deer Park

VISITOR INFORMATION

Twickenham Road, TW9

Website: www.richmond.gov.uk

Buses: 65, 190, R70

Train: Richmond

Richmond Old Deer Park Recreation Ground lies to the north of Twickenham Road, across the river from Syon Park and to the south of Kew Gardens. It stretches right up to the pretty river bank and is an important area for sports and events. It was originally part of the land connected to Henry VII's Richmond Palace and before that it was part of James I's 17th century deer park.

Now the pretty flat green is home to Richmond Athletic Ground and Rugby Club, a large swimming pool complex (see below), hard and grass tennis courts, a playground and several football and rugby pitches. The area is also the site for the Richmond Horse Show and funfairs and circuses. The walk along the riverfront, under Twickenham Bridge along Cholmondeley Walk to Richmond Bridge or up Old Palace Road into Richmond Green (see below) is one of London's prettiest riverside walks.

HIGHLIGHTS

- Riverside walk
- Heated outdoor swimming pool

Facilities

- Gym
- Leisure club
- Playground
- Rugby
- Squash
- Swimming pool
- Tennis

SQUASH CLUB AND GYM

Cannons Squash Club is located in the Richmond Athletic Ground in the Old Deer Park. It has five squash courts, a gym and a fabulous bar with floor to ceiling windows overlooking the rugby pitch. Richmond and London Scottish Rugby Clubs are based at the grounds, and you have commentator quality views of the matches. Website: www.cannons.co.uk.

SWIMMING POOLS

Springhealth Leisure Club, The Old Deer Park, Twickenham Road, tel. 020 8940 0561, website www.springhealthleisure.com.

This club has an indoor and heated outdoor pool with a large sunbathing area. On summer evenings the pool stays open until 21.00. There is a fully equipped gym, steam room and sauna and fitness classes. Day passes are available for non-members for £10. Membership is from £39 plus start up fee. Open Monday to Friday 06.30–19.45 or later (phone), Saturdays 08.00–18.00 and Sundays 07.00–18.00.

TENNIS

There are several tennis courts in the Old Deer Park. Bookings can be made through the Springhealth Leisure Club (above) and cost from £4.50/hour (adults).

Richmond Park

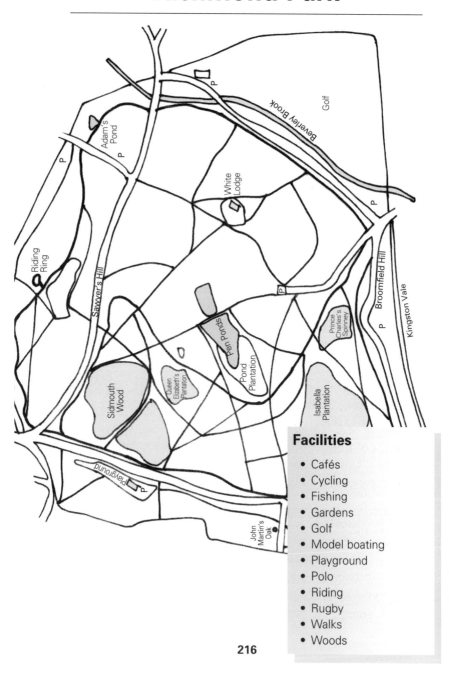

Facilities

- Cafés
- Cycling
- Fishing
- Gardens
- Golf
- Model boating
- Playground
- Polo
- Riding
- Rugby
- Walks
- Woods

216

Richmond Park is the biggest park in Europe, stretching eight miles at its widest point and covering 2,470 acres. Unlike the other Royal Parks, Richmond Park was never landscaped and is largely unchanged since medieval times, with ancient oaks, ponds, hills and rolling grassy spaces. It was used by successive monarchs for hunting until the 19th century. In 1637 Charles I built the brick wall around it to mark the territory and stop poachers. To this day, large herds of red and fallow deer roam free in the park. There are some of the best views of London, 12 miles of riding tracks, several enclosed woodlands, one of London's best woodland gardens, cafés, golf, polo, rugby, fishing, ponds and a playground.

This area has numerous parks in close proximity to each other, on either side of one of the prettiest stretches of river in London (see map). This includes Syon Park (see p244) (and Old Isleworth), Kew Gardens, Old Deer Park (see p214), Richmond Park (and Richmond Green), Ham Common (see p226) and nearby Marble Hill Park (see p172) and Bushy Park (see p32). There is enough for several weeks' worth of exploring.

HIGHLIGHTS

- View from King Henry VIII Mount
- Isabella Plantation: London's prettiest woodland garden (42 acres)
- Pembroke Lodge terrace
- Herds of deer
- Vast expanses of un-landscaped grassland

BEETLES

Richmond Park's population of the stag beetle, the largest beetle in the world, is of international importance. Over a thousand species of beetle have been recorded in the park, which is more than 25% of the British list. If you are interested in helping with a survey of the stag beetle contact jhatto@blueyonder.co.uk.

CAFÉS

There are two cafés in the park and several hatches around the car parks. Pembroke Lodge is by far the nicer of the two.

Pembroke Lodge

The Lodge is also available for corporate functions and weddings. The main attraction is its terrace (with outdoor seating) and gardens. In warm weather this is one of the most picturesque places for a Sunday roast. Inside is less enticing. The large windows in the restaurant overlook the southwest side of the gardens, but it is rather down at heel with bad acoustics. Cappuccino £1.30, tea £1.05, cream tea £3.75, cake £1.95, sandwiches from £1.95.

Tel. 020 8940 8207, website www.pembrokelodge.co.uk, email info@pembroke-lodge.co.uk. Open daily from 10.00 (except Monday, 10.30) to 17.30 or half an hour before dusk in winter. Hot lunches are served between 12.00–14.45 and roast lunches on a Sunday.

Pavilion Café

The rather run down Pavilion Café is next to the Richmond Park Golf Club, at the Roehampton entrance. It was built in 1923 at the same time as the first golf course. The café is a wooden building with a terrace.

Open Monday to Friday 09.30–15.30, Sundays from 07.30, Saturdays and Tuesdays from 08.00. Lunch is served 11.00–14.00.

BICYCLING

Richmond Park has a network of paths for cyclists and a hire shop that has bicycles to suit all ages. Richmond Park Cycle Hire is at Roehampton Gate.

Tel. 07050 209249, 07932 075347 or 020 7581 1188. Open every day 10.00–16.00.

DEER

Richmond Park is famous for its red and fallow deer. The numbers are kept to around 650 with selective culls in November and February. They feed on the numerous sweet chestnuts, acorns, beech mast and horse chestnuts in autumn to stock up for their lean winter. The British Deer Society provides information leaflets.

BDS, Beale Centre, Lower Basildon, Reading, Berks RG8 9NH. Tel. 07348 44094.

FISHING

Fishing is allowed (with a permit) in the Pen Ponds (see also below), which are well stocked with fish, including pike, carp, tench and roach. The application forms for permits are available from Holly Lodge, the main information centre in the park, tel. 020 8948 3209, and cost £16 per rod for the season (16 June–14 March).

FRIENDS OF RICHMOND PARK

The enthusiastic Friends of Richmond Park organise meetings and events regarding the running of the park. There are free guided walks on many Saturdays. These start at 10.00 and last for two hours. Membership costs £3 (single) and £5 (joint). Contact Brian Baker, 203 Park Road, Kingston-upon-Thames, KT2 5JY, tel. 020 8546 3109.

GATES

When Charles I moved to Richmond Palace in 1637 he built an eight-mile brick wall around the park to keep the game inside for his hunting. In order to avoid public outcry he also built six gates and several ladderstiles for access to the park. The wall and gates are still intact and enclose all 2,500 acres. Richmond Gate is the prettiest entrance. It was probably designed by Sir John Soane (see also p289, museum), who was the Deputy Surveyor of Woods and Forests and who also helped re-design Pembroke Lodge. Roehampton Gate is also one of the six original gates of the 1637 enclosure, although the present gates were erected in 1899. The Ladderstile Gate is interesting in name only. It was one of the last remaining ladderstiles constructed by Charles I in order to appease the public over his enclosure.

GOLF

There are two 18-hole golf courses in the park, the Prince's Course and Duke's Course. The Prince's Course was designed by J.H.Taylor and opened by the Prince of Wales in 1923, when he drove from the first tee. It was such a success that two years later a second was added, Duke's Course. Both are regarded as among Britain's finest public courses. The courses are 'pay and play' with no membership restrictions. The centre has affiliation with the Surrey Golf Union and the English Golf Union for those wishing to obtain an official handicap. There are competitions, a large golf shop and a 16-bay driving range.

Richmond Park Golf Courses and Driving Range, Roehampton

Gate, Priory Lane. Pro Shop, tel. 020 8876 1795. Lesson booking line: 020 8876 3205. Open 06.00 weekends and 07.00 weekdays. Email info@richmondparkgolf.co.uk, website www.richmondparkgolf.co.uk. Costs: weekend green fee £21, weekday £18, last two hours £6. Half price for under 16s and OAPs.

HOUSES

Pembroke Lodge was originally the park's molecatcher's cottage. It was quite an important job in the 18th century: William II's death in 1706 followed a fall from his horse as it tripped on a molehill in Kensington. The Lodge was later given to the Prime Minister, Lord John Russell, by Queen Victoria as a perk of the job. He lived here from 1847 until his death in 1878. His grandson, the philosopher Bertrand Russell, lived here from 1876 until 1894 and wrote of the 'wide horizons and unimpeded view of the sunset'. In World War II the crack Phantom Squad had their headquarters here, among them the actor David Niven. The current cafeteria has a view across the garden, a stunning terrace and pretty gardens.

The other important house in the park is White Lodge, built in 1727 for George I and used by the Royal Ballet School since 1955. This is situated near the pretty Pen Ponds (see below).

ISABELLA PLANTATION

Isabella Plantation is without a doubt one of the best reasons to visit Richmond Park. It was originally natural woodland and was enclosed and nurtured into a 42-acre 'woodland garden' in 1951. It is one of London's prettiest gardens, particularly in spring when the famous collection of rhododendrons, azaleas, daffodils, bluebells and magnolias are in flower. Even in winter and autumn there is colour, however, with bright yellow witch hazel, flowering heathers and the autumn colours of the trees.

The plantation is big enough to wander around without seeing anyone else, giving the atmosphere of a wild secret wood. A stream winds its way through the ancient oaks, beeches and sweet chestnuts and collects in three ponds with waterfowl. There are paths throughout, and seats carved out of tree trunks. The notice boards by the gates have information about walks and a monthly newsletter.

INFORMATION

The Park Office and information centre is based at Holly Lodge, off Sawyer's Hill within the park (see map and Lodges, below). It is open 09.00–16.00 from Monday to Friday, tel. 020 8948 3209. They do not win any prizes for being welcoming or helpful, however. Unless you want to view the pretty lodge itself you may be better off avoiding it altogether.

KING HENRY VIII MOUND

See Views, below

KITE FLYING

The best places for kite flying are the high points around Pembroke Lodge, also conveniently near a tea break.

MODEL BOATING

Model boats can be sailed in Adam's Pond near Sheen Gate.

PLAYGROUND

There is a children's playground at Petersham Gate.

POLO

The second ever polo match played in England was in Richmond Park, around 1865. The ground is near Roehampton Gate and is currently used by Ham Polo Club as an ancillary ground. It is used for many of their preliminary tournament rounds. Ham Polo Club is one of the oldest clubs in the UK, founded in 1926. For further details contact the club on 020

8334 0000, website www.hampoloclub.org.uk, email office@hampoloclub.org.uk.

PONDS

There are over 20 ponds in the park, but the prettiest are the Pen Ponds in the centre of the park. These were dug in 1746 and named after the deer pens. They have a large collection of swans, Canada geese, grebe and gadwalls. The ponds are generously stocked with fish, and fishing permits can be obtained (see Fishing, above). Model boats can be sailed on the pond near Sheen Gate, Adam's Pond.

RIDING

There are several riding stables and over 12 miles of riding tracks in the park. A free information leaflet and map called 'Riding in Richmond Park' is available from Holly Lodge and Pembroke Lodge restaurant. The schools listed are BHS approved and have a range of lessons for all ages and levels including rides through the park, group and individual lessons, intensive courses, jumping, stable management and dressage. Each school is based by a different park gate (see map).

Barnfield Riding School Livery Stables

Parkfields Road (off Park Road), Kingston-upon-Thames, Surrey KT2 5LL, tel. 020 8546 3616, website www.barnfieldriding.co.uk, email barnfield.riding@virgin.net.

A BHS and ABRS approved school for all ages and standards but specialising in nervous riders. The school also runs three-day adult intensive courses. Lessons are held in a flood-lit arena, or in the park.

Kingston Riding Centre

38 Crescent Road, Kingston-Upon-Thames, Surrey KT2 7RG, tel. 020 8546 6361, website: www.kingstonridingcentre.co.uk, email info@kingstonridingcentre.co.uk.

A BHS approved school with indoor and outdoor facilities including evening lessons and rest facilities for friends and parents.

Roehampton Gate Equestrian Centre

Priory Lane, London, SW15, tel. 020 8876 7089.

Within spitting distance of the park gate, this school includes a wide range of activities including BBQ rides, hacks, 'Own a Pony' day/week and birthday parties.

Stag Lodge Stables

Robin Hood Gate, Richmond Park, London, SW15 3RS, tel. 020 8974 6066, website www.ridinginlondon.com.

Situated at the gate and open Tuesday to Sunday this school has flood-lit facilities, early morning hacks and summer evening rides. There are also pony parties and 'Own a Pony' weeks.

RUGBY

The Rosslyn Park Rugby Football Club uses the three rugby pitches at Richmond Park for many of its matches. The club has teams of all levels from under sevens to senior national league and includes social teams and female teams. They are based at Priory Lane, Upper Richmond Road, Roehampton SW15 5JH, website www.rosslynpark.co.uk, email Admin@rosslynpark.co.uk, tel. 020 8876 6044.

TREES

The park is well known for its tree plantations, in particular for the many ancient oaks. The woodland plantations were mostly planted in the early 19th century and provided good cover for the hunting. Sidmouth Wood is the largest and is partly closed to the public as a bird sanctuary. The undergrowth of rhododendrons is, like in the Isabella Plantation (see above), particularly pretty in spring. The second largest plantation is Spankers Wood, near the White Lodge, which has several coniferous trees as well as the oaks and chestnuts.

The park's most famous tree is John Martin's Oak, at the end of Hornbeam Walk, near Ham Gate. Martin was a Victorian painter of disaster scenes. His painting of this oak tree hangs in the Victoria and Albert Museum.

The Veteran Tree Focus Group is compiling a list of all ancient trees. If you spot an ancient looking tree, and want it investigated by the 'tree squad' contact the tree manager on tel. 020 8831 6135.

VIEWS

From King Henry VIII Mount it is possible to see well over ten miles to the London Eye and St Paul's Cathedral in the east and across the Thames Valley to Windsor Castle in the west. It was from here that Henry VIII would watch the progress of the hunt. It is the highest point in the park and was probably a Bronze Age burial mound.

WALKS

The park staff organise a series of free guided walks throughout the year. Each walk lasts about an hour and themes include seasonal walks, migratory birds, skylarks and wildlife. Booking is essential. For further information contact the Park Office on 020 8948 3209.

NEAR THE PARK

Ham House (www.nationaltrust.org.uk/regions/southern, tel. 020 8940 1950)

Marble Hill Park (see p172)

Old Isleworth

Richmond High Street

Syon Park (see p244)

The River Thames and riverside walks

Wimbledon Common

Kew Gardens

HAM COMMON

Ham Common is a pretty nature reserve just outside the Ham Gate of Richmond Park. It was an area grazed by livestock until the 19th century. Since then woodland has formed. Its grassy glades, birch trees and brambles are home to an important wildlife collection including three species of woodpecker. There are pretty woodland walks and bridleways through the common. Ham Pond forms a focal point in the common across the road, and is also the site for the summertime Ham Fair. For information about practical workdays and volunteering contact Richmond BRCV on tel. 020 8332 1995 or the ecology officer on 020 8831 6135, website www.richmond.gov.uk.

RICHMOND RIVERSIDE WALKS

The riverside around Richmond is one of London's prettiest walking/cycling areas. It is easy to link several of the area's parks on a riverside walk. From Syon Park the path runs through Old Isleworth, and crosses the river at Richmond Lock. The path then runs alongside the Old Deer Park, under Twickenham Bridge into Cholmondeley Walk. In the short stretch between here and Richmond Bridge there are some of England's tallest plane trees. The tiny cobbled Old Palace Lane leads into Richmond Green past the remains of Richmond Palace. Alternatively the towpath continues beyond Richmond Bridge to Midhurst, the Terrace Gardens and Petersham Meadows, which lie opposite Marble Hill House. The Terrace Gardens can be followed up to the top of Richmond Hill, into Richmond Park.

Roundwood Park

Harlesden Road, Willesden, NW10 3HS

Tel. 020 8937 5622

Bus: 52, 98, 206, 226, N52

Tub/train: Willesden Junction, Dollis Hill

Roundwood Park is 22.4 acres (9.1 hectares) of pretty Victorian style gardens and open space. It is in the top 80 parks of Britain and is Grade II listed. The park was opened in 1895. In his opening speech the Chairman of the Parks Committee said that the architect of the park, Oliver Robson, had changed the sight of the park from 'a miniature Dartmoor... to a veritable Garden of Eden...' This vision has been maintained and the park has been a Green Flag winner for the past four years. There is a good view of London from the top of the grassy hill in the park as well a 1950s aviary, café, nature area, playground and a free netball/basketball pitch.

HIGHLIGHTS

- Aviary
- Café
- View of London

AVIARY

The Willesden and District Caged Birds Society established the aviary in 1956.

Facilities

- Aviary
- Bowls
- Café
- Netball/basketball
- Playground
- Wildlife reserve

There are budgerigars, cockatiels, canaries, golden pheasants and zebra finches, making the park alive with birdsong.

BOWLS

The Bowls Club was founded in 1924. They are keen to attract new members and beginners are welcome. There is a qualified coach for beginners as well as more experienced players. Games are played every day except Mondays from April to September. The club organises two coach trips each year and friendly games with neighbouring clubs. Tel. 020 7286 5472. Annual membership costs £60.

CAFÉ

Roundwood Lodge Café

This is a child-friendly café with an enclosed play area. Even on a cold wet afternoon, the café was warm and service was friendly. Food is standard but carefully prepared in the on-site kitchen. English breakfast £5.50, cappuccino £1.50, tea 50p, children's meals from £3, soup £3.50 and panini £3.50. There is a toilet for wheelchair users. The community exchange has clean second-hand clothes and toys to bring and exchange. Tel. 020 8838 1414. Open every day 10.00–16.00.

DRINKING FOUNTAIN

The fountain was erected to commemorate the opening of the park in 1895. It is one of the prettiest in London but is in need of renovation.

FISHPOND

The pond was built by the Willesden and District Aquarist Club in 1957.

GAZEBO

To mark the 100th anniversary of the park, a paved rose-lined walkway with a gazebo was built. The gazebo is a small open building with a roof and open sides.

NATURE AREA

The nature area has picnic tables and a notice board showing what animals, plants and insects are in the area. At one time, a pond in the area contained frogs and newts but this has been filled in for safety reasons. Look out for the foxgloves (*digitalis purpurea*) but mind the stinging nettles (*urtica dioica*).

NURSERY

The Happy Child Nurseries offer high quality day-care for children from three months of age. The building is an enclosed modern one-storey building, the inside is warm and brightly painted. Everywhere, there are smiling faces and the sound of children enjoying themselves. All staff are qualified and experienced in childcare. There is a 1:3 ratio of staff for the under two year olds and 1:6 ratio for the two to five year olds.

Open Monday to Friday 08.00–18.00. Prices start at £16.50/half day. Tel. 020 8961 3485 or 020 8579 8558 (head office), website www.happychild.co.uk.

PLAYGROUND

There is a small playground, but it is not as well equipped as the area around the café, although it does have a first aid point.

Southwark Park

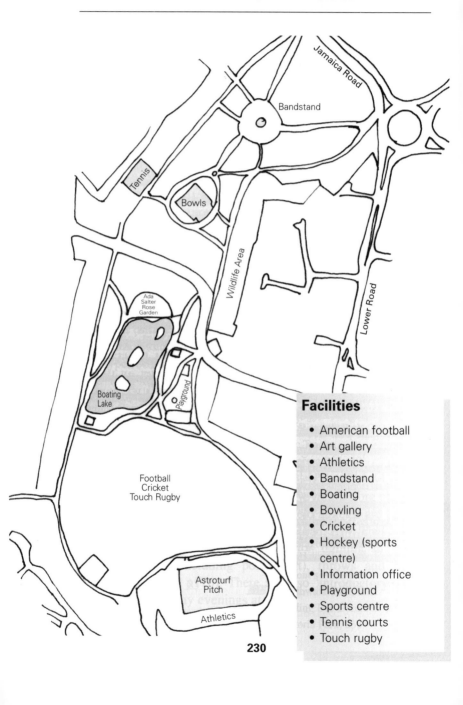

Jamaica Road

Bandstand

Tennis

Bowls

Wildlife Area

Lower Road

Ada Salter Rose Garden

Boating Lake

Playground

Football
Cricket
Touch Rugby

Astroturf Pitch

Athletics

Facilities

- American football
- Art gallery
- Athletics
- Bandstand
- Boating
- Bowling
- Cricket
- Hockey (sports centre)
- Information office
- Playground
- Sports centre
- Tennis courts
- Touch rugby

Jamaica Road/Lower Road, SE16

Bus: 1, 47, 188, 199, 225, 381

Car: Hawkstone car park and Gomm Road have free car parking

Tube: Canada Water, Surrey Quays

This beautifully restored 63-acre Victorian park is in an area of dense council housing. This park was opened in 1869 and facilities were added as funds became available. The cricket ground was opened in 1871, a bandstand in 1884 (transferred form the Great Exhibition), the boating lake in 1885 (Queen Victoria donated a pair of swans), football pitches in 1890, the bowling green in 1908 and a lido in 1923 (sadly closed in 1985).

The industrial revolution had brought urban squalor described vividly by the like of Charles Dickens in *Oliver Twist*. Southwark Park was the first park to be built exclusively for working people whose homes did not include a garden or much space in which to relax. Recently the park had become run down but with the aid of a £2.75m lottery grant has been fully restored to its Victorian splendour.

HIGHLIGHTS

- Ada Salter Rose Garden
- Free art gallery
- Free tennis courts
- Friendly information office

AMERICAN FOOTBALL

The London Os American Football Club has its home ground at Southwark Park. The club uses the astro-pitch in the centre of the athletics track run by Southwark Park Leisure Centre. The club has junior and senior teams and welcomes new members of all standards from the age of eight. Training takes place on Wednesdays and Sundays and the club plays from February to November. For further information either contact the club direct on tel. 020 7584 3323, 07956 379161, website www.londonos.org.uk, or contact the ground at London Os, Home Ground, Southwark Park Leisure Centre, Hawkstone Road, London SE16, tel. 020 7231 9442.

ART

The modern art gallery has free exhibitions throughout the year. There are also free workshops for children. Open 11.00–17.00 Wednesday to Sunday, website www.cafegalleryprojects.org, tel. 020 7237 1230.

ATHLETICS

There is a synthetic, 400m, seven-lane track at the Southwark Park Sports Centre (see below). The track was opened in 1980 and was home to the Herne Hill Harriers for several years. It is not currently used for any meetings. There are some field event facilities available and jumps. The central synthetic field is used by the London Os American Football Club (see above) and can be hired for hockey and football. For further information contact Southwark Park Sports Centre, Burbage Road, London SW24, tel. 020 7231 9442, website www.fusion-lifestyle.com (click on Southwark).

BANDSTAND

There is a programme of concerts in the bandstand in the summer as well as a firework display in November.

BOATING

The beautiful boating lake has boats for hire. There is a smart boating house at the gallery end of the lake.

BOWLING

The restored bowls club is open to anyone over 16. Games cost £2/hour/person including equipment. Open Monday, Wednesday and Friday 14.00–16.00 and Tuesday and Thursday 18.00–20.00. Tel. 020 7237 5671.

CAFÉ

The Good Food Deli Café

A park café is planned for 2006. At the moment, for an Illy coffee and freshly toasted panettone head to the Good Food Deli Café, a five minute walk from the Jamaica Road exit. This tiny café has just four tables but is next to St Mary Gardens, a mini park for picnics. There are take-aways and a catering service for parties. Cappuccino £1.50, tea £1, scrambled egg £3, pasta of the day £3.95, soup and toasted ciabatta £3.50, hot chocolate and marshmallows £2 and a bargain cup of tea with a sarnie £2.50.

Good Food Deli Café, 68 St Mary Church Street (first left off Brunel Road, turn right at the Ship Pub), website www.dpseager.com. Open Monday to Saturday 10.00–16.00 and Sundays 11.00–16.00.

FOOTBALL

The football pitches can be booked on the park hotline 020 7525 1050. For adults the cost is £42 and for under 16s £22.

FRIENDS OF SOUTHWARK PARK

The Friends of Southwark Park meet on the second Tuesday of each month and are active in preserving the park. There is also a children's group and volunteer environmental work.

GARDENS

A Wildlife Garden is currently being developed. The Ada Salter Rose Garden is a semi-circular rose garden on the south side of the lake. Dr Salter and his wife headed the Beautification Committee in the inter-war years that aimed to improve the grim environment of the area. The Rose Garden was named in memory of Ada Salter when she died in 1942. It is a quiet place to sit and watch the birds on the lake.

INFORMATION

The Park Ranger's office near the Gomm Road entrance has free leaflets, hot drinks machine, toilets and friendly advice about all that the park has to offer. Open Monday to Friday 09.30–16.30. Tel. 020 7232 2091.

PLAYGROUNDS

The new playground is built over the disused lido. It has all the latest rides with wood shavings for a soft landing. It is conveniently near the lake and gallery.

The Southwark Park Playroom is available free of charge to under fives from 12.30–16.00 Monday to Friday. Under eights are allowed during school holidays. The playroom has a new building in the south of the park and some fun new rides. Tel. 020 7231 3755.

SPORTS CENTRE

The Seven Islands Leisure Centre is on the east side of the park and has excellent facilities including an athletics track (south side of the park), Astroturf pitch, gym, 33m pool and solarium. There are many classes and activities based there including American football, hockey, running, aerobics and yoga. Pool £3.50, athletics £1, gym £5.35 or £36.50/month (including swimming). Open 07.00–22.00 Monday to Friday and 08.00–17.30 weekends. 100 Lower Road, tel. 020 7237 3296, website www.fusion-lifestyle.com.

TENNIS

There are two free tennis courts that anyone is allowed to use but there is no pre-booking service.

WALKS

The Healthy Walkers Club runs free weekly walks which leave from the Visitor Centre 11.00 on Thursdays and finish with a hot drink for everyone. Tel. 020 7232 2091.

St James's Park

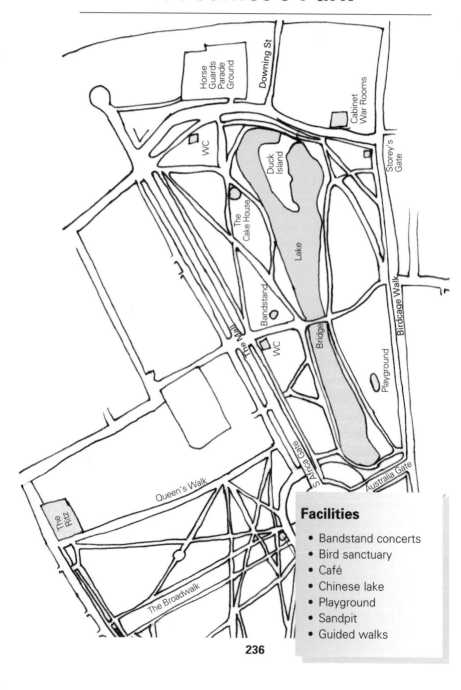

Horse Guards Parade Ground

Downing St

Cabinet War Rooms

WC

Duck Island

Storey's Gate

The Cake House

Lake

Bandstand

Birdcage Walk

The Mall

WC

Bridge

Playground

S Africa Gate

Australia Gate

Queen's Walk

The Ritz

The Broadwalk

Facilities

- Bandstand concerts
- Bird sanctuary
- Café
- Chinese lake
- Playground
- Sandpit
- Guided walks

VISITOR INFORMATION

St James's Park, SW1

Open 05.00–24.00

Tel. 020 7930 1793 Website www.royalparks.org.uk

Tube: St James's Park, Westminster, Green Park, Victoria

Bus: 3, 6, 8, 9, 11, 12, 14, 15, 19, 21, 22, 23, 24, 29, 38, 53, 77A, 88, 91, 139, 159, 453

Car: there are no car parks in the park

St James's Park takes its name from a 13th century hospital that was founded to look after 13 women suffering from leprosy. The hospital was dedicated to St James and was built on the marshy land that became the park. In 1532 Henry VIII turned the area into a deer park and built St James's Palace. James I further developed the area with a menagerie and duck pond in 1603. At this time there were elephants and crocodiles in the park. In 1667 pelicans and other exotic birds were introduced into the park.

When Charles II was exiled in France he enjoyed the garden at Versailles and when he was restored to the throne he had the park re-landscaped in a French style including a pitch to play the croquet-like game *paille-maille*. From this game the names of the Mall and Pall Mall were derived. During the reign of William III the first tea house was built and there were regular milk fairs where cows provided fresh milk to the locals. John Nash finally re-designed the park in its present form in 1827 for George VI. In 1837 the Ornithological Society built the Birdkeeper's Cottage by the lake that has helped to continue central London's tradition of exotic birds.

The park is an ideal place to stroll, picnic and bird-watch and is five minutes' walk from Big Ben and the Houses of Parliament. It is the oldest of London's Royal Parks and is also one of the prettiest, with 93 acres of shady weeping willows, sweeping lawns, a Chinese-style lake and many rare birds.

HIGHLIGHTS

- Bird watching and feeding the ducks
- View from the 1950s bridge across the lake
- Birdkeeper's Cottage surrounded by weeping willows

BIRDS

There are at least 17 species of birds using Duck Island in the lake to breed, including mute swans, Canada geese and pelicans. The Canada geese were introduced in the 18th century. They have thrived in the park and each lives for more than 20 years. Pelicans were first given to Charles II by the Russian ambassador in 1684 and have remained ever since. The pelicans are fed every day at 15.00 on the lawn near Duck Island. Other rare breeds include Bahama pintails, carrion crows, chiloe wigeons, golden eyes, grey wagtails, shovelers and willow warblers. The Royal Society for the Protection of Birds holds regular outings and talks, see their website www.janja.dircon.co.uk/rspb/.

CAFÉ

Inn the park

The newly refurbished café (the old Cake House) is housed in a beautiful building with a turf roof designed by the Glyndebourne Opera House architect Michael Hopkins. The restaurant has views across the lake and runs as a café by day and restaurant by night. There is indoor and outdoor seating and newspapers and magazines are available. Open 08.00–11.00 in summer and 08.00–22.00 in winter. Website www.innthepark.com. Situated west of Horse Guards Parade.

FRIENDS OF ST JAMES'S PARK

The Friends of St James's Park and The Green Park are active in preserving the heritage of old Westminster. They were founded in 1985 and have a current membership of over 400. There are regular dinners with guest speakers and private visits to landmarks and places of local interest, many of which are not easily accessible to the public. The society is keen to welcome new members. For information contact the Thorney Island Society, 39 Westminster Mansions, Great Smith Street, London SW1P 3BP, tel. 020 7222 2449.

INFORMATION

The St James's Park office stocks free leaflets and information about the latest events in and around the park. It is based at The Storeyard, Horse Guards Approach, London SW1A 2JB, tel. 020 7930 1793, website www.royalparks.org.uk, and is open Monday to Friday 09.00–16.00.

LAKE

The lake lies at the heart of the park, spanning 4.5 hectares with fresh water 1.2 metres deep. It is surrounded by weeping willows and packed with birds. At the Whitehall end of the lake is Duck Island, the park's bird sanctuary.

MUSIC

The bandstand has regular free concerts on Saturday and Sunday afternoons from the end of June to the end of August, including brass, concert, youth and military bands from all over Britain.

NIGHT

St James's Park doesn't close until midnight, allowing full appreciation of the lake's underwater lighting and of the lamp-lit Birdcage Walk and the Mall.

PLAYGROUND

There is a playground and sandpit for under elevens on the south side of the park near the lake and Birdcage Walk.

QUEEN'S BIRTHDAY PARADE

The Queen's Parade takes place in the Mall. Tickets are available to the public through a ballot process, tel. 020 7414 2479, website www.army.mod.uk/ceremonialandheritage.

STATUE

The 'grand old Duke of York who had ten thousand men' is the 19th century Duke of York, whose statue stands on a 38m Tuscan column at the top of the steps connecting the Mall to Waterloo Place.

VIEWS

The 1950s iron bridge across the lake is a good viewing spot for the park. Spencer House (1756) also has super views of the park. It was built by the Earl and Countess Spencer who had eloped together. It is still owned by the Spencer family of the late Diana, Princess of Wales. It is only open on Sundays for guided tours in every month except January and August. Tel. 020 7499 8620 for recorded information given in a strict matronly style: no refreshments, no photography, no smoking, no advance booking for individuals and no children under 10! Adults £6.

WALKS

The Royal Parks team runs regular free guided walks throughout the year. These include Horse Guards Parade, seasonal walks and nature walks. Booking is essential, contact the Parks Office on 020 7930 1793.

The Jubilee Walk is a signposted 12.7-mile walk through the centre of London, passing through St James's Park. For details see the website www.jubileewalkway.com.

NEAR THE PARK

Cabinet War Rooms – recently renovated, the nerve centre of Britain's war effort (King Charles Street).

This underground bunker was closed three days after D-Day in 1945 and not opened again until 1980. The 21 rooms include Churchill's bedroom and cabinet room as well as unusual things like the specially designed extra quiet typewriters, Churchill's favourite champagne and some sugar lumps saved for a quieter moment. There is a good value basement café.

Open every day 09.30–17.15, tel. 020 7930 6961, website www.iwm.org.uk (main Imperial War Museum site). Adults £7 including audio guide, children under 16 free.

Buckingham Palace: the Duke of Buckingham built Buckingham Palace, which was bought by George III in 1761. John Nash remodelled it for George VI and since 1837 it has been the monarch's official residence. The changing of the guard occurs daily at 11.30. From 1 August to 28 September parts of the palace are open to the public. Tickets cost £12 for adults and £30 for family tickets. The website www.royal.gov.uk has information on the history of the monarchy and all the royal residences as well as on-line ticket sales.

Waterloo Place has statues and buildings for all interests including John Nash's Carlton Gardens. Statues of famous people include Florence Nightingale, Edward VII and Captain Robert Falcon Scott.

The Green Park – see p90.

Stationers Park

VISITOR INFORMATION

Mayfield Road or Denton Road, N4

Train: Haringey

Tube: Finsbury Park

Stationers Park is one of Haringey's newest parks, northwest of Finsbury Park. It was opened in 1987 and occupies 3.7 acres on hilly ground which was the site of the Stationers School. The park has been carefully planned and landscaped and is one of the most interesting small parks in London. It is on an improbably steep hill which commands views across and out over the top of London. There are tennis courts, a basketball pitch, an adventure playground, picnic areas, ponds and water features.

HIGHLIGHTS

- Adventure playground
- Water features

BASKETBALL

There is an open access basketball pitch at the top of the park near the adventure playground.

BIRDS

The park attracts many birds including green woodpeckers, greenfinches and grey wagtails.

Facilities

- Basketball
- Tennis courts
- Playgrounds
- Water features

FRIENDS OF STATIONERS PARK

The Friends of Stationers Park organise events and meetings about the park and its development. Contact friendsofpark@blueyonder.co.uk or tel. Elma or Adrian on 020 8348 6222.

PLAYGROUNDS

The park has a wooden adventure playground and an enclosed playground for younger children.

TENNIS

There are two tennis courts in the park, both free of charge and run a 'turn up and play' basis. Saturday lessons are available from 10.00–13.00, tel. Terry Anderson 020 8340 1449.

TREES

The park is dominated by three large Lombardy poplars and is bordered by silver birches, maples and hornbeams. There are weeping willows by the ponds.

WATER FEATURES

The park takes advantage of its gentle slope with a small lake at the top supplying landscaped winding rivers, waterfalls over natural rock formations and several ponds. The sound of water is everywhere. There are many aquatic plants including rare reeds and rushes, and aquatic wildlife includes an important population of frogs.

NEAR THE PARK

Alexandra Park – see p1.

Finsbury Park – see p77.

Parkland Walk – see p83.

Syon Park

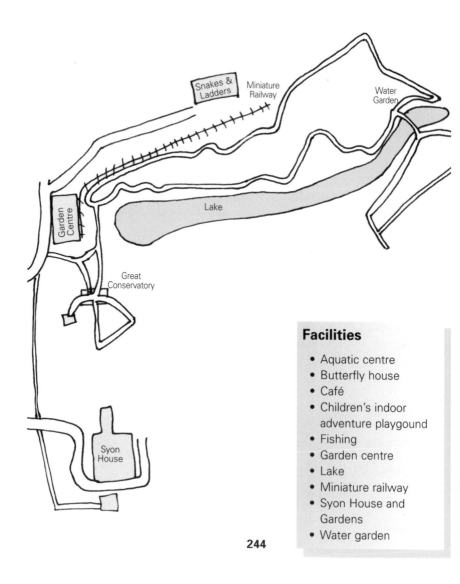

Facilities

- Aquatic centre
- Butterfly house
- Café
- Children's indoor adventure playgound
- Fishing
- Garden centre
- Lake
- Miniature railway
- Syon House and Gardens
- Water garden

VISITOR INFORMATION

Brentford, Middlesex, TW8 8JF

Tel. 020 8560 0882, email info@syonpark.co.uk, website
www.syonpark.co.uk.

Bus: 237 or 267 to Brentlea Gate bus stop

Train: Waterloo to Kew Bridge then bus, or

Tube: Gunnersbury (District line), then bus

Car: free car parking, entrance is from Park Road, Isleworth

Syon Park is one of the last of London's major private estates. It is owned by the 12th Duke of Northumberland and is three miles from Osterley Park (see p182). The house has one of the countries finest Adams interiors. The gardens include a remarkable 19th century glasshouse that inspired Joseph Paxton's Crystal Palace, a beautiful lakeside and woodland walk and Capability Brown's famous garden landscaping.

The house is on the site of a 16th century abbey founded by King Henry V for the Bridgettine Order (St Bridget of Syon), the name deriving from Mount Zion in the Holy Land. Henry VIII suppressed this abbey in 1539. The nuns eventually settled in Devon and are the oldest surviving religious community of women. They still have the iron cross and pinnacle from the original abbey gateway, and apparently never surrendered the keys or seal! The estate was taken over by the 9th Earl of Northumberland and has remained in the same family since.

The house and gardens are set in 200 acres of landscaped parkland. It is free to enter the park, giving views of the house and one of the lakes. Entrance to the house and gardens is charged (see below). The park has several other attractions (all private enterprises), including the very popular 'snakes and ladders' children's indoor adventure playground, England's oldest garden centre (opened in 1861), the London Butterfly

House and the Aquatic Experience. If you want to see the London Butterfly House here you'd better be quick. Their lease runs out in September 2005 and the Duke is apparently planning a conference centre and five-star hotel in its place...

HIGHLIGHTS (ADMISSION CHARGE)

- Syon House with the fine 18th century Robert Adam interior
- The garden's lakeside walk, among wandering peacocks and ancient trees
- The Great Conservatory: the beautiful glasshouse that inspired Crystal Palace
- The children's activities at Snakes and Ladders, the Butterfly House and Aquatic Centre

ADVENTURE PLAYGROUND

Snakes and Ladders is a supervised giant indoor adventure playground for children up to 12 years old; it has a café. Open daily 10.00–18.00 (last admission 17.15). Tel. 020 8847 0946 www.snakes-and-ladders.co.uk. Cost: from £3 (under fives).

AQUARIUM

The Aquatic Experience is open daily 10.00–18.00 April to September and 10.00–17.00 October to March. Tel. 020 8847 4730, website www.aquatic-experience.org. Cost: adults £4, children £3.50 and families £12.50.

BUTTERFLIES

The London Butterfly House is open daily 10.00–17.00 (summer) and 10.00–15.30 (winter). Tel. 020 8560 0378, website www.butterflies.org.uk. Cost: adults £4.95, children £3.95 and families £15.

CAFÉ

The café is an uninspiring square room with old carpeting, peeling paint and no views. Coffee £1.30, tea £1.05, sandwiches £2.99, soup of the day £2.50.

FISHING

Syon Park Trout Fishery offers a day ticket fly-fishing for rainbow trout from £22/day. Open daily (except 25 December). Tel. 020 8568 6354 or 07956 378138, website www.alburyestate.com.

GARDEN CENTRE

Wyevale Garden Centre is open Monday to Saturday 09.00–18.00, Sunday 10.30–16.30. Tel. 020 8568 0134.

HOUSE AND GARDENS

House, gardens, conservatory £6.95 adults, £5.95 child, £15 family (2A, 2C).

Gardens and conservatory £3.50 adult, £2.50 child, £8 family.

House open 26 March–2 November 11.00–17.00 on Wednesday, Thursday, Sunday and bank holidays. Gardens open daily (except 25 and 26 December) 10.30–17.30. Mini-steam railway open weekends and bank holidays from April to October.

No dogs are allowed in the house or gardens (except guide dogs).

Thames Barrier Park

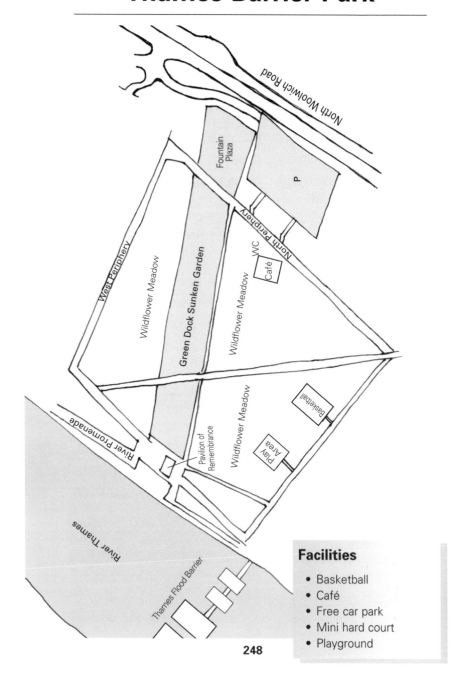

North Woolwich Road

Fountain Plaza

P

West Periphery

North Periphery

Wildflower Meadow

Green Dock Sunken Garden

Wildflower Meadow

WC

Café

Wildflower Meadow

Basketball

River Promenade

Pavilion of Remembrance

Play Area

River Thames

Thames Flood Barrier

Facilities

- Basketball
- Café
- Free car park
- Mini hard court
- Playground

248

Barrier Point Road (off North Woolwich Road), E16 2HP

Website www.thamesbarrierpark.org.uk, tel. 020 7511 4111

Train: DLR to Canning Town or Silverlink to North Woolwich

Tube: Canning Town (Jubilee Line) (20 minute walk)

Bus: 69, 474 to and from Canning Town, 161, 472 to Eastmore Street

Car: free car park off A13

This is London's best modern park. It is the first new riverside park to be built in the last 50 years. Its 22 acres of landscaped gardens overlooking the Thames Barrier were once derelict disused docklands. Now this stunning park has won countless awards for its design as well as its horticulture. The Thames Barrier's shell-like structures raise and lower massive gates to protect central London from the tides of the North Sea. It is London's answer to the Sydney Opera House. The park has an excellent view of the Barrier, a delightful café, an award-winning sunken garden, playground and riverside walk.

HIGHLIGHTS

*   Superb café
*   Award-winning sunken garden
*   Spectacular view of the Thames Barrier

CAFÉ

Pavilion Café

The Pavilion Café and Visitor Centre is a wonderful place to sit and drink coffee. It has a funky modern design with three sides of floor to ceiling glass, wood block flooring and outside decking overlooking the gardens and Thames Barrier. The manager is a self-declared coffee addict and spent five months perfecting the house blend – it was worth it. This is a relaxed restaurant with park café prices. Cappuccino 90p, tea 70p, coke 50p. Tel. 020 7511 4111, Open Thursday to Saturday10.00–16.00 and often every day (phone).

GARDEN

The Green Dock is a sunken garden with a flood-lit fountain plaza at one end and the Pavilion of Remembrance at the other. The fountain has 36 water jets, which in summer spray water in computer-controlled intervals. The garden has pretty topiary in the shape of waves mingled with rosemary and lavender. There are cleverly built banks of clipped hedges growing out of the concrete.

INFORMATION

The Visitor Centre in the café is well stocked with free leaflets about the park, the surrounding area and transport options, website www.thamesbarrierpark.org.uk, tel. 020 7511 4111.

MEMORIAL

The 26-foot high Pavilion of Remembrance is a memorial to the people of Newham who died in the Blitz. It was designed by Andrew Taylor. Its roof has a perfect circle of light similar to the Pantheon in Rome.

PLAYGROUND

The playground has a range of games for all ages. At the entrance there are brightly painted carved wooden animals to welcome children, including a crocodile, owl, fox, rabbit and birds. There is a rope bridge and slide as well as swings, climbing frames and a see-saw.

Next to the enclosure is a mini hard court for basketball/netball practice and a goal net for hockey/football.

THAMES BARRIER

The Thames Barrier forms a major flood defence system to protect London from rising water and North Sea tidal surges. It was opened in 1984 by the Queen and consists of ten massive gates, powered by hydraulics housed in distinctive stainless steel shells. The four main gates are each 20 metres tall, weigh 3,700 tonnes and are capable of withstanding a load of 9,000 tonnes. The Barrier has a small information centre on the south side of the river (opposite the park) that has a working model of the barrier, a video of the construction and a café. This is also a good place from which to start the Thames Path walk into central London.

Note: the Thames Barrier Information Centre is on the opposite side of the river to the park. There is no direct access across the river from the centre to the park but the excellent Woolwich Foot Tunnel is within walking distance (1.5 miles), as is the free Woolwich car ferry (tel. 020 8921 5786). There are cruises around the barrier from Greenwich by Campion Cruises (tel. 020 8305 0300) or from the Embankment with Thames Cruises (tel. 020 7930 3373). Thames Barrier, 1 Unity Way, Woolwich SE18, website www.environment-agency.gov.uk, tel. 020 8305 4188. Train from Charing Cross to Charlton Station (15 minute walk or buses 177 or 180). Tube: North Greenwich (45 minute walk or buses 472 or 161). Information Centre open April to September 10.30–16.00 and October to March 11.00–15.30.

Tooting Bec Common

Tooting Bec Common is a wide open space of nearly 92 hectares (221 acres), the largest in the borough. It is not a manicured park: flat grassland and scrub lie between small areas of wood. There are tennis courts, two ponds, football pitches, a playground, an athletics track and one of the oldest and biggest lidos in the country.

HIGHLIGHTS

* Athletics track
* Lido – the biggest and oldest in London

ATHLETICS

The Tooting Bec Athletic Track and Stadium is open to everyone from casual use to high-level competitions. It has a high quality eight-lane synthetic track which is

Facilities

* Athletics
* Café
* Fishing
* Football pitches
* Lido (swimming)
* One O'Clock Club
* Ponds

flood-lit on Wednesday evenings. There is a small gym, changing rooms and common room with vending machines. The Herne Hill Harriers running club is based at the track and caters for all standards from ten year olds to veterans. The club organises a large number of events including cross country runs (in winter in Brockwell Park, see p23), training sessions, competitions, and indoor events. For further information about the Harriers check www.hernehillharriers.co.uk or phone the club on the number below. Tooting Bec Athletics Track, Tooting Bec Road, SW16, tel. 020 8871 7171. Open Monday to Friday 09.00–21.00, weekends 09.00–19.00, website www.runtrackdir.com. Cost: gym £15/month or £2.80/day plus £10 induction, track £78/year or £2/session.

CAFÉ

Tooting Bec Café

The Tooting Bec Café is near the tennis courts and playground. It is a little run down and service is with a scowl but prices are low. Mug of coffee 80p, tea 70p, English breakfast £3.75, hamburger £1.10, egg on toast 90p, crisps and chocolate bars 40p. There is a children's menu from £2.25 for egg and chips. Open every day 09.00–17.00 (but closing time is variable, at the discretion of the owner), tel. 0208 673 5980.

FOOTBALL AND RUGBY

There are six football pitches that can be booked for weekend matches. Morning kick off is at 10.30 and afternoon at 14.30. There are shower and changing facilities available and pitches cost approximately £48. The central booking number for the pitches is tel. 020 8876 7685 (also covers Wandsworth Common).

FISHING

There is fishing at the lake, with plenty of perch and carp. A season ticket costs £50. Contact the park's yard on 020 8871

6347 for further information or the 'Fine Line' fishing shop, 299 Mitcham Road, tel. 020 8672 1699.

INFORMATION

The general enquiries office is housed in the park's yard, tel. 020 8871 6347.

PLAYGROUNDS

There is a well-equipped playground conveniently located next to the duck pond and tennis courts, open every day dawn to dusk. There is another playground for younger children, unfortunately covered in graffiti, near the Cavendish Road entrance. This also has a One O'Clock Club, 'Triangle', tel. 020 8673 4106, which is a friendly, free drop in centre for under fives from 13.00–16.00 Monday to Friday.

SWIMMING

The Tooting Bec Lido is the biggest and oldest outdoor public pool in London. It was built in 1906 and is 94 metres long with over 30, 000 square feet of water. Its deep end is 2.1 metres and the shallow end is 0.9 metres. The lido is surrounded by trees planted on an embankment formed from the excavated soil and there is a café and a paddling pool.

It is located in the common on the Tooting Bec Road, tel. 020 8871 7198. The lido is open to the public from the end of May to the end of August 06.00–19.30 and in September 06.00–17.00. It is possible to swim all year round (including Christmas Day) by joining the South London Swimming Club, website www.slsc.org.uk, tel. 07985 141532 or contact the lido directly.

TENNIS

There are six smart tennis courts near the playground and café. These are managed from a small hut next to the courts and cost £4.75/hour. Membership is available for £13.50/year which allows advanced booking, tel. 020 8876 7685 (central sports booking line).

YOUTH CLUB

There is a graffiti-covered youth club next to the One O'Clock Club near the Cavendish Road entrance to the common, tel. 020 8675 6945 or contact the Youth Service on 020 8871 7553.

Victoria Park

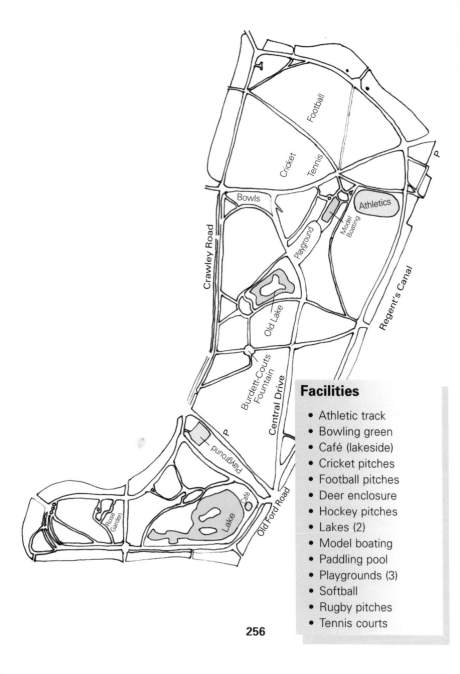

Football

Cricket

Tennis

Bowls

Athletics

Crawley Road

Playground

Model Boating

Regent's Canal

Old Lake

Burdett-Coutts Fountain

Central Drive

P

Playground

Old Ford Road

Café

Lake

Rose Garden

Facilities

- Athletic track
- Bowling green
- Café (lakeside)
- Cricket pitches
- Football pitches
- Deer enclosure
- Hockey pitches
- Lakes (2)
- Model boating
- Paddling pool
- Playgrounds (3)
- Softball
- Rugby pitches
- Tennis courts

VISITOR INFORMATION

Old Ford Road, E3

Tel. 020 8533 2057 (not overly helpful)

Friends website: www.victoria-park.org.uk

Tube: Mile End (nearest), Bow Road, Bethnal Green

Train: Cambridge Heath, Hackney Wick

Bus: 8, 26, 30, 55, 236, 253, 276, 277, 333, 388, S2

Victoria Park was designed in 1840 by James Pennethorne (son-in-law of John Nash of Regent's Park fame). Some 30,000 locals had signed a petition to Queen Victoria asking for a park following growing concern about the highest mortality rate in London amongst the local silk weavers and dryers who were living in over-crowded squalor. Their wishes were granted and in 1845 the 88-hectare (217 acre) Victoria Park was opened to the public. It was dubbed the Regent's Park of the East End, complete with a Speakers Corner where the likes of George Bernard Shaw spoke. The park was visited by its namesake, Queen Victoria, in 1873 and later by the Queen Mother in 1990 as part of her birthday celebrations.

There are two lakes; the West Lake has free fishing and the Model Boating Pond has the oldest model boating club in the country. The sports facilities include tennis courts, football, hockey and rugby pitches and bowling. There are several listed historical buildings, including the two alcoves from the original London Bridge, a lavish drinking fountain and several gate lodges. Regent's and Hertford Union Canals run along one side of the lake, making a 'countryside walk' from Islington to the park an easy possibility.

HIGHLIGHTS

- Model boating club – the oldest in England
- Numerous sports pitches
- Playgrounds
- Lakes
- Regent's Canal: for walking, cycling, fishing or boating

ATHLETICS

The athletics track is near the deer enclosure and the One O'Clock Club. It has five lanes and is 400m long. Although it is a little over-grown it is marked for renovation (or removal). The pavilion was destroyed in an arson attack in 2002 and there are no equipment, changing facilities or floodlighting at the track. It is only used for casual training at present and there is no charge. In its better days (it was built in the 1920s) it regularly drew crowds of several thousand people for its meetings and in 1933 Albert Cooper set the world record for the 3000m walk on the track. It became the base for the Victoria Park Harriers (see below under Running) for many years, but they now use the Mile End Park athletics facilities (p176). Tel. 020 8985 1957, or contact Victoria Park Harriers on 020 7254 4546.

BIRDS

There are many ducks, herons, geese and swans around the lakes and canals.

BOWLING

The bowling green is near Queen's Gate and does not have to be booked in advance.

CAFÉ

The Lakeside Pavilion Café

The Lakeside Pavilion Café sells home-cooked food at low prices. All day breakfast £3.99, BLT £1.90, tea 50p, coffee 60p, warmed scone and jam 40p, carrot cake 70p. There is a fine view of the lake and the 35 foot fountains. Open every day 10.00–17.00.

CANALS

The park is bordered on two sides by Regent's Canal (in the southwest) and the Hertford Union Canal. Where the two canals meet, an old glue factory, Bow Wharf, has been converted into restaurants and Jongleurs Comedy Club. The Regent's Canal towpath makes a good walk from Maida Vale and Little Venice through to Camden and on to Islington. At Islington the path detours around a long tunnel before rejoining the canal leading on to Victoria Park. (See also p175, Mile End Park).

CRICKET

The Victoria Park Community Cricket League is based at the park. It was formed in the early 1990s to encourage and involve players of all standards in competitive cricket. They play two competitions, a two division league and a knock-out cup. Standards range from good club standard to beginners. Matches are eight-a-side, 16 overs and generally take place every Tuesday and Wednesday evening (in season) at about 18.00. Some individual teams also play 11-a-side friendlies on a Sunday. All-weather nets are available for use off season. For further details email secretary@vpccl.co.uk.

The teams that take part in the league include the Victoria Lounge Cricket Club, tel. Alastair Dunning 07740 58867), website www.victorialounge.users.btopenworld.com the Old Fallopians (www.oldfallopians.co.uk) and the Pacific Cricket Club (www.pacificccc.co.uk).

DEER

There is a small animal enclosure near the One O'Clock Club and adventure playground with fallow deer, rabbits and fowl.

DRINKING FOUNTAIN

The magnificent 54-foot gothic drinking fountain was given to the park in 1861 by Baroness Burdett-Coutts and designed by Henry Darbishire. It needs renovating and so is fenced-off but has pretty carvings of cherubs riding dolphins and a domed clock-towered roof.

FISHING

The Western Lake has free fishing for carp, perch, roach and tench.

FOOTBALL

Games are held near Central Drive. The ground is home (rather bizarrely) to the Clissold Park Rangers, www.cpr-fc.co.uk. This team was formed in 1996 and moved from Clissold Park to better grounds at Victoria Park a few years ago.

FRIENDS OF VICTORIA PARK

The Friends form an important link between the council and the users of the park. For further details contact Simon Bulpin on 07961 339041, website www.victoria-park.org.uk.

GARDEN

The enclosed Old English Garden is a pretty garden near the adventure playground. There are box hedges, clipped yews and crazy paving paths winding among lavenders and roses.

LONDON BRIDGE

Two alcoves from the original London Bridge were brought to the park in 1860 when the bridge's houses were being removed.

Although they look fairly unimpressive their pedigree is interesting. They are situated opposite the cricket pitch.

MODEL BOATING

The Victoria Model Steam Boat Club is one of the oldest model boating clubs in England. It was founded in 1904 by local enthusiasts and has met at the Boating Lake, near the Crown Gate East, ever since. The club was one of the six founding members of the Model Power Boat Association, the country's governing body for model boating, and is listed in the *Guinness Book of Records* as the oldest club of its kind. The season begins on Easter Sunday (meeting at 10.30) and meets every second Sunday until October. Regattas start at 10.30 or 11.00 and include Straight Running (without remote control), Hydroplane and Radio Control.

Membership is open to anyone, regardless of ability, but the regattas are only open to adults and children over the age of ten (park regulations). The club has a current membership of about 70 people. For further details contact Keith Reynolds, 81 Worple Road, Laleham, Staines, Middlesex TW181HJ, tel. 01784 458692, email ReynoldsVMSC@aol.com, website www.mpba.org.uk (this is the main site for the Model Power Boat Association so scroll down to Victoria Model Steam Boat Club listing).

PLAYGROUNDS

There are three playgrounds in the park. The best is the excellent adventure playground near the One O'Clock Club and the deer enclosure. There are hilly areas, giant slides, swings, climbing frames and an enormous paddling pool. The nearby One O'Clock Club has a small area for younger children including a sandpit. This is open Monday to Friday from 12.30–16.00. The third, and least nice, playground is near the Gore Gates, with neglected swings, slides and rusty climbing frames.

RUGBY

Victoria Park has the only rugby pitch in Tower Hamlets, which serves around 1,000,000 people! It is currently used by Millwall Park Albion Rugby Club, for senior matches. The new Tower Hamlets Community Rugby Development Officer, Paul Cooper, is trying to start up a new under 18s club in the borough (yet to be named). This would include weekly mini and touch rugby. For further details contact Paul Cooper on tel. 07904 114139 or email bowrugby@yahoo.co.uk. For details on booking the pitch contact the central town hall number, 020 7364 5000 and ask for sports pitch bookings and information for Victoria Park (currently John Walsh).

RUNNING

The Victoria Park Harriers and Tower Hamlets Athletic Club (VPHTHAC) have their headquarters on the edge of the park. The two clubs were combined in 2001, bringing together well over 100 years of club history. Their aim is to provide a friendly environment for the local community to get involved in athletics, track and field and road running. Membership is open to anyone over the age of nine, regardless of ability. There are two types of members: road runners and track and field athletes. The road runners (who run in Victoria Park at 19.00 on Tuesdays and Thursdays) are based at St Augustine's Hall, Cadogan Terrace, E9 5EG, on the edge of Victoria Park. The hall is open to members five days a week and has changing rooms, showers, a gym, a circuit training hall and a bar. Circuit training is at 19.00 every Monday.

For further details see the website www.vphthac.org.uk, email info@vphthac.org.uk. The track and field athletes are based at the Mile End Stadium on Rhodeswell Road, E14. They meet at 18.30 on Tuesdays and Thursdays for training in sprints, hurdles, jumps (including pole vault), throws and middle distance (see also p176). There are also 'introductory' hurdle sessions on Monday evenings at 18.30.

TENNIS

There are four hard tennis courts midway between Queen's Gate and St Mark's Gate.

The courts cost £3.90/hour and cannot be booked in advance: just turn up and play.

TREES

There are 4, 500 trees in the park including many rare species such as a Kentucky coffee tree (*gymnocladus dioica*), a bitter orange and a Chinese privet. There are many London planes bordering the canal, oaks and horse chestnuts, cherries and hawthorns. The Arboricultural Department has three walks for those interested in the trees, each with a leaflet and map, tel. 020 7364 5012.

WALKS

The Tower Hamlets Healthy Walkers meet every Wednesday for a one- to two-mile walk. They start at the Crown Gates at 11.45, tel. 020 7364 3196.

NEAR THE PARK

Regent's Canal (see p177, Mile End Park)

Limehouse Basin: opened in 1820 as London's gateway to England's canals

Mile End Park (see p175)

Wandsworth Common

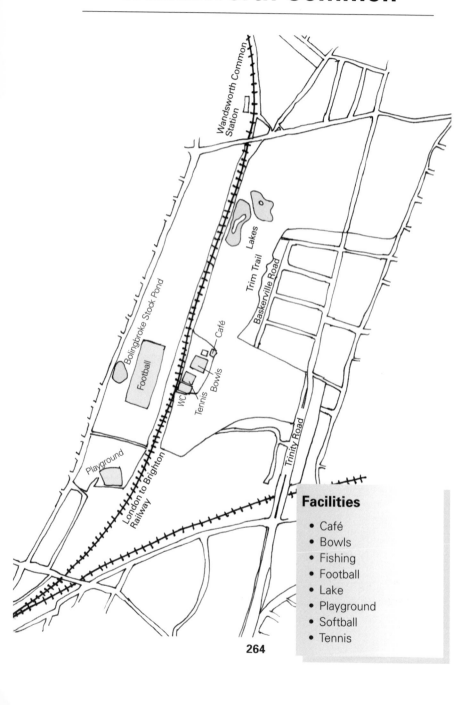

Wandsworth Common Station

Trim Trail

Lakes

Baskerville Road

Bolingbroke Stock Pond

Café

Football

Bowls

Tennis

WC

Trinity Road

Playground

London to Brighton Railway

Facilities

- Café
- Bowls
- Fishing
- Football
- Lake
- Playground
- Softball
- Tennis

VISITOR INFORMATION

Dorlcote Road, SW18

Tel. 020 8718 8688, website www.wandsworth.gov.uk, email
parks@wandsworth.gov.uk

Train: Wandsworth Common

Car: pay and display only

The borough of Wandsworth has over 650 hectares of open
space. Wandsworth Common consists of 73 hectares (175
acres) of land divided by the London to Brighton railway line.
There are sports pitches, tennis courts, fishing, a playground
and a nature study centre.

HIGHLIGHTS

- Common Ground Café Bar
- Nature Study Centre
- One O'Clock Club

BOWLS

The bowls pitch is surrounded by beautifully maintained flower
beds with a club house overlooking the pitch. Woods and slips
can be hired from the tennis hut. Sessions cost £1.50. For
further information contact the central sports booking team on
020 8876 7685.

CAFÉ

Common Ground Café Bar

Situated off the Dorlcote Road this is more of a family friendly
restaurant than a park café. The front has sunny tables in a
conservatory and the back has sofas, newspapers and a play-

corner. Cappuccino £1.70, tea £1.25, steak sandwich and chips £6.95, English breakfast £6.50, scones and cream £3.25, soup of the day £3.95. Open Monday to Friday 09.30–17.30 and weekends 10.00–17.30. Tel. 020 8874 9386.

FISHING

Wandsworth Common Lake is restocked yearly with fish, including some large carp, roach and tench. Season tickets are available for £50 and require a passport photo and rod licence (season June to March). Contact the Town Hall, tel. 020 8871 6000 or the Fine Line fishing shop, 299 Mitcham Road, tel. 020 8672 1699.

FOOTBALL

There is a football pitch on the west side of the common near the Bolingbroke Stock Pond. The pitch is available for hire and costs about £40 per session. For details regarding booking contact the central sports booking line at Barn Elms, tel. 020 8876 7685.

NATURE

The Nature Study Centre has a range of workshops, guided walks and talks throughout the year for both adults and children. These include field trips to discover the Wandsworth wildlife, including stag beetles, frogs, bats and birds.

Open Sundays 14.30–16.30. Tel. 020 8871 3863, email naturestudycentre@wandsworth.gov.uk. Bat help-line 020 7627 8822; frog help-line 01986 784 518; tree section 020 8871 6372; tree emergencies 020 8871 6000.

PLAYGROUND

Bolingbroke One O'Clock Club has a smart wooden building rather like a ski chalet. It is open to all children under the age of five and their carers. There is a small playground next to the club. Open Monday to Friday 13.00–16.00. Tel. 020 7228 6674, or contact the central play and community services number 020 8871 8820.

SOFTBALL

There are several softball clubs based at Wandsworth Common, including the London Breakers and the Saints. Both play in the London Softball Federation, the largest league of its kind in the country. The London Breakers have their own website, www.breakerssoftball.com. For further details of these clubs (and others in London) check Baseball Softball UK at www.baseballsoftballuk.com: click on 'softball' then on 'team finder', then 'London'. Alternatively visit the London Softball Federation website www.londonsoftball.co.uk.

TENNIS

There are four smart tennis courts, next to the bowls pitch. In winter the courts are run on a 'turn up and play' basis. During the summer months it is possible to register for telephone booking. Registration details are available from the attendant's hut next to the courts.

Waterlow Park

VISITOR INFORMATION

Swains Lane/Highgate Hill, N6

Tube: Archway, Highgate

Car: pay and display on Highgate Hill

Bus: 210, 271, 143

Tel. 020 7272 2825 (lodge for conservation information)

The beautiful grade II listed Waterlow Park has 29 acres of grassy slopes, a café, lakes, a playground and fabulous views of London. Sir Sydney Waterlow, Lord Mayor of London 1872–73, gave the small park to the people of London, 'a garden for the gardenless'. His statue in the park shows him admiring his gift while smoking his pipe and holding a key to the park. Currently, £1.2 million of Heritage Lottery money is being spent on improvements including the restoration of the 17th century Terrace Garden. Lauderdale House runs popular children's art, dance and music classes.

HIGHLIGHTS

- Lauderdale House
- The Italian Café
- Fine old trees
- Beautiful gardens
- Nearby Highgate Cemetery
- Views across London

Facilities

- Arts centre
- Aviary
- Bat walks
- Café
- Gardens
- Highgate Cemetery
- Lakes
- Playground
- Tennis

ART AND THEATRE

Lauderdale House runs free arts and crafts exhibitions throughout the year. There is also a range of art and dance classes for children of all ages. Prices for the classes start at £40 for ten weeks. Every Saturday touring companies bring a different production to the stage ranging from puppets to more traditional theatre for three to eight year olds. Tickets cost £3.50 or £2.50 for concessions. Throughout the year, there are concerts of all types of music. Tel. 020 8348 8716, website www.lauderdale.org.uk. Open Tuesday to Friday 11.00–16.00 and weekends noon until dusk.

BATS

During the summer months there are free evening walks advertised on the notice boards around the park. There are 16 species of bat in London with beautiful names such as natterer and pipistrelle. The tiny pipistrelle bat weighs just 4g but has a wingspan of 20cm and is able to eat 3, 500 insects in one night! Keen-beans bring their own bat detectors to distinguish the squeaks of different bats, but the walks are interesting for everyone. For further information contact the Bat Conservation Group (www.bats.org.uk), tel. 020 7627 2629 (the London Bat Group run the walks) or the Wildlife Trust on 020 7261 0447, website www.wildlifetrust.org.uk.

BIRDS

The Aviary once housed a large number of birds but is currently being restored.

CAFÉ

Lauderdale Café

This good value, unpretentious café has indoor and outside seating with views over the park. The café forms part of the 16th century house and has a large terrace overlooking the park. The enthusiasm of the Italian boss sets the tone of the place. It is one of our favourite cafés in London. Tea/cappuccino 95p, cakes from £1.20. Open 09.00–18.00 Tuesday to Sunday, tel. 020 8341 4807.

JAZZ

There is an annual jazz festival every summer that is advertised on the park's notice boards.

LAKES

The park has several lakes of varying size which are a haven for wildlife, including nesting birds, and dense plantations of willow, oak, azaleas and rose beds. Fishing is not permitted.

LAUDERDALE HOUSE

The 16th century Lauderdale House was home to the Duke of Lauderdale before he moved to Ham House in Richmond. It was later home to Nell Gwynne, who brought up her son by the King there. The house is now a community arts centre which provides a wide range of courses in art, dance, drama and music (see above). It is also a popular venue for wedding receptions. Website www.lauderdale.org.uk, tel. 020 8348 8716, open 11.00–16.00 Tuesday-Friday and variable weekends.

PLAYGROUND

There is a small playground for toddlers.

TENNIS

There are two hard tennis courts at the top of the park, commanding fine views of London. Play in winter is on a 'turn up and play' basis. During summer the attendant can provide details of registration for court booking.

TREES

The park has a fine population of densely planted trees, many of which are originals from the estate. These include oak, copper beech, willow, cedar of Lebanon and lime.

NEAR THE PARK

Highgate High Street with its pretty 18th century houses.

The Flask pub, where William Hogarth sketched the locals.

HIGHGATE CEMETERY

Highgate Cemetery, designed by Stephen Geary, is divided into East and West by Swains Lane. The Friends of Highgate Cemetery give guided tours of the beautiful older western section every day. Entering the huge enclosure, barred from the road by massive iron gates, is like stepping into another world. The towering mausoleums, hovering crumbling angels, gothic shrines and gravestones lie ivy-clad within thick native woodland alive with birds and wildlife. Karl Marx (1883) and George Eliot (1880) are in the newer eastern side and Michael Faraday (1867) and Christina Rossetti (1894) are in the west. Swains Lane, N6, tel. 020 8340 1834, website www.highgate-cemetery.org. The east side is open for strolling every day from 10.00–16.00 at a cost of £3. Visiting the west requires a guided tour, weekdays 12.00, 14.00, 16.00 and weekends hourly from 11.00 until closing.

Weavers Fields

Kelsey Street, Bethnal Green, E1

Tube: Bethnal Green (closest), Whitechapel, Shoreditch

Information: 020 8533 2057 (Victoria Park)

This is an award-winning neighbourhood park in the heart of Bethnal Green, a short way from the delights of Brick Lane, Spitalfields Market and the Columbia Road flower market. It is one of London's most vibrant, multi-cultural communities, home to a large Bangladeshi community and their restaurants. The park is a large flat square of green, surrounded by pretty terraced housing. There is a small playground, a local adventure playground and an excellent café.

HIGHLIGHTS

* Adventure playground
* Award-winning café

CAFÉ

Café Eat2

The award winning Eat2 café is one of the highlights of the area. It is housed on the ground floor of a large grade II listed building which was previously a school. The building was renovated and opened by the Queen in 2000 as the Weavers Restaurant Trust. The trust runs the café as a training centre for catering and

Facilities

* Café
* Dog walking
* Playgrounds

hospitality that includes qualifications and help with employment. It is open to anyone including unemployed people and people with disabilities. From the customer's perspective this means a well-run, friendly, good value café. There are pretty, round mosaic-inlaid tables, with high backed, velvet lined chairs and frescoed walls and ceilings. The café overlooks the park. Tea 50p, cappuccino 75p, full breakfast £3.25 (including vegetarian option), lunches and specials.

Kelsey Street, Bethnal Green, London E2 6HD. Tel. 020 7613 3694, fax 020 7613 5950. Open Monday to Friday 09.30–15.30. Lunch 12.30–14.30, afternoon tea 14.30–15.30. Website www.wrtrust.org.uk, email info@wrtrust.org.uk.

PLAYGROUNDS

There is an enclosed wooden adventure playground in the park. Open Tuesday to Friday 15.30–18.30 and Saturday 12.00–17.00. Tel. 020 7729 1295.

There is also a small enclosed playground for younger children in front of the café.

NEAR THE PARK

Brick Lane: home to some of the best Indian cooking in London as well as a famous Sunday market; the surrounding streets (Bacon, Cheshire, Cygnet and Sclater) come alive with stalls selling just about everything.

Columbia Road Flower Market: 08.00–13.00 every Sunday. This is one of the best and most colourful flower markets in London, with the street overflowing with colour and noise.

Bethnal Green

Museum of Childhood is a branch of the Victoria and Albert Museum and has a large display of historic toys, dolls and dolls' houses. Admission is free. Cambridge Heath Road E2, tel. 020 8983 5200, website www.museumofchildhood.org.uk, Bethnal Green tube. Open Monday to Thursday and Saturday and Sunday 10.00–17.50.

Spitalfields Market is a five-acre covered fruit, flower and vegetable market. It has a large underground area that was once one of London's most important banana ripening areas. Commercial Street, E1 (between Brushfield and Lamb Streets), tel. 020 7377 1496, Liverpool Street tube. Open Monday to Saturday 04.00–10.00.

Christchurch Spitalfields is Nicholas Hawksmoor's astonishing masterpiece. Its huge 225ft tower and spire are visible all around. Brushfield Street, E1, tel. 020 7859 3035 (Friends of Christchurch Spitalfields). Open Monday to Friday 12.30–14.30.

Smaller Green Spaces

BUNHILL FIELDS

Bunhill Fields is an ancient dissenters' graveyard of four acres, managed as a public space since 1867. The name probably derives from 'Bone Hill', reflecting the 120,000 bodies buried here between 1315 and 1867. It lies between the City Road and Bunhill Row, close to the heart of the city, and yet is a world away from it. It contains the tombs of some of the great Non-Conformists including William Blake (1827), Daniel Defoe (1731) and John Bunyan (1688). Stone paths flanked with railings run among the tall London plane trees and alongside the tightly packed crumbling memorials and tombs.

In the centre there is a small information office and an attendant for arranging viewings of the graves. From here the path opens out onto a wide lawn ringed with benches and trees. Most of the graves are enclosed but viewings can be arranged by telephoning the Park Ranger. The spiked gate at the east corner was a defence against body snatchers. The house, museum and chapel of John Wesley (1703–91), founder of the Methodists, are just across the road at 46 City Road. Bunhill Row was where Milton lived and wrote *Paradise Lost* and *Paradise Regained*. The large green space to the south of Bunhill Fields is the parade ground and cricket field of the Honourable Artillery Company, the oldest regiment in England. It is the largest open space in the city of London, but is unfortunately closed to the public.

John Wesley House, Museum and Chapel, tel. 020 7253 2262. The chapel is open on Sundays from 12.00–14.00. The house is open Monday to Saturday 10.00–16.00 and Sundays 12.00–14.00 and is closed Thursday 12.45–13.30 and public and bank holidays.

THE COLLEGE GARDEN (ABBEY GARDENS)

This secret garden is next to Westminster Abbey, the tallest gothic building in Europe. It is a haven of peace, next to the noise of Parliament Square. For more than 900 years it has been a cultivated garden, originally used to feed the monks in the abbey. It is the oldest garden in England and certainly one of the prettiest. The garden has a large lawn with two London planes and several rarer species of tree around the edge of the garden. These include a fig tree (*ficus carica*) and a double pink cherry tree (*prunus lanzan*).

In the far corner is the 'Crucifixion' by Enzo Plazzotta (1921–81), hidden behind a white mulberry tree (*morus alba*). There is a tiny knot garden in place of the original herb garden (*herbarium*) where medicinal herbs were grown. At the end of the garden is a round pond with a modern fountain, adding to the tranquillity of the garden. Concerts are held in the summer months, advertised on the notice boards around the abbey.

Tel. 020 7222 5152. Open Tuesday to Thursday 10.00–16.00. Entrance is via Deans Yard. Admission is free but donations are appreciated. Website: www.westminster-abbey.org.

ELTHORNE PARK

This six-acre park is a small Islington favourite and the grounds are well maintained. There is a free all-weather football pitch, a playground, a 'trim trail' and a peace garden. The latter is dedicated to Philip Baker (1889–1982), who won the Nobel Peace Prize in 1959 and co-founded the World Disarmament Campaign. Located off Hornsey Rise Road, near Archway tube.

FINSBURY CIRCUS

Finsbury Circus is a pretty circular garden in the heart of the City of London. It is home to the City's only bowling green and club, which dates from 1925 and is the largest open space in the City of London. The recently restored Pavilion is now an excellent bar and restaurant, with huge windows overlooking the green and the summer-time matches. The circus is ringed with office buildings but feels like a secluded oasis far from the surrounding bustle. There are free summer-time bandstand concerts, regular bowling matches and award-winning gardens.

The Pavilion Wine Bar and Restaurant serves sandwiches and drinks upstairs in the modern bar overlooking the green (ask for a window table); sandwiches £5.95, cappuccino and tea a steep £2.25. The restaurant is downstairs in a windowless but cosy basement with main courses from £12.95. Open Monday to Friday 11.00–23.00, tel. 020 7628 8224. Also nearby is Bunhill Fields (see p275) and Spitalfields Market (Commercial Street).

Tube and train: Moorgate or Liverpool Street.

The circus is just off London Wall, not far from Petticoat Lane Market on Middlesex Street and Wentworth Street (open Sundays).

KNOT GARDEN

The Knot Garden is a tiny green oasis with the sound of a fountain blocking that of traffic as it hurtles towards Lambeth Bridge. This tiny garden was once the graveyard of St Mary-at-Lambeth Church (1370) where Charles I and II's gardeners, the two John Tradescants, are buried. This father and son team were keen 17th century collectors of plants from all over Africa, North America, Russia and the rest of Europe. Since 1977 the church has housed the first Museum of Garden History. This excellent small museum has one of the first lawn mowers (and a child's miniature replica) as well as a brief history of garden design.

Of particular interest is the history of the 'knot garden'. In Tudor times, relative stability enabled houses to be built for comfortable living rather than the earlier fortresses built to withstand battle and deflect invaders. Tudor houses had bigger windows with gardens for pleasure. 'Knot' gardens have elaborately shaped geometric designed hedges best looked at from above. The drawing rooms of the new houses were often on the first floor to allow the full beauty of the knot gardens to be appreciated by the occupants.

Lambeth Place Road, tel. 020 7401 8865, website www.museumgardenhistory.org. Open every day 10.30–17.00 from March to November. Admission £3. The shady churchyard is free and it is possible to see the garden for free through a gateway. The museum has a café and an excellent gift shop (good for presents for gardeners).

MOUNT STREET GARDENS

The pretty Mount Street Gardens are one of Mayfair's hidden gems. Enclosed by tall buildings, they remain quiet and secluded even though they are just around the corner from Grosvenor Square (see p285). The gardens are built on an ancient burial ground. There are shady London planes, grass, benches and two beautiful churches: the Church of the Immaculate Conception by J.J. Scoles (1844) (tel. 020 7493 7811) with its Pugin high altar; and the 18th century Grosvenor Chapel, on South Audley Street.

The nearest tube is Bond Street (near Grosvenor Square and Berkeley Square).

POSTMAN'S PARK

This is one of London's smallest and prettiest parks. It is a stone's throw from St Paul's Cathedral, off King Edward Street, EC1, and sits like a hidden green courtyard among the surrounding buildings. The park forms the churchyard of the 18th century Guild Church of St Botolph's, although there has been a church on the site for over 1,000 years. There are some gravestones stacked against walls, bright flower beds among the clipped grass, a small round fish pond and fountain and an empty plinth which once supported Michael Ayrton's bronze 'Minotaur' before it was relocated. The park was recently used in the film 'Closer'.

The park is also home to one of London's most moving memorials: the Watts Memorial. Watts was a 19th century painter who campaigned and eventually paid for a memorial to heroic ordinary people. An entire wall, under a timber alcove, is lined with art nouveau tiles recording individual acts of bravery. For a coffee (or a meal) go to Smiths of Smithfield with its huge sofas, great service and views of the market.

Near the park

Hatton Garden: for some serious diamond hunting and a browse around the Leather Lane market.

Smithfield Market, Charterhouse Street, open Monday to Friday 05.00–09.00.

Smiths of Smithfield, 66 Charterhouse Street, tel. 020 7251 7950.

St Paul's Cathedral is five minutes' walk away.

St Botolph's Guild Church is well worth a visit.

RANELAGH GARDENS

The gardens were opened in 1742. In the middle was a large rococo rotunda built by William Jones. It was 150ft long and was heated by a large fireplace near where Mozart was said to have played. It was the place to go, and Edward Gibbon said at the time it was 'the most convenient place for courtships of every kind'. Canaletto painted it. Sadly in 1803 it was pulled down.

The 66 acres were re-designed by John Gibson in about 1860. The neighbouring Royal Chelsea Hospital was founded by Charles II in 1682 as a home for veterans of the army who had become unable to continue service. It was designed by Wren, who was the King's Surveyor-General of Works.

Bus: 11, 137, 239. Tube: Sloane Square. The gardens have a tennis court: see notice board for booking details.

RICHMOND GREEN

Richmond Green is one of the most unexpected and pretty squares in London. Although close to the bustle of Richmond's high street (the Quadrant), it feels a world away. Old trees and fine Georgian houses surround the green, overlooked by the famous Richmond Theatre and two excellent pubs. Cricket matches are played on summer evenings and at weekends.

The roads leading off the square from the south and west formed part of the 17th century Richmond Palace and include Old Palace Terrace, Maids of Honour Row (western edge) and Old Palace Yard, accessed via a surviving palace gateway. The 19th century Old Palace Lane leads straight out onto the river near Richmond Bridge. Richmond Lock is a convenient place to cross (on foot) to visit Old Isleworth and Syon Park (see p244).

ST GEORGE'S GARDENS

This peaceful oasis behind Coram's Fields (see p57) was an 18th century burial ground. It was laid out as a public garden in 1882. The area is tucked out of sight off Handel Street. The narrow paths wind their way among flowerbeds under the shady branches of London planes. Ancient gravestones lean on the surrounding walls. It is one of the quietest corners of this part of London.

Tube: Russell Square. Located off Handel Street and Heathcote Street, near to Coram's Fields.

ST JOHN'S WOOD CHURCH GROUNDS

This small park is conveniently next to Lord's Cricket Ground. It was originally a graveyard of the neighbouring church. Now it offers a shady area to picnic, a playground and a small nature reserve. Just outside the gates on Wellington Place is a kiosk café where well-informed taxi drivers and park-goers stop for bacon sandwiches and cups of tea.

ST MARY ISLINGTON

This small green space is off the busy café-packed Upper Street. The church has a full programme of services, activities for children, walks and courses. The Crypt Café has good value food and regular art exhibitions. The garden has tall London plane trees, seats and a drinking fountain. The fountain shoots out water from a lion's mouth and was donated by the Brewer's company in 2001.

Website: www.stmaryislington.org, tel. 020 7226 3400.

The alpha course is a ten-week introductory course on Christianity that starts in a local café and aims to be informal, fun and open to all. (www.alphacourse.org).

VICTORIA TOWER GARDENS

This small green strip of lawn runs down the edge of the Thames from the Victoria Tower of the Palace of Westminster to Lambeth Bridge. It has a small playground at the Lambeth Bridge end with a slide and swings. Emmeline Pankhurst, the leader of the militant suffragettes, has a bronze statue in her remembrance at the entrance near the House of Lords.

The Victoria Tower was the largest highest square structure in the world when it was built in 1860; it is taller than Big Ben's Clock Tower at 336ft. It has a spiral staircase with over 500 steps but the view from the roof is a just reward for the sprightly. The 11 floors are now used for the Records Office.

The garden is a quiet haven with a riverside walk and spectacular views of the London Eye. The centrepiece of the garden is a unique Victorian Gothic drinking fountain, the Buxton Memorial. It marks the freeing of slaves in 1834 after the abolition of slavery. It is two storeys high with a brightly coloured tiled roof.

WANDSWORTH PARK

This small park is a strip of grassy space with a shady riverside walk near Putney Bridge. The park is just 20 acres but has a football pitch and playground. This grade II listed park has been open to the public since 1903 having been landscaped into a park from previous land used for allotments. Lt. Col. J. Sexby, the first superintendent of London's parks, laid out the grounds.

Football

The football pitch costs from £38/session. Sports booking line 020 8876 7685, information line 020 8871 6347.

Information

The latest update on the park's facilities is supposed to be available from the Council but they have not proved helpful. Check the website www.wandsworth.gov.uk. Tel. 020 8871 6347.

Squares and Inns of Court

BERKELEY SQUARE

Berkeley Square is one of Mayfair's 'Great Squares' but there are few reasons to visit it now. Until the traffic is banned it will be little more than a polluted, noisy roundabout. The London plane trees are described as being the oldest and finest in London, but there are many nicer places to view them. There are fine Georgian houses on the west side of the square. The pretty Mount Street Gardens are nearby (see p278).

CAVENDISH SQUARE GARDEN

This pretty shaded square is two minutes' walk from the crowds of Oxford Circus. It is a good place to read or picnic and conveniently has an underground car park below it (£5/hour). The present gardens were laid in 1971 but the square dates from 1770. The year before the two Palladian style villas on the square were linked with an arch built over Dean Mews by Louis Osman. More recently a Jacob Epstein sculpture of the Madonna and Child (1953) was added to the arch.

The original garden had a huge statue of William, Duke of Cumberland (1721–65), but today only the plinth remains. There is, however, a grand statue of William Cavendish Bentinck. Many famous people have lived in the square including Lord Asquith the Prime Minister, Princess Amelia the daughter of George II, and the artists Frances Cotes and George Romney.

FITZROY SQUARE

Fitzroy Square is one of the prettiest squares in London. It sits in the shadow of the British Telecom Tower in the interesting district of Fitzrovia, to the west of Tottenham Court Road. The square was built in the 18th century by the 1st Baron Southampton, a descendant of Charles II. It is pedestrianised and peaceful, with wide stone paving surrounding a central enclosed garden. This circular garden has a gentle undulating design with large plane trees at each corner and a sculpture by Niami Blake, 'View' (1977), which celebrated the Queen's Silver Jubilee. The south and east sides have wonderful 18th century Adam brother terraces.

For 200 years the square had strong artistic and literary connections with number 29 being home to both George Bernard Shaw and Virginia Woolf, and number 33 the home of Roger Fry's Omega workshops. Gardens open to the public from 1 May to end of September, Monday to Friday 12.00–15.00, care of Frontager's Garden Committee.

GORDON AND TAVISTOCK SQUARES

These twin squares lie near each other and are only a ten minute walk from Euston Station. Both squares were built in the 19th century by Thomas Cubitt. Tavistock Square has a pretty statue of Mahatma Gandhi (1869–1948) by Fredda Brilliant (1968). A copper beech tree was planted in 1953 by Pandit Nehru, the then Prime Minister of India. There are several other memorial trees: a cherry tree planted in 1967 in memory of the victims of Hiroshima and a field maple planted in 1986 by the League of Jewish Women. There are also twin bronze busts of the famous surgeon Dame Louisa Aldrich-Blake, one looking out over the top of the railing, the other back into the park.

Tavistock Square is noisier than the nearby Gordon Square and both are a little bleak in the winter. The British Medical Association is based on the east side of the square, on the site of James Burton's Tavistock House. This was where Dickens wrote, amongst other novels, *Bleak House* and *A Tale of Two Cities*. The Jewish Museum is housed on the north side of the square in Adler House and the west side has pretty Georgian terracing. Gordon Square is a quieter square and surrounded by closely planted trees. It is just around the corner from the

University of London and one of London's largest Waterstones bookshops which has a large academic section.

GROSVENOR SQUARE, W1

Grosvenor Square is the second largest square in London (the largest being Russell Square). It was laid out in 1725 as an 'Italian style' wilderness but has gradually transformed into a formal setting. The square is impressively proportioned and the six acres of flat open grassland are a popular area for lunchtime picnics.

Its western side is dominated by the United States Embassy and the giant American eagle. At the eastern end of the square is a small garden memorial to the September 11 terrorist attack in New York. Sir William Reid Dick's memorial to President Roosevelt lies on the central axis, incorporating fountains and bedding. Opposite this is a memorial to the RAF Eagle Squadron. This part of Mayfair's strong association with the United States has led to it being known as 'Little America'. The nearby 18th century Grosvenor Chapel, on South Audley Street, is worth visiting. This is opposite the quieter, prettier and less well known Mount Street Gardens (see p278).

RUSSELL SQUARE

Russell Square is London's largest square and is the prettiest of Bloomsbury's public squares. It was built by the Duke of Bedford, a Russell, in the early 19th century. The square was recently restored with iron railings and ornamental gates enclosing the pretty gardens of brightly coloured flowers. There is a central computer-controlled fountain, a statue of the Duke of Bedford, a pergola circling the horseshoe path, and many large old London plane trees.

The west side includes some of the original houses by James Burton and the east side is dominated by the 19th century redbrick and terracotta Russell Hotel. There is a lively Italian café in the square, and Bedford Square is also close by: this has a preservation order and is one of the finest 18th century squares in London, one of the few complete Georgian squares left in Bloomsbury (the garden, unfortunately, is private). The British Museum is also nearby.

The Russell Square Café was recently refurbished and has large windows overlooking the fountain and plane trees. There is cosy indoor seating for the winter and a terrace for warm weather. Tea 80p, cappuccino £1.10, English breakfast £3.50, omelettes £3.50 and pasta £2.50. Café open: summer Monday to Friday 07.00–18.00 and weekends 07.30–17.00, winter Monday to Friday 07.00–17.00 and weekends 07.30–17.00. British Museum, Great Russell Street, tel. 020 7636 1555, website www.thebritishmuseum.ac.uk.

ST JAMES'S SQUARE

Pretty St James's Square is another tiny 17th century gem. It is tucked away between Regent's Street, St James's, Piccadilly and Pall Mall, in a quiet peaceful nook. The colourful flower beds and shady trees are surrounded by elegant 18th century buildings, including Chatham House, home to the Hoare banking family for over 100 years and Prime Ministers Chatham, William Pitt and Gladstone. A large bronze equestrian statue of William III sits in the centre of the square. The square is near the delights of St James's Street, including Berry Bros. & Rudd, the wine merchants, and St James's Palace.

INNS OF COURT

The Inns of Court were established in the middle ages for the training and lodging of lawyers. There are four surviving: the Inner and Middle Temple, Lincoln's Inn and Gray's Inn. Even today barristers must be accepted by one of the Inns of Court on completion of their training. The Inns are governed by Masters of the Bench (Benchers) who call the successful students to the bar. Although the Inns are private property they are open during weekdays for the public to enjoy. They form a tranquil oasis amid the modern surroundings. The atmosphere is pure 17th century London and gives a fascinating glimpse into the world of the barristers and law-makers.

The Temple

The Temple (consisting of the Middle and Inner Temples) is perhaps the best known of the Inns, if only because of its visibility from the Embankment. Despite its location between Embankment and Fleet Street, its atmosphere is one of a tranquil Oxbridge college. Groups of beautiful 17th century buildings surround courts and gardens and are linked with discreet alleys.

There is much to be seen, including the circular Temple Church (1185), Wren's King's Bench Walk and the Middle Temple Hall. The 12th century Temple Church is the Inn's oldest building and is the City's only complete building of the early Gothic style. It was built by the Knights Templar, an order of 'soldier-monks' who built their churches in the circular fashion of the Holy Sepulchre in Jerusalem. The pretty King's Bench Walk passes immaculate 17th century houses, two of which are attributed to Wren. The walk leads to the Middle Temple Hall, which has a famous oak hammer-beam roof under which Shakespeare's *Twelfth Night* was first performed in 1601.

The Refreshers bar/café/restaurant is on the ground floor of the library building on Middle Temple Lane (in the heart of the area). It feels rather like a private club but is open to the public. Inside there are large comfy sofas and armchairs, a friendly bar and café and newspapers. Breakfast is served from 08.00, lunch until 14.00 and dinner until 21.00.

Inner Temple, Crown Office Row, King's Bench Walk, EC4, tel. 020 7797 8250.

Middle Temple, Middle Temple Lane, EC4, tel. 020 7427 4800.

Temple Church, tel. 020 7353 3470.

Middle Temple Hall, usually open Monday to Friday

10.00–12.00 and 15.00–16.00.

Refreshers Café, tel. 020 7427 4826, open Monday to Friday 08.00–21.00.

Lincoln's Inn

Lincoln's Inn is to the north of the Temple, behind the Law Courts. Both the Inn and the nearby Lincoln's Inn Fields are worth exploring. The entrance to the Inn is through a red brick 16th century gatehouse. Here the neat gardens and stretches of lawns are surrounded by a series of beautiful buildings. The garden includes rows of cherry trees, clipped lawns, roses and maples. The Inn's 17th century chapel has had a £2 million restoration. It has an unusual open undercroft with finely carved pillars and bosses, original pews and stained glass including, in one window, the arms of 228 Treasures of the society. It is open to the public 12.00–14.30 Monday to Friday and for services.

Lincoln's Inn Fields lies on the western edge of the Inn. This pretty seven-acre square is one of the city's largest green spaces, and has some of the tallest plane trees in London. There are three tennis courts, a netball pitch, and a café. The café is a marquee style building overlooking the tennis courts. The coffee is good but unfortunately they do not serve pastries. Risotto £6.45, sandwiches from £2.00, breakfast £4.25, specials £5.45. The Sir John Soane Museum and the Museum of the Royal College of Surgeons are on the square.

Lincoln's Inn Fields, WC2, tel. 020 7405 1393.

Café, tel. 020 7404 1414, email cafeinthepark@yahoo.co.uk. Open every day11.00–20.00 (21.30 in the summer).

Gray's Inn

Gray's Inn lies off Holborn. The long central Field Court garden is open from 12.00–14.30 from Monday to Friday and is a beautiful retreat from 21st century London. As in the other Inns there are seats among the clipped lawns, lavender and tall plane trees. At the north end there is a raised grass terrace, looking down the long straight gardens and the young oak avenue. On the terrace there is a memorial to Sir Francis Bacon (1564–1626), who lived here for 30 years, with an inscription from his *Advancement of Learning* (1605).

Gray's Inn, Gray's Inn Road, WC1, tel. 020 7458 7800. Open Monday to Friday 12.00–14.30.

Near the Inns of Court

Royal Courts of Justice: tel. 020 7947 6000, open Monday to Friday: 09.00–16.00. Closed Aug/Sept.

Sir John Soane Museum: tel. 020 7405 2107, website www.soane.org.uk, open Tuesday to Saturday 10.00–17.00 and 18.00–21.00 first Tuesday in month.

Museum of the Royal College of Surgeons: tel. 020 7405 3474. Admission is free, open 10.00–16.00 Monday to Friday, website www.rcseng.ac.uk. After a £3m two-year refurbishment project the Hunterian Museum re-opened in February 2005. It is packed with art treasures, antique surgical instruments, the history of both the college and of surgery and the Hunterian Collection of 3,000 specimens.

The Best For...
(see also the index)

Best for **Adventure Playgrounds**: Battersea Park, Burgess Park, Kensington Gardens

Best for **Animals**: Battersea Park, Regent's Park, Richmond Park (deer)

Best for **Art Galleries**: Battersea Park, Kensington Gardens

Best for **Australian Rules Football**: Clapham Common, Regent's Park

Best for **Baseball**: Finsbury Park

Best for **Bats**: Highgate Wood, Holland Park, Waterlow Park

Best for **Beekeepers**: Regent's Park

Best for **Beetles**: Bushy Park, Highgate Woods, Richmond Park

Best for **Bird Watching**: Alexandra Park, Hampstead Heath, Richmond Park, Highgate Wood, Queen's Wood, Regent's Park (waterfowl)

Best for **Boating**: Battersea Park, Hyde Park, Regent's Park

Best for **Bowls**: Dulwich Park, Hampstead Heath, Wandsworth Common

Best for **Butterflies**: Alexandra Park, Syon Park Butterfly House

Best for **Cafés**: Clapham Common, Highgate Wood, Queen's Wood, Kennington Park, Parliament Hill

Best for **Budget Cafés**: Chiswick Park, Tooting Bec Common, Weavers Fields

Best **Restaurant-Style Cafés**: Kensington Gardens, St James's Park (in the park), Wandsworth Common

Best **Café for Modern Design**: Thames Barrier Park, Holland Park, St James's Park

Best **Coffee**: Battersea Park, Kennington Park, Thames Barrier Park

Best for **Children**: Coram's Fields, Kensington Gardens, Queen's Park, Hampstead Heath

Best for **Cricket**: Blackheath, Chiswick Park, Highgate Wood

Best for **Cycle Hire**: Battersea Park, Dulwich Park, Richmond Park

Best for **Fireworks**: Alexandra Park, Battersea Park, Primrose Hill (see Regent's Park)

Best for **Fishing**: Bushy Park, Hampstead Heath, Osterley Park

Best for **Football**: see index!

Best for **Fountains**: Bushy Park, Kensington Gardens, Regent's Park

Best for **Garden Centres**: Alexandra Park, Bishop's Park, Syon Park

Best for **Gardens**: Hampton Court, Holland Park, Kensington Gardens, The Hill Garden (Hampstead Heath), Golders Hill Park, Regent's Park Secret Garden (and Rose Garden)

Best for **Go-Karting**: Burgess Park, Mile End Park

Best for **Golf**: Queen's Park, Gunnersbury Park, Regent's Park, Richmond Park

Best for **Gyms**: Battersea Park, Richmond Old Deer Park and the Paddington Recreation Ground

Best for **Hockey**: see index!

Best for **Houses**: Chiswick House, Greenwich Park, Gunnersbury Park (run down), Holland Park (Leighton Hs), Hampstead Heath (Fenton Hs, Kenwood), Marble Hill Park, Osterley Park, Syon Park

Best for **Ice-Skating**: Alexandra Park, Hampton Court (Christmas only)

Best for **Kite Flying**: Clapham Common, Hampstead Heath (Parliament Hill), Primrose Hill (see Regent's Park), Richmond Park

Best for **Massage**: Paddington Recreation Ground

Best for **Mazes**: Crystal Palace Park (free), Hampton Court (entrance fee)

Best for **Model Boating**: Kensington Gardens, Victoria Park

Best for **Museums**: Crystal Palace Park, St James's Park, Hyde Park, Kensington Gardens, Greenwich Park, Mile End Park (Barnardo)

Best for **Observatories**: Greenwich Park, Hampstead Heath

Best for **Open Space**: Clapham Common, Hampstead Heath, Richmond Park

Best for **Opera**: Hampstead Heath, Holland Park

Best for **Paddling Pools**: Clapham Common, Hampstead Heath, Paradise Park (fountain)

Best for **Riding (Horses)**: Bushy Park, Hyde Park, Richmond Park

Best for **Riverside**: Battersea Park, Greenwich Park, Marble Hill Park, Richmond Park, Syon Park, Thames Barrier Park

Best for **Robert Adam architecture**: Osterley Park, Syon Park, Hampstead Heath (Kenwood)

Best for **Roller-Blading**: Hyde Park

Best for **Rugby**: see index

Best for **Running**: Dulwich Park, Hampstead Heath, Holland Park, Richmond Park

Best for **Shopping**: Dulwich Park, Hampstead Heath, Hyde Park, Richmond Park

Best for **Skate-Boarding**: Alexandra Park, Bishop's Park, Clapham Common

Best for **Softball**: Clapham Common, Finsbury Park, Regent's Park, Wandsworth Common

Best for **Sports Centres**: Battersea Park, Bushy Park, Crystal Palace Park

Best for **Swimming**: Bushy Park, Brockwell Park, Hampstead Heath, Tooting Bec Common

Best for **Tennis**: Hampstead Heath, Hyde Park, Clissold Park, Regent's Park, Waterlow Park, Southwark Park (free)

Best for **Theatre**: Holland Park, Regent's Park, Waterlow Park

Best for **Trees**: Brompton Cemetery, Bushy Park, College Garden, Greenwich Park

Best for **Views**: Alexandra Park, Crystal Palace, Greenwich Park, Hampstead Heath, Primrose Hill, Richmond Park, Waterlow Park

Best for **Walks**: Diana Princess of Wales Walk (p168), Jubilee Walk (p240), Parkland Walk (p83), Regent's Canal (p177)

The Biggest: Richmond Park

The Smallest: The Knot Garden

The Most Secret: College Garden, Secret Garden (Regent's Park)

Index